Frontiers in African Business Research

Series Editor
Almas Heshmati, Jönköping International Business School,
Jönköping, Sweden

This book series publishes monographs and edited volumes devoted to studies on entrepreneurship, innovation, as well as business development and management-related issues in Africa. Volumes cover in-depth analyses of individual countries, regions, cases, and comparative studies. They include both a specific and a general focus on the latest advances of the various aspects of entrepreneurship, innovation, business development, management and the policies that set the business environment. It provides a platform for researchers globally to carry out rigorous analyses, to promote, share, and discuss issues, findings and perspectives in various areas of business development, management, finance, human resources, technology, and the implementation of policies and strategies of the African continent. Frontiers in African Business Research allows for a deeper appreciation of the various issues around African business development with high quality and peer reviewed contributions. Volumes published in the series are important reading for academicians, consultants, business professionals, entrepreneurs, managers, as well as policy makers, interested in the private sector development of the African continent.

More information about this series at http://www.springer.com/series/13889

Gouranga G. Das · Rukundo Bosco Johnson
Editors

Rwandan Economy at the Crossroads of Development

Key Macroeconomic and Microeconomic Perspectives

Editors
Gouranga G. Das
Department of Economics
Hanyang University
Ansan-Si, Gyeonggi-do, Korea (Republic of)

Rukundo Bosco Johnson
Department of Economics
School of Economics
University of Rwanda
Kigali, Rwanda

ISSN 2367-1033   ISSN 2367-1041 (electronic)
Frontiers in African Business Research
ISBN 978-981-15-5048-5   ISBN 978-981-15-5046-1 (eBook)
https://doi.org/10.1007/978-981-15-5046-1

© Springer Nature Singapore Pte Ltd. 2020
This work is subject to copyright. All rights are reserved by the Publisher, whether the whole or part of the material is concerned, specifically the rights of translation, reprinting, reuse of illustrations, recitation, broadcasting, reproduction on microfilms or in any other physical way, and transmission or information storage and retrieval, electronic adaptation, computer software, or by similar or dissimilar methodology now known or hereafter developed.
The use of general descriptive names, registered names, trademarks, service marks, etc. in this publication does not imply, even in the absence of a specific statement, that such names are exempt from the relevant protective laws and regulations and therefore free for general use.
The publisher, the authors and the editors are safe to assume that the advice and information in this book are believed to be true and accurate at the date of publication. Neither the publisher nor the authors or the editors give a warranty, express or implied, with respect to the material contained herein or for any errors or omissions that may have been made. The publisher remains neutral with regard to jurisdictional claims in published maps and institutional affiliations.

This Springer imprint is published by the registered company Springer Nature Singapore Pte Ltd.
The registered company address is: 152 Beach Road, #21-01/04 Gateway East, Singapore 189721, Singapore

To the fondest memory of my Parents, who instilled within me the value of development without divisiveness, and replenished my credence that the world—despite odds–will always emerge a better place for all.

—Gouranga

To my Wife and our two Boys, who have always been beside me on the academic trajectory

—Johnson

Foreword

> *The Greatest Escape in human history is the escape from poverty and death. ... Building on the Enlightenment, the Industrial Revolution, and the germ theory of disease, living standards have increased by many times, life spans have more than doubled, and people have fuller and better lives than ever before. The process is still going on.*
>
> —Angus Deaton. Page 23, In 'The Great Escape: Health, Wealth, and the Origins of Inequality'. Princeton University Press.

The quote above by a Nobel Laureate in Economics is apt one to start this foreword as it highlights that salient feature of economic development is a continuous process despite ups and downs. In less than three decades, Rwanda has managed to undergo an impressive economic and social transformation, serving as a model for many African countries which aspire to a true renaissance. Coming from far away, after a 3-year civil war that destroyed existing economic and social infrastructure, Rwanda is now experiencing robust economic growth, a sharp reduction in poverty, and an improvement in infrastructure. However, despite significant progress, much remains to be done to put the economy on the path of sustainable development.

From this point of view, the book offers a nice tale about how a developing country could turn failure into real success and what should be done to maintain growth momentum. It also brings hope to many countries around the world, currently facing civil wars and conflicts, that with enlightened leadership, strong determination, and disciplined people, success is possible.

The book begins by assessing the macroeconomic framework to give an idea of the main economic challenges facing the country, focusing mainly on investment as a basis for economic activity and on the financing needed to achieve higher growth.

Given the key role of the private sector in job and wealth creation, the book focuses on the performance of Rwandan companies, especially SMEs, supporting the analysis with success stories on which the country could build on to achieve higher economic performance.

Since no success could be achieved without the existence of an appropriate ecosystem and a good legal framework, the book attaches great importance to the role of entrepreneurial culture in stimulating investment and innovation and to the role of tax incentives in shaping the economic structures and channeling investments to priority areas.

What is appealing about the book is that it uses concrete examples of success to show how developing countries could achieve economic transformation and promote sustainable growth. The book also shows the way forward to consolidate good economic performance and meet existing challenges.

There is much to learn from Rwanda's experience on how to transform negative feelings and anger into a determination to fuel development and progress. This edited book is a valuable addition in the area of growth and development economics with commendable blends of theory and practice.

I would like to thank the editors for this compilation of research papers, the contributors for offering us a complete analysis of the Rwandan economy, and advise readers to browse the 13 chapters of the book to learn more about the resurgence of Rwanda.

February 2020

Imed Drine, Ph.D.
Lead Economist
Country Strategy and Cooperation Department
Islamic Development Bank
Jeddah, Saudi Arabia

Associate Professor of Economics
University of Sousse
Sousse, Tunisia

Preface and Acknowledgements

The book is a timely and relevant study on the aspects of development of the Rwandan economy and the underlying drivers that could shape the evolution of the economy, polity, and society. This is more pertinent in considering the Government of Rwanda's Strategic Road Map (SRM) for Economic Development, the National Strategy for Development 2017–2024. In other words, given the plans and road map adopted by the Republic of Rwanda, we need to investigate what are the implications for those agendas, identify the "pillars" of success, and highlight the policies that need to be formulated for effective implementation of those high-profile objectives. This book is the outcome of a high-profile conference held in Kigali, Capital of Rwanda. The conference entitled "4th International Conference on Eastern Africa Business and Economic Watch (4th EABEW—2019)" was held during June 12–14, 2019 at the College of Business and Economics, University of Rwanda. The theme of the research was "Inclusive Growth and Sustainable Socio-Economic Transformation." What could be more appropriate theme than discussing sustainable and inclusive development in the context of less-developed economies aspiring to make progress in the fast-track highway of socio-economic and structural transformation.

The volume is rich because, as the section plans show, it covers both micro-level and macro-level analysis. Given the fact that the world economy is inflicted with problems of macroeconomic adjustments, conflicts, trade wars, and rise of protectionism, the current economic scenarios in the developing and least-developed economies are not so promising in an interconnected world. Thus, the necessity of "global" as well as "national, local, or regional" problems and policy dimensions are crucial. This book—taking Rwanda as a case in hand—is important in the context of African continent undergoing structural changes.

The essays comprise contributions on various microeconomic and macroeconomic policy angles that are crucial for a less-developed economy to embark on a road to recovery to converge with the desired trajectory. Organization of the book is based on three major themes: (i) Macroeconomic Constraints: Monetary Policy,

Investments, and Population; (ii) Firms' Performance, SMEs, and Role of Entrepreneurship; and (iii) Entrepreneurship and Business Performance: Strategies and Policies.

The conference papers are further revised and updated to offer a collection of 12 empirical studies that have an overall focus on macroeconomic policies such as savings among the rural poor; sustained investments in and development of capital markets; role of entrepreneurial sustainability; role of innovations for firms' performance; healthcare reforms; the benefits of technology, policy incentives such as tax benefits for promoting growth, and strategic considerations such as marketing or positioning strategies; export strategies; and productivity enhancement via processing and profit sharing.

It enhances the readers' knowledge about the factors that influence inclusive growth on a sustained basis via better technologies and innovations favoring productivity, firm performance, and their positive externalities in the food, nutrition, and health sectors. As it covers top-down and bottom-up approaches and strategies for development, the insights are truly pragmatic and realistic for policy interventions necessary for Rwanda's gradual transitioning from agriculture to an industrial transformation.

The topics are oriented to development and growth in investments, business and entrepreneurial growth, innovation, and others. The main methods of interest include the quantitative techniques used such as the econometric models, and the results they portray to the readers. All topic suggested in the book are of interest as they are diverse and linked to the development agenda of Rwanda' development strategy. The readers will derive new analytical techniques used in the chapters, the methodologies used in the different chapters of the book, and most importantly the policy recommendations aimed at supplementing the existing policy frameworks for Rwanda's growth.

The book will be read by various scholars, students, and the public in Rwanda. It can be used as "reference" book for any Development Economics course, graduate course, or for research only courses. In particular, the book addresses the issues under the following major areas: Macroeconomics, Microeconomics, Business and entrepreneurship, Firm performance and innovation, Economics of Development.

Ansan-Si, Gyeonggi-do, Korea (Republic of)	Gouranga G. Das
Kigali, Rwanda	Rukundo Bosco Johnson

Acknowledgements With no exception, alike other works, this book is the outcome of collective effort of many people. It's our pleasure to offer our sincerest thanks to those whose inspiration, help, and advice have shaped this work. The contributors are researchers and academics from diverse backgrounds, and thus their contributions have made this book a "salad-bowl" of multiple ingredients with wide range of perspectives. First of all, the conference was organized with the valuable support of the Global Labor Organization (GLO) and their intellectual stalwarts, fellows, and other personnel. Without their moral and intellectual support, this book would not have seen the daylight. Special thanks are due to Almas Heshmati—the Academic Lead of the GLO Research Cluster on "Labor Markets in Africa" and the GLO Fellow/s, who have given us the opportunity to edit this volume and imbibed within us a spirit of "can-do" attitude, without which any "development" story is a wishful thinking. His continuous encouragement was a *tour-de-force* behind this edited volume. Second, we are grateful to the contributors for their intellectual fervors that ignited our minds. Thirdly, we thank the reviewers as their contributions are as valuable as the authors. Special thanks are due to William N. Achauer of Springer (Germany) for his continued support and unstinted help despite his busy schedules. His unfailing support was quite a source of encouragement. Also, special mention must be made to Anil Chandy for shaping this effort into a feasible project. Anushangi Weerakoon needs special mention too for her promptness in offering help while we were struggling against the time. All these high-quality publication assistances make this project a truly valuable one.

Last but not the least, without constant enthusiasm of family members and their emotional support in difficult times, we wouldn't have been able to complete this book, and persevere. No words could possibly express the gratitude for moral support of them. We owe special debts to them.

Blurb

This volume represents a cornucopia of research studies coming out of an international conference held in Kigali, Rwanda in 2018. The essays comprise contributions on various microeconomic and macroeconomic policy angles that are crucial for a less developed economy to embark on a road to recovery to converge with the desired trajectory. The topics encompass a broad range of issues like the role of savings, capital formation, human capital, innovations, entrepreneurship, profit-shifting by multinational corporations, small and medium enterprises (SMEs), and firms' strategies for achieving sustained and balanced growth. The chapters are organized under three major themes based on the commonality of areas that they cover: (i) Macroeconomic Constraints: Monetary Policy, Investments, and Population; (ii) Firms' Performance, SMEs, and Role of Entrepreneurship; and (iii) Entrepreneurship and Business Performance: Strategies and Policies. It has a collection of 12 empirical studies that have an overall focus on macroeconomic policies such as savings among the rural poor; sustained investments in and development of capital markets; role of entrepreneurial sustainability; role of innovations for firms' performance; healthcare reforms; the benefits of technology, policy incentives such as tax benefits for promoting growth, and strategic considerations such as marketing or positioning strategies; export strategies; and productivity enhancement via processing and profit sharing. With contributions from 27 authors, the studies bring forth knowledge about the factors that influence well-being via better technologies and innovations favoring productivity, firm performance, and their positive externalities in the food, nutrition, and health sectors. Given the wide-ranging coverage of top-down and bottom-up approaches and strategies for development, the book offers insights for policy interventions necessary for Rwanda's gradual transition from agriculture to an industrial transformation via manufacturing and service-led development without smokestack industries.

Praise for *Rwandan Economy at the Crossroads of Development*

"The editors and contributors are to be congratulated for the publication of this interesting new volume. Over a quarter of a century ago, the world's attention focused on the Rwandan tragedy. But in more recent times the attention has switched to the country's dynamic economic performance as one of the fastest growing economies in Sub-Sahara Africa. The 12 studies in the volume cover many important topics, from macroeconomic management to innovation and healthcare."
—Hal Hill, *Australian National University, H.W. Arndt Professor of Southeast Asian Economies, Crawford School, College of Asia and the Pacific, Australian National University.*

"In a short span of 25 years, Rwanda has witnessed a striking transformation from an economy torn by conflict to a success story in development. This book provides an engaging discussion and perceptive analysis of the constraints on, and possibilities of development over the next quarter century. Its macroeconomic perspective supported by microeconomic analysis is unusual, yielding policy lessons not only for Africa but also for Least Developed Countries elsewhere in the world. It will be valuable reading on the Rwanda economy for research scholars and policy practitioners in development. The editors have done a commendable work in bringing out this volume."
—Deepak Nayyar, *Emeritus Professor of Economics, Jawaharlal Nehru University, New Delhi, Honorary Fellow, Balliol College, Oxford, and former Vice Chancellor, University of Delhi.*

"The volume contains an array of contributions employing sound economics research to address selected topics on Rwanda's development. The collection's analyses focus on issues ranging from long-term development prospects vis-à-vis persistent socioeconomic challenges, to options for realizing the country's ambitious National Strategy for Transformation. The book will serve as a valuable reference for scholars, policymakers, and readers interested in African development."

—Amelia U. Santos-Paulino, *Chief, Investment Research Section, Division on Investment and Enterprise, Deputy Editor, Transnational Corporations Journal,United Nations Conference on Trade and Development (UNCTAD), Geneva, Switzerland.*

"There has been considerable interest in the developmental lessons from the Rwandan economic experience, both among scholars and among the policy community. The Rwandan economy has performed well in many dimensions in recent years, and widely regarded as a success story of a country coming out of conflict. This volume by both Rwandan and international scholars bring together what we know about the Rwandan economic development experience. It will be valuable reading for both academics and policy makers. The authors deserve credit for compiling this collection."

—Professor Kunal Sen, *Director, United Nations University, World Institute of Development Economics Research, Helsinki, Finland.*

"I recommend this book for all those interested in the economic development of the least developed economies of the world. The microeconomic studies of the factors that contribute to survival and growth of small and medium enterprises in Rwanda are especially valuable. Based on a database of 49,000 small and medium enterprises (SMEs) in the region in and around Kigali, there are multiple chapters that examine the factors that contribute to survival and growth of SMEs in Rwanda, including tax incentives, education, training and mentoring, financial discipline, family relationships in the business, networks and others. There are chapters that focus on: what influences SME productivity; and process and product innovations in SMEs. Researchers, students and policy-makers would all benefit from the insights of these studies."

—David G. Tarr, *Consultant and Former Lead Economist, The World Bank.*

Contents

1   **Introduction and Overview** 1
     Gouranga G. Das and Rukundo Bosco Johnson

Part I   Macroeconomic Constraints: Monetary Policy, Investment, and Population

2   **An Analysis of Savings Among Rural Poor Households in Rwanda**... 21
     Aristide Maniriho, Edouard Musabanganji, and Philippe Lebailly

3   **Economic Modeling of Capital Markets and Sustainable Investments in Rwanda**................................. 43
     Fidèle Mutemberezi and Christian N. Mbabazi

4   **The Working of Monetary Policy Transmission Mechanisms in Rwanda: An Econometric Analysis Using the Equilibrium Model** 55
     Ferdinand Nkikabahizi, Veneranda Hategekimana, and Edouard Musabanganji

5   **Population Growth's Effect on Economic Development in Rwanda**... 73
     Daniel Ruturwa Sebikabu, Eric Ruvuna, and Martin Ruzima

Part II   Firm's Performance, SMEs and Role of Entrepreneurship

6   **Innovation and Firms' Performance in the Rwandese Manufacturing Industry: A Firm-Level Empirical Analysis** 99
     Etienne Ndemezo and Charles Kayitana

7   **Business Networks and Small and Medium Enterprise Growth in Rwanda**... 115
     Olivier Mugwaneza and Olof Brunninge

8	Cost-effectiveness of Optimizing a Network of Drone-Aided Healthcare Services in Rural Rwanda........................	139
	Chinasa I. Ikelu and Eugene C. Ezin	
9	Effect of Transfer Pricing on Profit Shifting by Multinational Companies in Developing Countries: A Case of Rwanda	149
	Daniel Twesige, Faustin Gasheja, Jonas Barayendema, and Alexis Uwamahoro	

Part III Entrepreneurship and Business Performance: Strategies and Polices

10	Determinants of Entrepreneurship Sustainability Among Family Businesses in Rwanda: Case of Small and Medium Family Businesses in Kigali.....................................	171
	Alexis Uwamahoro and Daniel Twesige	
11	Assessing the Role of Positioning Strategy on Market Performance of Soft Drink Manufacturing Enterprises (SDMES) in Rwanda....................................	191
	Nimusima Pereez, Karuhanga Nathan, Mukarutesi Dative, Gasana Charles, Kampire Charity, and Turyamushanga Labson	
12	Determinants of Productivity of Rwandese Food and Beverage Processing Sector: Do Tax Incentives Matter?	217
	Etienne Ndemezo and Jean Bosco Ndikubwimana	
13	Tax Incentives and Growth of SMEs in Rwanda: A Case Study of Small and Medium Enterprises in Nyarugenge District	231
	Daniel Twesige, Faustin Gasheja, and Jonas Barayendema	

Author Index...	249
Subject Index...	257

Contributors

Jonas Barayendema School of Business, College of Business, University of Rwanda CBE, Kigali, Rwanda

Olof Brunninge Jönköping International Business School, Jönköping, Sweden

Kampire Charity University of Rwanda, College of Business and Economics, Butare, Rwanda

Gasana Charles University of Rwanda, College of Business and Economics, Butare, Rwanda

Gouranga G. Das Department of Economics, Hanyang University, Ansan-Si, Gyeonggi-do, Korea (Republic of)

Mukarutesi Dative University of Rwanda, College of Business and Economics, Butare, Rwanda

Eugene C. Ezin Institut de Formation et de Recherche en Informatique (IFRI), Universite de Abomey Calavi, Cotonou, Republic of Benin

Faustin Gasheja School of Business, College of Business, University of Rwanda CBE, Kigali, Rwanda

Veneranda Hategekimana Faculty of Commerce, Catholic University of Rwanda, Huye, Rwanda

Chinasa I. Ikelu Institut de Mathematiques et de Sciences Physiques (IMSP), Porto Novo, Republic of Benin

Rukundo Bosco Johnson Department of Economics, School of Economics, University of Rwanda, Kigali, Rwanda

Charles Kayitana Department of Marketing and Human Resources, University of Rwanda, Kigali, Rwanda

Turyamushanga Labson Department of Business Studies, Faculty of Arts and Social Sciences, Kabale University, Kabale, Uganda

Philippe Lebailly Unity of Economics and Rural Development, Gembloux Agro-Bio Tech, University of Liège, Liège, Belgium

Aristide Maniriho Unity of Economics and Rural Development, Gembloux Agro-Bio Tech, University of Liège, Liège, Belgium;
School of Economics, University of Rwanda, Kigali, Rwanda

Christian N. Mbabazi World Bank Research Group, Kigali, Rwanda

Olivier Mugwaneza School of Business, University of Rwanda, Kigali, Rwanda

Edouard Musabanganji School of Economics, College of Business and Economics, University of Rwanda, Kigali, Rwanda

Fidèle Mutemberezi School of Economics, University of Rwanda College of Business, Kigali, Rwanda

Karuhanga Nathan University of Rwanda, College of Business and Economics, Butare, Rwanda

Etienne Ndemezo Department of Economics, University of Rwanda, Kigali, Rwanda

Jean Bosco Ndikubwimana Department of Applied Statistics, University of Rwanda, Kigali, Rwanda

Ferdinand Nkikabahizi School of Economics, College of Business and Economics, University of Rwanda, Kigali, Rwanda

Nimusima Pereez University of Rwanda, College of Business and Economics, Butare, Rwanda

Eric Ruvuna Department of Economics and Management, Business and Development Studies Faculty, Kibogora Polytechnic, Nyamasheke, Rwanda

Martin Ruzima Institute of Policy Analysis and Research - Rwanda (IPAR-Rwanda), Kigali, Rwanda

Daniel Ruturwa Sebikabu Department of Applied Statistics, School of Economics, University of Rwanda, Kigali, Rwanda

Daniel Twesige School of Business, College of Business, University of Rwanda CBE, Kigali, Rwanda

Alexis Uwamahoro School of Business, College of Business, University of Rwanda, Kigali, Rwanda

Abbreviations

ADF	Augmented Dickey–Fuller
AEDs	Automated External Defibrillators
AEO	African Economic Outlook
AERC	African Economic Research Consortium
AfDB,	African Development Bank
ANOVA	Analysis Of Variance
ARDL	Autoregressive Distributed Lag
ATE	Average Treatment Effect
BK	Bank of Kigali
BLR	BRALIRWA
CDM	Clean Development Mechanism
CMA	Capital Market Authority
CTL	Crystal Telecom
EAC	East African Community
ECM	Error Correction Model
EDPRS	Economic Development and Poverty Reduction Strategy
EQTY	Equity Bank Group Ltd.
FDI	Foreign Direct Investments
GDP	Gross Domestic Production
IMR	I&M Bank Rwanda
IPAR	Institute for Policy Analysis and Research
ISIC	International Standard Industry Classification
KCB	Kenya Commercial Bank
KPMG	Klynveld Peat Marwick Goerdeler
LM	Lagrange Multiplier
MINECOFIN	Ministry of Economics and Finance
MINICOM	Ministry of Commerce
MNCs	Multinational Corporations
MPTM	Monetary Policy Transmission Mechanism
NERPNET	Education Research and Policy Network

NGO	Nongovernmental Organizations
NISR	National Institute of Statistics of Rwanda
NLFS	National Labor Force Survey
NMG	National Media Group
OECD	Organization for Economic Cooperation and Development
OLS	Ordinary Least Squares
PCA	Principle Component Analysis
PPH	Postpartum Hemorrhaging
R&D	Research and Development
RRA	Rwanda Revenue Authority
RSE	Rwanda Stock Exchange
RSEL	Rwanda Stock Exchange Limited
SDG	Sustainable Development Goals
SDMEs	Soft Drink Manufacturing Enterprises
SEM	Structural Equation Model
SMEs	Small and Medium Enterprises
SPSS	Statistical Product and Service Solutions
SRM	Strategic Road Map
SSA	Sub-Saharan Africa
TFP	Total Factor Productivity
UHC	Universal Health Coverage
UNDP	United Nations Development Program
UNECA	UN Economic Commission for Africa
USL	Uchumi Supermarket Ltd
VAT	Value-added Tax
VECM	Vector Error Correction Model
VUP	Vision 2020 Umurenge Program
WHO	World Health Organization

List of Figures

Chapter 3

Fig. 1	Trends in African IPOs (2011–15). *Source* Africa Capital Markets Watch (2015)	46
Fig. 2	Graphical illustration of investments	49
Fig. 3	Graphical illustration of the number of shares	50
Fig. 4	Graphical illustration of turnover	50
Fig. 5	Graphical illustration of market capitalization	51

Chapter 5

Fig. 1	Population growth	85
Fig. 2	Real GDP	86
Fig. 3	Population growth rate	86
Fig. 4	Economic growth rate	87
Fig. 5	CUSUM	91
Fig. 6	CUSUM square	91

Chapter 6

Fig. 1	Number of firms according to size. *Source* Authors' computations using the World Bank Enterprise Surveys: Rwanda 2006	107
Fig. 2	Average number of employees as per firm size. *Source* Authors' computations using the World Bank Enterprise Surveys: Rwanda 2006	108
Fig. 3	Age of firms according to size. *Source* Authors' computations using the World Bank Enterprise Surveys: Rwanda 2006	108
Fig. 4	Capacity utilization of firms as per size. *Source* Authors' computations using the World Bank Enterprise Surveys: Rwanda 2006	109

Chapter 8

Fig. 1   An architectural structure of a distribution plant and several destination centers. *Source* Author's representation using SmartPLSSmartPLS 144

Chapter 9

Fig. 1   Income tax contributions by the telecommunication sector. *Source* RRA systems, income tax returns for the period 2010–17 152

Fig. 2   Income tax contributions by the mining sector. *Source* RRA systems, income tax returns for the period 2010–17 152

Fig. 3   Income tax contributions by the construction sector. *Source* RRA systems, income tax returns for the period 2010–17 153

Fig. 4   Income tax contributions by the banking sector. *Source* RRA systems, income tax returns for the period 2010–17 153

Fig. 5   Conceptual framework. *Source* Author's framework 158

Fig. 6   Histogram and density display of the residuals generated by the model. *Source* Authors' output 161

Chapter 13

Fig. 1   Conceptual framework of the study. *Source* Author's formulation (2019) 239

List of Tables

Chapter 2

Table 1	Pairwise correlations of the key variables in the study.	28
Table 2	Sample distribution by welfare categories and regions.	29
Table 3	Descriptive statistics and definitions of the variables used.	30
Table 4	One-sample T-test for the savings.	33
Table 5	Two-sample T-test with equal variance of savings by sex.	34
Table 6	Two-sample T-test with equal variance of savings by age group.	34
Table 7	The 2SLS regression estimates. Factors affecting savings among rural poor households.	35

Chapter 3

Table 1	Results of the vector autoregression estimates.	53

Chapter 4

Table 1	Stationary tests—the augmented Dickey–Fuller (ADF) unit root tests.	62
Table 2	Stationarity tests—the augmented Dickey–Fuller (ADF) unit root tests.	63
Table 3	ADF test on the residuals of the cointegrating model.	64
Table 4	Summary of correlation coefficients.	67
Table 5	Summary of the expected signs.	68
Table 6	Findings and prior signs.	69

Chapter 5

Table 1	Summary statistics.	87
Table 2	ADF units root test's results.	88
Table 3	ARDL bound test's results.	88

Table 4	ARDL long-run findings (GDP as the dependent variable)	89
Table 5	ARDL (2, 2, 2, 2, 2) short-run findings, ΔGDP as the dependent variable	89
Table 6	Diagnostic statistics test's results	91

Chapter 6

| Table 1 | Effects of innovation engagements on innovation output: a generalized Tobit regression | 110 |
| Table 2 | Effects of innovation output on financial performance: the two-stage least squares method | 111 |

Chapter 7

| Table 1 | Networks and addressing the existing growth challenges | 129 |
| Table 2 | List of abbreviations | 134 |

Chapter 8

Table 1	Units of blood shipped	145
Table 2	Distance covered	145
Table 3	Blood supply value	145
Table 4	Cost of the blood	145
Table 5	Demand for blood	146

Chapter 9

Table 1	Variance inflation factor values for each predictor coefficients	160
Table 2	Model summary on the determinants of profit shifting	161
Table 3	Significance of the model for determining profit shifting (ANOVA[a] Table)	162
Table 4	Determinants of profit shifting	162
Table 5	Transfer pricing factors and taxable income	163
Table 6	Anova test results	164
Table 7	Determinants of profit shifting	164

Chapter 10

Table 1	Effects of training and mentoring entrepreneurs on a business' sustainability all tables need to be mentioned in text	182
Table 2	Association between family involvement and sustainability	183
Table 3	Relationship between good family relationships and sustainability	183
Table 4	Relationship between financial resources and a business' sustainability	184
Table 5	Financial discipline and a business' sustainability	185

Table 6	Relationship between education level and a business' sustainability	186
Table 7	Relationship between innovations and a business' sustainability	186

Chapter 11

Table 1	Resource measurement	200
Table 2	Capabilities measurement	200
Table 3	Correlations for Resources and Capacities and the quality of the positioning strategy	201
Table 4	Resources and capacities and market performance	202
Table 5	Positioning strategy measurements	203
Table 6	Positioning strategy measurements (continued...)	204
Table 7	Positioning strategies and market performance measurement	205
Table 8	Positioning strategies and market performance measurement (continued...)	207
Table 9	Correlations between positioning strategies and market performance Correlations	210
Table 10	Positioning strategies and market performance	211

Chapter 12

Table 1	Determinants of capacity utilization of food manufacturing firms in Rwanda	225
Table 2	Determinants of capacity utilization of beverage manufacturing firms	228

Chapter 13

Table 1	Type of industry all tables need to be mentioned in text	241
Table 2	Respondents' views on understanding the tax laws in Rwanda	241
Table 3	Respondents' views on awareness about the tax incentives available in tax laws	242
Table 4	Distribution of respondents by tax incentives enjoyed by SMEs	242
Table 5	Level of SMEs' sales and profits	243
Table 6	Level of investments in SMEs' assets	243
Table 7	Model summary	244
Table 8	Estimated coefficients of the model	244

Chapter 1
Introduction and Overview

Gouranga G. Das and Rukundo Bosco Johnson

"At the heart of Rwanda's capital sits the Kigali Convention Centre, a $300m monument that lights up the night with the national colours of blue, yellow and green. It symbolizes modernity and prosperity in a country that has bounced back from a genocide in 1994 when perhaps 500,000 people, mostly Tutsis, were killed. As impressive as the skyline are Rwanda's economic statistics. In the past decade the economy has expanded by 8% a year. The share of people classified as poor has fallen by seven percentage points since 2011, to 38% in 2017," The Economist (August 17, 2019).

1 Background and Motivation

Problems in developing and less developed nations are so diverse and at the same time so unique that once we begin to look deep, the research becomes enormous in scope. The stated objectives of any nation—for climbing up the development ladder—are development, growth, employment creation, health and education, addressing climate change, improving the business climate for competing in global markets, and ultimately achieving a high standard of living for its citizens (see for example, Clark 2007; Lewis 1954, 1955; Rodrik 2005-to name a few).

In fact, this year's Nobel Memorial Prize in Economic Sciences (2019) awarded for "evidence-based" policymaking with field experiments is a ripe occasion to celebrate persistent efforts in researching economic development in Africa, Asia, and Southeast Asia. Despite methodological debates (Deaton and Cartwright 2018, Deaton 2019;

G. G. Das (✉)
Department of Economics, Hanyang University, Ansan-Si, Gyeonggi-do, Korea (Republic of)
e-mail: dasgouranga@gmail.com

R. B. Johnson
Department of Economics, School of Economics, University of Rwanda, Kigali, Rwanda
e-mail: rukujohn@yahoo.com

© Springer Nature Singapore Pte Ltd. 2020
G. G. Das and R. B. Johnson (eds.), *Rwandan Economy at the Crossroads of Development*, Frontiers in African Business Research,
https://doi.org/10.1007/978-981-15-5046-1_1

Reddy 2013), one thing that comes out from this award is the preponderant role of "development economics research" as a field for understanding specific problems in different countries, the impediments that inhibit the growth of the "poor" economies, and the necessity of deriving policy dialogues for fixing "the nuts and bolts" of anti-development traps via strategies and visions for growth and prosperity (Bardhan 2019; Duflo 2017; Lin and Monga 2011; Heshmati et al. 2015). However, the concept of development is broad and overarching with multiple objectives going beyond growth measured by national income indicators (Basu 2001; OECD 2018; Rodrik 2008; Sen 1988; Stiglitz 1998). Identifying "growth miracles" or "growth debacles" and analyzing the root causes either for success and/or failure are important for drawing valuable lessons for policymakers. This book—in the context of Rwanda—is an honest attempt toward that end.

An analysis of the economy and policy recommendations emanating from empirical and theoretical research either following a top-down or a bottom-up approach provides important insights for future course of action for policymakers. Emphasis on sustained economic growth and development, and the factors inhibiting or facilitating economic growth have gained traction in voluminous literature (Acemoglu and Robinson 2012; Aghion and Howitt 2009; Barro 1997; Barro and Sala-i-Martin 2004; Clark 2007; Das 2012; Galor 2012; Islam 1995; Nayyar 2013, 2019; Rodrik 2005). All these studies signify that although there are overlapping factors such as the role of the state, institutions, geography; disease traps and skill scarcity, state failure and macroeconomic stability, and access to the market and globalization through trade and investment are crucial for bridging empirics with history and that there is no "unifying framework" that fits the narrative of each individual country. In other words, what is true in the Asian context is not parallel in connection to the African experience, and there are also intra-African heterogeneities in explaining each episode of development (Hickey et al. 2019; Nayyar 2013; Rodrik 2008; Tausch and Heshmati 2012). Literature has volumes of studies focusing on the Africa growth and development experience. The general themes evolve around the ideas of the roles of the government and governance, entrepreneurship, financial openness, openness, and human capital (health and education) (AfDB 2017, 2019; Bhattacharyya 2009, Binns et al. 2012, Chitonge 2014; Collier 2007, 2009; Das and Drine 2020; Drine et al. 2013; Fofack 2014; Fosu 2012, 2015; Heshmati 2017; Okonjo-Iwela 2014; World Bank 2011; Young 2005; among others).

The focus of the literature is on aspects such as the business environment or ease of doing business; determinants of growth and impediments to growth and development; lack of good quality institutions; developing firms' capabilities via entrepreneurship; lack of entrepreneurial capabilities and industrialization policy; management challenges confronted by African firms; the impediments in connecting with global business networks; reaping technological benefits, structural diversification with shared prosperity (often dubbed as inclusive growth); and appropriate technology and barriers to its adoption (Das 2015; Das and Drine 2020; Ndulu et al. 2008; Ramirez-Pacillias et al. 2017; Robson and Lury 2011; Stiglitz and Lin 2013; Stiglitz et al. 2013; UNECA 2013). The themes that emanate from these strands of research are broad and applicable to a wide range of countries in Africa. For example,

Collier (2007) states some "agendas" such as stopping conflict; overcoming the natural resource trap; removing the impasse via reforms; changes in trade and aid policies; and focusing on strategies and prioritizing "goals". As Okonjo-Iwela (2014) states in the context of Nigeria, "the great challenges present great opportunities, and that the chance to reposition an economy can be a springboard for steadier, more diversified long-term growth"; this is valid for Rwanda as well as also for economic reforms in Africa.

However, explaining the phenomenon of great divergence and convergence (or catching up) globally or regionally in Asia, Africa, or Latin America requires a wealth of information at the micro-level in a specific country. Although the voluminous literature has enriched our understanding of the African context, country-specific studies dealing with these issues in the context of a particular country require more probing for improving the business climate, institutional improvements, and the resultant performance of an economy. The overarching research questions in the African context are: Why do some countries produce more output per capita than the others? Why some countries remain laggards, what undergird their low-level performances, and what needs to be done to improve this? The quest for explanations to these ever-lasting research questions helps us explore different facets following a no "one-size-fits-all" approach. This is where the contribution of this book lies as it discusses a host of factors in the context of Rwanda "deemed the African region's economic miracle" (Nweze 2018, p. 2).

Before embarking discussion on the focus of this volume, let us consider the strategy for economic development undertaken by the Government of Rwanda to drive home the significance of the thematic issues. As documented in the country's Economic Development and Poverty Reduction Strategy 3 (EDPRS3) for Vision 2050 and the strategic roadmap and the National Strategy for Transformation (NSTI) achieving economic development is built on three pillars—economic transformation, social transformation, and transformational governance—for addressing important issues such as industrial transformation, job creation, and employment generation over the period 2017–2024 and beyond till 2050 in the long term. NSTI covers the SDGs' targets, African Union Agenda 2063 and its implementation for first 10-year plan (2014–23) for a globally integrated Africa with peace and prosperity, and the East African Community (EAC) Vision 2050. Specific objectives under these three pillars include poverty reduction for inclusive growth, export promotion, developing a knowledge-based economy, infrastructure development, promoting service sector-led growth, healthy population for a better quality workforce, better institutions for transparency and accountability, job creation, and employment growth.

The first pillar, economic transformation, aims at inclusive growth and development with the participation of the private sector based on knowledge and natural capital. The pillar for social transformation includes developing a skilled, educated, and healthy Rwandan workforce for stable living standards and prosperity with poverty eradication. The governance pillar's purpose is creating a conducive institutional framework with a sound base of justice, cooperation, regional cooperation, transparency, and accountability for strengthening foreign policy and partnerships between the government, the private sector, NGOs, and the people. Identifying local conditions and country-specific features, such as human capital, population, self-reliance, public policy, regulations, and regional integration of the economies of the countries in sub-Saharan Africa and Eastern and Southern Africa, is important for considering broad-based development beyond traditional measures (Fofack 2014; Fosu 2013, 2015; Hickey et al. 2019; Johnson 2016). Identifying policy syndromes and addressing these are necessary but the same lessons from the "role models" such as Ghana, Botswana, or our case—Rwanda—cannot be exported and applied off-the-shelf in general (Aryeetey et al. 2012; Fosu 2015; Rodrik 2008). As Lavers (2016) analyzed, the Vision 2020 Umurenge program (VUP) has been a "key part of the development strategy that aims to promote social stability and the legitimacy of the ruling coalition through rapid socioeconomic development." Its aim is addressing the crisis due to distributional problems (high inequality and incidence of poverty) and achieving stability for economic development.

With the African continent being at the heart of the discussion for its "emerging" image in development via structural transformation, the narratives on Rwanda—a country with cycles of ups and downs in the history of its gradual transformation after the genocide in 1994—is a legitimate and topical one as can be seen in the quote at the beginning of this chapter. Growth in Rwanda has been attributed to liberalization in the agricultural sector (tea and coffee), an export boom, improved productivity via an investment boost, good performance of the mining and construction sectors, and tourism. Due to reforms and last several years' development in the financial and business sectors, Rwanda was successful in improving its rank in the "Doing Business Report" to 45 in 2017 from 148 in 2012, with the third rank in the "Index of Economic Freedom." With a decline in the poverty rate (from 59% in 2000 to 39% by 2014 and Gini index to 0.43 in 2017 from a high 0.52 in 2006) and achievements on other fronts, the objective of reaching a high-middle-income status by 2035 needs more concerted efforts and development strategies for regaining the momentum via resource mobilization, boosting domestic savings, skill formation, and productive investments (Pritchett et al. 2017). According to the World Bank (2011) "While public investments will continue to support the growth over the medium-term, Rwanda needs to strengthen its nascent private sector to stay on a high growth trajectory in the long-run."[1]

Policy reforms and good governance facilitated the structural diversification of the Rwandan economy along with job creation, with benefits spilling over to social impacts such as reduction in poverty and inequalities. The Rwandan economy is projected to grow at a rate of 8% in 2020, up from 7.8% in 2019, while real GDP growth, thanks to services growth (4.1%) and growth in the manufacturing and industry sectors (1.5%) moved up to 6.1% in 2017.[2] The "Made in Rwanda" policy along with other reforms was instrumental in achieving this. On the demand side, household consumption and investments were prime drivers with 5.8% and 2.9% of GDP, respectively (AEO 2019).[3]

---

[1] https://www.worldbank.org/en/news/press-release/2019/06/25/rwanda-economic-update.
[2] https://www.afdb.org/en/countries/east-africa/rwanda/rwanda-economic-outlook.
[3] https://www.afdb.org/en/countries/east-africa/rwanda/rwanda-economic-outlook.

This growth was "broad-based" and contributed by agriculture, services, construction, and manufacturing sectors resulting in a structural transformation in the country (The World Bank 2019).[4] Ggombe and Newfarmer (2017) attribute this sweeping growth since the genocide and civil war devastated the economy to multitude of factors such as the government's effective policy interventions for a structural transformation, foreign investments, export growth, developing "industries without smokestacks," a coherent policy framework, and international policy coordination to support such growth. In fact, for sustained growth, the country needs to engage itself in global value chains in agriculture, mining, and manufacturing. As Frazer and Van Biesebroeck (2019) show, there are differences across small and large exporting firms in terms of product diversification, market penetration, and direction of exports as well as its composition.

As Rwanda envisages an annual two-digit growth and is targeting to be a middle-income economy by 2035, and achieving a high-income status by 2050, there is a need to invest more in research-based development aspects that will render sustainable growth. This is important as it can help alleviate many of the persistent challenges observed across sub-Saharan Africa. No doubt, this is a challenging and fertile area as the focus areas of this volume have gained much traction in current literature, and several recent studies have addressed a wide array of topics related to industrialization in Africa and the role of macroeconomic and microeconomic reforms. More than 70% of the Rwandan population's main activity is agriculture which has been growing at 5.5% annually in recent years. However, the country is turning toward industry and services with huge investments in infrastructure to enhance growth and social welfare. Investments are expected to contribute significantly to increasing productivity and competitiveness; diversified tourism; business and financial services; information and technology; innovations; and construction, extractive industries, and processing industries.

These thematic orientations listed above are assumed to drive studies and research undertakings that will inform policymakers about the key trends for growth. Hence, this book is a timely and relevant study of the aspects of Rwandan economy's development and the underlying drivers that could shape the evolution of its economy, polity, and society. It is also pertinent to consider the Government of Rwanda's Strategic Road Map (SRM) for economic development. In other words, given the plans and roadmap adopted by the Republic of Rwanda, we need to investigate the implications of these agendas, identify the "pillars" of success, and highlight the policies that need to be formulated for effective implementation of high-profile objectives. This book adds value by organizing research studies which investigate key hindrances and offer policy insights into the necessary steps that can be taken to address these impediments to growth. This volume is also rich because as the section plans show it covers both micro-level and macro-level analyses. Given that the world economy is facing problems of macroeconomic adjustments, conflicts, trade wars, and rise of protectionism, the current economic scenario in developing and least-developed economies is not so promising in an interconnected world. Thus, "global"

---

[4] https://www.worldbank.org/en/news/press-release/2019/06/25/rwanda-economic-update.

and "national, local, or regional" problems and policy dimensions are crucial. This book—taking Rwanda as a case—is important in the context of the African continent which is undergoing structural changes. The book will inform the public and policymakers about the various development aspects which the country has put at the forefront of its development strategy.

It is worthwhile to note that this volume represents a cornucopia of research studies coming out of an international conference entitled "4th International Conference on Eastern Africa Business and Economic Watch (4th EABEW—2019)" on the theme "Inclusive Growth and Sustainable Socio-Economic Transformation." It was held during June 12–14, 2019 at the College of Business and Economics, University of Rwanda. The essays comprise contributions on various microeconomic and macroeconomic policy angles that are crucial for a less developed economy to embark on a road to recovery to converge with the desired trajectory. The topics encompass a broad range of issues like the role of savings, capital formation, human capital, innovations, entrepreneurship, profit shifting by multinational corporations (MNCs), small and medium enterprises (SMEs), and firms' strategies for achieving sustained and balanced growth (Achtenhagen and Brundin 2016). It has a collection of 12 empirical studies that have an overall focus on macroeconomic policies such as savings among the rural poor; sustained investments in and development of capital markets; role of entrepreneurial sustainability; role of innovations for firms' performance; healthcare reforms; the benefits of technology, policy incentives such as tax benefits for promoting growth, and strategic considerations such as marketing or positioning strategies; export strategies; and productivity enhancement via processing and profit sharing. It has contributions by 11 authors. The studies aim at increasing our knowledge about the microeconomic and macroeconomic factors that influence well-being via investments in better technologies and innovations favoring productivity, firm performance, and their positive externalities in the manufacturing, hi-technology, food, nutrition, and health sectors.

2 Overview and Summary of the Studies

We now present a summary of the contributions in this book. The volume includes this introductory chapter and 12 other chapters contributed by 11 authors. The chapters are thematically arranged under three categories. This collection of 12 selected empirical studies enhances our understanding of the constraints on development that Rwanda is facing, how these obstacles can be overcome, and the need for a policy framework. This will help in informing debates on addressing persistent problems and their alleviation via policies such as nudging behaviors for boosting savings; capital formation; developing capital markets; promoting entrepreneurial abilities and growth of SMEs; and firms' positioning strategies, business networks, and the role of foreign firms. As the studies are inter-related, they provide a comprehensive account of the state of the economy and some of the most challenging issues that could obstruct Rwanda's pursuit of its development agenda. Being complementary in nature, the discussions in the book provide a broad canvas with wide strokes exploring the determinants of development, entrepreneurship, growth of business, job creation, family business, SMEs growth, etc. and their roles, finding causal effects, and policy implications. Given the wide-ranging coverage involving top-down and bottom-up approaches and strategies for development, the book offers insights for policy interventions necessary for Rwanda's gradual transitioning from agriculture to an industrial transformation via manufacturing and service-led development without smokestack industries.

The chapters are organized under three major themes depending on the commonality of areas that they cover: (I) *Macroeconomic Constraints: Monetary Policy, Investments, and Population*; (II) *Firms' Performance, SMEs, and Role of Entrepreneurship*; and (III) *Entrepreneurship and Business Performance: Strategies and Policies*.

The volume includes three essays related to problems of savings, sustainable investments via the capital market, and the role of monetary policy for economic growth in Rwanda. One study explores the role of population growth as a source of productivity growth via human as well as financial development while another study explores the role of innovations in firms' performance in the manufacturing sector in Rwanda which finds that quality upgradation via product and process innovations is crucial for domestic as well as global performance. Two chapters investigate the role of networks for developing SMEs in the country and their applications in important healthcare services for rural welfare in Rwanda. Another chapter highlights the role of multinational companies in an open economy context. It shows that often transfer-pricing arrangements entail profit shifting, and hence counteract with national strategies for developmental objectives. This chapter calls for regulations through laws or legislations to prioritize national goals for economic development. Two articles consider tax incentives for productivity and growth of particular SMEs in rural Rwanda. Their findings confirm that tax incentives affect sustainable growth via development of SMEs in some rural districts and evidence exists in the case of the food and beverage processing sectors, and for 4,900 SMEs in the agricultural, industrial, and service sectors.

Two articles discuss the role of "positioning strategies" on manufacturing enterprises' market performance and explore the underlying factors shaping sustainability of entrepreneurs especially in the domain of family businesses.

This volume will inform public policymakers, academicians, the public sector, and the Rwandan population about the key areas for growth and development through the extensive research carried out in Rwanda. As Rwanda envisages an annual two-digit growth and is targeting a middle-income economy status by 2035 and a high-income status by 2050, there is need to invest more in research-based developmental aspects that will render sustainable growth.

The aim of the studies included in the first part of this volume is increasing our understanding of the factors that influence savings, capital formation, and monetary policy for influencing the policies for investments with a focus on households. The studies in the second part cover aspects of firms' performance and innovations via entrepreneurship. These studies also explore the role of networks and synergies with technology such as the use of drones in the healthcare sector. The third section focuses on business performance and the role of entrepreneurship for firms' success and positioning. It also analyzes tax incentives and their effects. In summary, the volume focuses on several key factors underlying the Rwandan economy's prospects of development. In what follows, we summarize the content and contributions of individual chapters.

2.1 Part I: Macroeconomic Constraints: Monetary Policy, Investments, and Population

This part comprises four chapters which, inter alia, address some of the major macroeconomic constraints facing Rwanda. Learning from the fundamentals of Keynesian macroeconomics and the micro-foundations of a consumption, this part provides rationale for considering the macroeconomic factors underlying economic transformation of a nation. The trade-off between consumption and savings is a problem that households face. Also, following the Solovian paradigm and other neoclassical theories of economic growth and development, we know that investments (physical capital formation) are essential for a country's growth.

Chapter 2 considers this important theoretical perspective in the context of rural poor households in Rwanda using data from the 5th round of the Household Living Survey. The results show positive effects of savings. However, an important unconventional finding of this chapter is that as opposed to income and wealth, consumption is correlated positively with savings, which leads to important policy recommendations because this pertains to socioeconomic development inducing income and saving behavior among poor households. This chapter is insightful as it addresses rural poverty alleviation as consumption and savings are two sides of the same coin—income and wealth.

In a similar vein but in the macroeconomic context, Chap. 3 discusses the importance of developing capital markets which are supported by both public and private sectors for accelerating growth via sustainable investments in Rwanda. This is an econometric study using simulations via the impulse-response function to prove that developing the capital markets is necessary for long-run sustained growth in Rwanda. The next Chap. 4 brings an important dimension to the analysis by considering the role of monetary transmission mechanisms which are important channels where nominal and real interest changes (via the Fisher effect) affect investments for growth in Rwanda. Using a sophisticated econometric technique and a cointegration analysis for a dataset of 15 years, this chapter shows that the monetary and exchange rate policy is crucial for economic growth. This is quite pertinent for the central bank's interest rate policy and for financial development-led growth in Rwanda.

On a different note, Chap. 5 adds value to existing knowledge by discussing demographic changes and trends in Rwanda. By analyzing a 40-year-long dataset it explores the role of population dynamics in economic development via capital formation. The findings are important for policies pertaining to human, physical, and financial capital development. Needless to say, economic growth cannot happen without these underlying dynamics as the population forms the backbone of a country and considering its welfare is policymakers' main concern. In brief, these four chapters call for paying greater attention to socioeconomic development via policies and projects for influencing savings behavior, incentives to invest, development of financial capital, manipulating monetary policy for inducing financial development, and the interaction between real side (population dynamics) and financial development for promoting growth.

2.2   Part II: Firms' Performance, SMEs, and Role of Entrepreneurship

This part has contributions related to micro-aspects like firms' performance, role of entrepreneurial capabilities, and development of SMEs. The study in Chap. 6 is a valuable addition to the area of firms' innovations and performance both domestically and for international competitiveness for becoming an engine of growth. It is also important as far as the national innovation systems and strategies are concerned because public policy should embrace these for generating jobs, employment, and also for industrialization. Using the World Bank's data, the authors find that product and process innovations are important for product sophistication and for launching new products. Interestingly, from a trade policy perspective the study finds that foreign technology licensing via technology transfers is crucial for upgrading quality and recognizing financial success. This is significant from the perspective of a trade and industrial policy nexus for growth of the Rwandan economy via product complexity and diversification. However, this is not an isolated phenomenon because it is related to developing business networks and their impact on SMEs' growth, especially in employment creation and inclusive growth.

Chapter 7 adds to our knowledge by considering these two aspects. Taking existing literature in the context of the experience of developed and emerging engines of growth, this chapter finds that developing networks facilitate SMEs' growth in a complementary way as networks promote syncretism by bringing all players together. The study follows a case study approach and underscores the importance of policies promoting business networks through an improved business climate to address growth challenges facing SMEs, which, in turn, could lead Rwanda to a higher level of development.

In Chap. 8, we find an important value addition for applications of network services in the context of healthcare services through the state-of-the-art "drone" technology. This has important policy implications for human capital formation via developing technology-aided healthcare facilities in rural Rwanda. It offers an analytical optimization model (transportation model using integer linear programming) that such a technology could enormously benefit human capital formation via a reduction in maternal mortality rates through the transshipment of blood at low costs. This chapter has tremendous value in terms of the healthcare policy linked to a "new" technology via innovations.

Chapter 9 adds another dimension to the book by considering development in the context of multinational companies in Rwanda. As is evident in international trade literature, transfer pricing is one of the avenues that MNCs use for avoiding taxes in the host economy. Considering 72 MNEs and using quantitative research with the agency and accounting theories, the authors find a positive correlation between intra-group transactions, and a negative relationship between such transactions and taxable incomes along with finance costs. This chapter advocates putting in place a policy for controlling such practices by enacting laws or legislations for such practices in Rwanda. This is important from the perspective of policies promoting inward-bound FDI and its impact on industrial development via domestic industries as well as for the objectives of national development. In sum, the chapters in this part of the book analyze factors such as innovations; developing business networks; growth of SMEs and the challenges that they face; using modern technologies for effective networks for rendering quality healthcare services; and regulations for transfer-pricing practices by foreign multinationals.

These two sections' contributions encompass a variety of key issues and they also identify a number of challenges and their possible implications for addressing these issues via policy interventions. This brings us to the final section, which has studies on entrepreneurship strategies, case studies of business performance, and government's tax incentives.

2.3 *Part III:* **Entrepreneurship and Business Performance: Strategies and Policies**

This concluding section is a collection of four chapters. The first, Chap. 10, provides an interesting case study of entrepreneurship sustainability of Rwanda's family businesses. In particular, it considers the case of small and medium family businesses under SMEs (4,900 SMEs). Given that most of the businesses in Rwanda are family-owned, this is important from the perspective of family and household welfare. Its findings are that a business' sustainability depends on innovations, management, and training of family members, mentorship, financial discipline, and conducive familial relationships. However, its most important finding is that education's role as an explanatory factor in business sustainability is much less important than was expected although factors such as innovations, good family structures, training and mentorship via management, and financial prudency are crucial determinants. This offers important insights for policies pertaining to education and mechanisms for policy action to transform education into good practices for effectiveness.

Chapter 11 takes soft drink manufacturing enterprises (SDMEs) as a case study to highlight the role that positioning strategies play. This is a novel approach which uses the typology of the positioning strategy in the context of two industrial enterprises. Variations in their performance are attributed to product quality, customization, cultural symbols, prices, and environmental changes. The study recommends that in keeping with the roadmap for achieving the ambitious goal of achieving middle-income status by 2050, these SDMEs need to revamp themselves for developing capabilities for addressing these challenges and augmenting their financial positions. This is important for other nascent or developing SMEs as well. Hence, this chapter adds to existing knowledge.

Chapter 12 considers similar aspects in the context of the food and beverage processing sectors but extends in another valuable direction by incorporating the role of tax incentives for productivity in these sectors. The policy recommendations are that non-tax measures are more important for capacity utilization and productivity, and hence boosting these sectors. In other words, for these sectors to develop it is necessary to generate sufficient demand, and on the supply side, it is important to provide raw materials, develop specialized technologies, provide tax incentives, and working capital. This is important as these sectors generate jobs and employment as they are linked to tourism and other services.

The concluding Chap. 13 carries the previous chapter's value addition in the case of SMEs in the district of Nyarugenge. Its findings reinforce the findings that tax incentives do play a positive role in SMEs' growth. However, different forms of tax incentives such as VAT refunds, compensating for wear and tear, and losses are crucial for designing tax-incentive policies and fiscal measures for promoting growth based on SMEs. This is an important insight not only for the district in which the study is based but it could be further analyzed and replicated in other districts across regions, which will help in exploring other factors underlying such problems. In a nutshell, this section offers valuable policy insights about the development of SMEs, family businesses via public support such as tax benefits or incentives and adopting positioning strategies for marketability and supporting adequate demand.

3 Epilogue

This book is comprehensive and wide ranging and is an up-to-date account of the Rwandan economy which is facing challenges despite being a star performer among African nations. Often, it has been dubbed as an "economic miracle" in the region (Nweze 2018). This book's value addition is that it analyzes several dimensions both at the micro- and macro-levels and offers policy implications which can be strategized to sustain this miracle.

For industrialization in Africa, "industries without smokestacks" (that is, agri-businesses, agricultural supply chains, tourism, ICT-based services, and logistics and infrastructure) are emergent industries. Developing firms' capabilities with heterogeneities, learning effects, and scale economies are an important part of the industrial policy with novel disruptive technologies with small adoption cycles with fast adoption lags. Innovations and the spread and adoption of the Internet and digital technology have overwhelming ripple effects across any economy and the world in terms of connectivity, organizing socioeconomic activities, trade networks, data and information flows, and even in shaping identities. The emergence of organically evolved functionalities is crucial for expanding capabilities. In many developing nations, the state often lacks the capability to implement human development policies and sustained improvements in performance by spreading digital benefits which depend on a host of factors like investments in education and training; this research explores these aspects in the African context.

The *policy recommendations* of this edited volume and from extant literature include the following:

(i) *Savings and capital markets*: encouraging socioeconomic development policies and strategies for enhancing a balance between savings and consumption are necessary, especially for rural households. To that end, for raising investment rates, public and private support is necessary for boosting investment-led growth. Monetary policy is an important instrument because it affects interest rates and also GDP via foreign capital flows through the exchange rate (Chaps. 2, 3 and 4).

(ii) *Human capital and population*: population growth is not necessarily detrimental to growth and development (Chap. 5). In fact, it affects financial development and results in economic progress. This is in line with Michael Kremer's historical account (1993) or the anti-Malthusian perspective that population growth could bring about technological changes and have a positive impact on the economy if it is properly managed.[5]

(iii) *Innovations and productivity at the micro-level* (Chap. 6): innovations are a prime driver of industrial diversification and growth. Product as well as process innovations feed on one another leading to new products and product sophistication and quality-ladder effects on products, inputs, and intermediates resulting in improvements in total factor productivity (TFP) at the firm level thanks to heterogeneities in technology as well as skill differences. A study by Atlas of Economic Complexity 2015–2016 shows that Rwanda mainly exports travel and tourism (28.72%), ICT (22.13%), and gold (19.3%).[6] However, tea, coffee, and tin comprised 80% of the exports. High transportation costs and limited knowledge for diversifying production were "key constraints" for this structural diversification (Hausmann and Chauvin 2015).

(iv) *Entrepreneurial capabilities and positioning strategies for sustainable business*: level of education as well as innovations and the involvement of family

---

[5] Michael Kremer is one of the three recipients of the Nobel Memorial Prize in Economic Sciences in 2019.

[6] https://atlas.cid.harvard.edu/explore?country=187&product=undefined&year=2017&productClass-HS&target=Product&partner=undefined&startYear=undefined.

members in the management, training, financial discipline, and leadership are crucial for family businesses to be successful and for achieving entrepreneurship sustainability. Not only this, but also positioning strategies at the corporate and business levels are crucial for success in market competition, performance, facing environmental challenges, addressing customers' needs, and improving product quality thus creating jobs and employment for skilled professionals to be absorbed in the workforce (Chaps. 10 and 11).

(v) *Entrepreneurship, tax incentives, and SMEs as growth engines* (Chaps. 7, 12 and 13): growth of SMEs and development of business networks are important for their contribution to economic progress, expanding capabilities, and job creation. These work in a complementary fashion to facilitate SMEs, employment creation, and sustained growth. Apart from this, the government's tax incentives (and some non-tax measures) are crucial for boosting SMEs, their capacity utilization, and diversification. Sustainable growth depends on a host of factors including innovations, environmental challenges, positioning strategies, health and skill formation of human capital, productive investments, and policy designs encompassing tax incentives and regulations controlling multinationals' transfer-pricing motives.

(vi) *FDI for firms' performance*: openness to trade and FDI is necessary for external competition as a strong inducement for domestic firms to become more resilient and efficient. However, multinational companies' transfer-pricing or profit-shifting motives need to be regulated by enacting laws or legislations via the Rwanda Revenue Authority (RRA). Thus, internal or local policies as well as external factors need to be balanced for domestic development (Chap. 9).

(vii) *Technology for Broad-based effects such as health and well-being*: for developing human capital and supporting population-led growth for a better quality workforce, it is imperative to develop good healthcare services. Investments in and development of sophisticated technologies such as the drone technology or even robotics are important for optimizing healthcare benefits via cost reduction and efficiency enhancements. Although this book shows the benefits of drone application in the case of blood delivery, this could be replicated in the context of other countries and services aimed at sustainable development via shared prosperity (Chap. 8).

This book brings issues of concerns that need to be addressed despite success stories in Rwanda to the limelight. There are concerns about "measuring" the indicators such as poverty rate, inflation, and other national account statistics (The Economist 2019). There are also concerns about fiscal and monetary policies as well as stabilization programs addressing adequate savings, investments, and the monetary policy for long-term developmental goals.

However, as a "starter" this book could be a case study or a "role model" which the laggard African economies could emulate. In this sense, this book makes an important contribution for policymakers, advanced undergraduate students doing seminar courses and projects, and for academic researchers. Further, NGOs and their practitioners and policymakers in charge of formulating development planning and growth strategies will find the book a useful background study. This book could also enrich readers in terms of "general" lessons derived from development theory and practice irrespective of Africa's geographical boundaries. In other words, drawing lessons from African case studies, especially Rwanda, the knowledge accrued could be valuable for backward or underdeveloped economies in Latin America, Middle East, and South and Southeast Asia because their contexts might be different, but they share some commonalities in terms of "development issues and growth challenges" undermining their efforts. Quite pertinently, as mentioned in Sect. 1, as the current Nobel Memorial Prize in Economic Sciences is awarded for "evidence-based policymaking" in development economics, the importance of such an analysis is even more significant.

Although no field experiments are reported in this volume the case studies are good surveys in this regard. For orchestrating all these, the Rwandan government which is at the helm of policymaking needs to create a policy space with greater coordination and come up with policies for sustained growth via investments in productive sectors. Expertise in designing taxes and monetary and industrial policies is also needed. As has been discussed in Rusuhuzwa (2012), leadership is an important component in a long list of doable things and "although Rwanda still has challenges in its economic development due essentially to structural problems, the country has achieved very good results and has built a solid foundation for its development in the long term." Although it is a small, landlocked nation with scarcity of resources and belongs to the bottom billion (Collier 2007), Rwanda's strong growth in the last few years shows its potential to launch a truly dynamic agenda for inclusive and sustained prosperity. Quoting Adam Smith (1755): "Little else is requisite to carry a state to the highest degree of opulence from the lowest barbarism, but peace, easy taxes, and a tolerable administration of justice; all the rest being brought about by the natural course of things. All governments which thwart this natural course, which force things into another channel, or which endeavor to arrest the progress of society at a particular point, are unnatural, and to support themselves are obliged to be oppressive and tyrannical." This book is a step toward stimulating an informed debate in this direction.

References

Acemoglu, D., & Robinson, J. (2012). *Why nations fail*. USA: Crown Business.
Achtenhagen, L., & Brundin, E. (Eds.). (2016). *Entrepreneurship and SME management across Africa: Context, challenges, cases*. Singapore: Springer.
Aghion, P., & Howitt, P. (2009). *The economics of growth*. Cambridge, MA: MIT Press.
AfDB. (2017). *Africa economic outlook 2017: Entrepreneurship and industrialization*. Abidjan: African Development Bank Group.
AfDB (2019). Africa economic outlook 2019. Macroeconomic performance and prospects. Jobs, growth, and firm dynamism.
Barro, R. J. (1997). *Determinants of growth: A cross country empirical study*. Cambridge MA: MIT Press.

Barro, R. J., & Sala-i-Martin, X. (2004). *Economic growth* (2nd ed.). Cambridge MA: MIT Press.

Bardhan, P. (November 4, 2019). Development economics after the Nobel Prize. Retrieved November 5, 2019, from https://www.3quarksdaily.com/3quarksdaily/2019/11/development-economics-after-the-nobel-prize.html.

Basu, K. (2001). On the goals of development. In G. Meier & J. Stiglitz (Eds.), *Frontiers of development economics: The future in perspective*. Washington, DC: The World Bank.

Bhattacharyya, S. (2009). Root causes of African under development. *Journal of African Economies, 18*(5), 745–780.

Binns, T., Dixon, A., & Nel, E. (2012). *Africa: Diversity and development*. London: Routledge.

Clark, G. (2007). *A farewell to alms: A brief economic history of the world*. Princeton and Oxford: Princeton University Press.

Chitonge, H. (2014). *Economic growth and development in Africa: Understanding trends and prospects*. London: Routledge.

Collier, P. (2007). *The bottom billion: Why the poorest countries are failing and what can be done about it*. New York, USA: Oxford University Press.

Collier, P. (2009). *Wars, guns, and votes: Democracy in dangerous places*. New York, USA: Harper Collins.

Das, G. G. (2012) Globalization, socio-institutional factors and North-South knowledge diffusion: Role of India and China as southern growth progenitors. *Technological Forecasting and Social Change, Elsevier, 79*(4), 620–637.

Das, G. G. (2015). Why some countries are slow in acquiring new technologies? A model of trade-led diffusion and absorption. *Journal of Policy Modeling, 37*(1), 65–91.

Das, G. G., & Drine, I. (forthcoming, 2020). Distance from the technology frontier: How could Africa catch-up via socio-institutional factors and human capital? *Technological Forecasting and Social Change. Elsevier, 150*. https://doi.org/10.1016/j.techfore.2019.119755.

Deaton, A., & Cartwright, N. (2018). Understanding and misunderstanding randomized controlled trials. *Social Science and Medicine, 210*, 2–21.

Deaton, A. (2019). Randomization in the tropics revisited: A theme and eleven variations. In Forthcoming in F. Bédécarrats, I. Guérin, & R. François (Eds.), *Randomized controlled trials in the field of development: A critical perspective* (pp. 1–25). Oxford University Press. https://scholar.princeton.edu/sites/default/files/deaton/files/deaton_randomization_revisited_v2_2019_01.pdf.

Drine, I., Nabi, M. S., & Aissa, M. S. B. (2013). Financial openness and technology catch-up: Empirical evidence from the mediterranean basin. *Review of Market Integration, 5*(1), 43–69. https://doi.org/10.1177/0974929213496503.

Duflo, E. (2017). The economist as plumber. Richard T. Ely Lecture. *American Economic Review, B.107*(5), 1–26.

Fofack, H. (2014). The idea of economic development: Views from Africa. WIDER working paper 2014/093.

Fosu, A. K. (2012). The African economic growth record, and the roles of policy syndromes and governance. In A. Noman, K. Botchwey, H. Stein, & J. Stiglitz (Eds.), *Good growth and governance in Africa: Rethinking development strategies*. Oxford: Oxford University Press.

Fosu, A. (2013). Country role models for development success: The Ghana case. In A. Fosu (Ed.), *Achieving development success. Strategies and lessons from the developing world* (pp. 265–283). UK: Oxford University Press.

Fosu, A. K. (2015). Growth and institutions in African development. In K. Augustin (Ed.), *Growth and institutions in African development* (Chapter 1, pp. 1–17). New York: Routledge Studies in Development Economics.

Frazer, G., & Van Biesebroeck, J. (2019). The extent of engagement in global value chains by firms in Rwanda (English). Policy Research working paper; no. WPS 8979. Washington, DC: The World Bank Group. http://documents.worldbank.org/curated/en/617871565698066427/The-Extent-of-Engagement-in-Global-Value-Chains-by-Firms-in-Rwanda.

Galor, O. (2012). *Unified growth theory*. NJ, USA: Princeton University Press.

Ggombe, K., & Newfarmer, R. (2017). Rwanda: From devastation to services-first transformation. WIDER working paper 2017/84. Helsinki: UNU-WIDER.

Hausmann, R., & Chauvin, J. (2015). Moving to the adjacent possible: Discovering paths for export diversification in Rwanda. http://www.tinyurl.com/y5xbtsp7.

Heshmati, A. (Ed.). (2017). *Studies on economic development and growth in selected African countries*. Singapore: Springer.

Heshmati, A., Maasoumi, E., & Wan, G. (Eds.). (2015). *Poverty reduction policies and practices in developing Asia*. Singapore: Springer.

Hickey, S., Lavers, T., Seekings, J., & Niño-Zarazúa, M. (2019). *The politics of social protection in Eastern and Southern Africa*. UK: Oxford University Press.

Islam, N. (1995). Growth empirics: A panel data approach. *The Quarterly Journal of Economics, 110*(4), 1127–1170.

Johnson, O. E. G. (2016). *Economic diversification and growth in Africa: Critical policy making issues*. London: Palgrave Macmillan.

Lavers, T. (2016). Understanding elite commitment to social protection. Rwanda's Vision 2020 Umurenge Programme. UNU-WIDER working paper 2016/093. Forthcoming in Hickey et al. (eds.) 2019 See above.

Lewis, A. (1954). Economic development with an unlimited supply of labour. *The Manchester School, 22,* 139–191.

Lewis, A. (1955). *Theory of economic growth*. Milton Park: Routledge.

Lin, J., & Monga, C. (2011). Growth identification and facilitation: The role of the state in the dynamics of structural change. *Development Policy Review, 29*(3), 264–290.

Nayyar, D. (2013). *Catch up: Developing countries in the world economy*. Oxford: Oxford University Press.

Nayyar, D. (2019). *Resurgent Asia: Diversity in development*. United Kingdom: Oxford University Press.

Nweze, C. (August 2018). The unprecedented economic growth and development of Rwanda. Policy Brief. Institute for Politics and Society. Retrieved November 7, 2019, from www.politikaspolecnost.cz.

Ndulu, B. J., O'Connell, S. A., Bates, R. H., Collier, P., & Soludo, C. C. (Eds.). (2008). *Political economy of growth in Africa, 1960–2000*. Cambridge: Cambridge University Press.

OECD. (2018). *Beyond GDP: Measuring what counts for economic and social performance*. Paris: OECD.

Okonjo-Iwela, N. (2014). *Reforming the unreformable. Lessons from Nigeria*. MA, Cambridge, USA: MIT Press.

Pritchett, L., Sen, K., & Werker, E. (2017). *Deals and development: The political dynamics of growth episodes*. Oxford: Oxford University Press.

Ramirez-Pacillias, M., Brundin, E., & Markowska, M. (2017). *Contextualizing entrepreneurship in emerging economies and developing countries*. London: Edward Elgar.

Reddy, S. G. (2013). Randomise this! On poor economics. *Review of Agrarian Studies, 2*(2). http://www.ras.org.in/randomise_this_on_poor_economics.

Robson, P., & Lury, D. A. (2011). *The economies of Africa*. London: Routledge.

Rodrik, D. (2005). Growth strategies. *Handbook of Economic Growth, 1*(1), 967–1014.

Rodrik, D. (2008). *One economics, many recipes: Globalization, institutions and economic growth*. Princeton: Princeton University Press.

Rusuhwza, T. K. (2012). Rwanda: Leadership for economic growth and development. In E. Aryeetey, S. Devarajan, R. Kanbur, & L. Kasekende (Eds.), (2012). *The Oxford companion to the economics of Africa*. New York, USA: Oxford University Press.

Sen, A. (1988). The concept of development. In H. Chenery, & T. N. Srinivasan (Eds.), *Handbook of development economics* (Vol. 1). North Holland: Elsevier.

Smith, A. (1755). Lecture in 1755, quoted in Dugald Stewart, Account of the life and writings of Adam Smith LLD, Section IV, 25.

Stiglitz, J. (1998). An agenda for development in the twenty-first century. In B. Pleskovic & J. E. Stiglitz (Eds.), *Annual World Bank Conference on Development Economics 1997*. Washington, D.C.: The World Bank.

Stiglitz, J., & Lin, J. (Eds.). (2013). *The industrial policy revolution I: The role of government beyond ideology*. Palgrave Macmillan: New York.

Stiglitz, J., Lin, J., Monga, C., & Patel, E. (2013). Industrial policy in the African context. Policy research working paper 6633. Washington, DC: The World Bank.

Tausch, A., & Heshmati, A. (2012). *Globalization, the human condition and sustainable development in the 21st century: Cross-national perspectives and European implications*. London: Anthem Press.

The Economist (August 17, 2019). The devil in the details. https://www.economist.com/middle-east-and-africa/2019/08/15/has-rwanda-been-fiddling-its-numbers.

UN Economic Commission for Africa (UNECA). (2013). *Making the most of Africa's commodities: Industrializing for growth, jobs and economic transformation*. Addis Ababa: UNECA.

World Bank (2011). *Improving the odds of achieving the MDGs: Heterogeneity, gaps and challenges. Global monitoring report 2011*. Washington, DC: World Bank.

Young, A. (2005). The gift of the dying: The tragedy of AIDS and the welfare of future African generation. *Quarterly Journal of Economics, CXX, 2,* 423–466.

Part I
Macroeconomic Constraints: Monetary Policy, Investment, and Population

Chapter 2
An Analysis of Savings Among Rural Poor Households in Rwanda

Aristide Maniriho, Edouard Musabanganji, and Philippe Lebailly

Abstract A household's savings are considered a primary source of investments which drive economic growth and development. This study identifies the determinants of private savings among poor rural households in Rwanda. It uses data from the 5th round of the Integrated Household Living Conditions surveys conducted in Rwanda every 4 years. It specifies a simultaneous equations model and does the estimations using the 2SLS method to account for missing variables and a possible correlation between some covariates and the error term, which is complemented with a T-test and correlation analysis. The results of the T-test show that savings among poor rural households are significantly positive. The econometric estimates show that in contrast with existing literature, income and all other forms of wealth are factors which do not influence the savings of poor rural households, while consumption is positively correlated with savings. We recommend that socioeconomic development programs, projects, and policies that aim at improving income and consumption levels thus affecting savings among poor rural households should be enhanced.

Keywords Household's savings · Investments · Rural poor · Economic growth · Economic development · Rwanda

JEL Classification Codes D14 · E41 · O12 · R20

1 Introduction

Due to the absence of efficient credit and insurance markets, household savings are a crucial determinant of welfare in developing countries. Without savings, households have only a few other mechanisms to smooth out unexpected variations in their

---

A. Maniriho (✉) · P. Lebailly
Unity of Economics and Rural Development, Gembloux Agro-Bio Tech, University of Liège, Liège, Belgium
e-mail: Aristide.Maniriho@uliege.be; manirihoaristide1@gmail.com

A. Maniriho · E. Musabanganji
School of Economics, University of Rwanda, KK 737 Kigali, Rwanda

© Springer Nature Singapore Pte Ltd. 2020
G. G. Das and R. B. Johnson (eds.), *Rwandan Economy at the Crossroads of Development*, Frontiers in African Business Research,
https://doi.org/10.1007/978-981-15-5046-1_2

incomes, and so shocks may leave permanent scars such as interrupting the process of human capital accumulation at the early stages (Attanasio and Székely 2000). For long, the issue raised by scholars related to whether the poor can save. Karlan et al. (2014) proved that poor individuals and households save or invest using either formal or informal instruments that are highly risky, not cost-effective, and with a low range of functions.

Private savings among households influence economic development and lead to improvements in welfare in developed as well as developing economies since they have a significant effect on the circular flow of income in the economy (Kasongo and Ocran 2017; Karlan et al. 2014). Households make good profits from their savings (Brata 1999; Obayelu 2012) which enable them to hedge against unpredictable events; provide access to productive and valuable assets; help them avail of funds for their investments; enable retired people to afford goods and services; permit people to afford decent homes and accommodation; and improve their loan repayment abilities, school fees, and healthcare payments (Kasongo and Ocran 2017; Karlan et al. 2014). Melese and Ejigu (2016) highlight that savings make people financially independent even when they stop working. Western countries have strong economic growth and development as a result of increasing investment rates, which are significantly influenced by high private saving rates. A high rate of investments is therefore considered the primary effect of increasing private savings (Ciftcioglu and Begovic 2010). Parallel to the increase in savings in Europe, savings rates have also doubled in East Asia, but stagnated in sub-Saharan Africa, Latin America, and the Caribbean countries (Loayza et al. 2000a, b). Lack of appropriate financial sectors in most African countries serves as a salient spur for individuals to save and ultimately turn these savings into loans for borrowers (Kelly and Mavrotas 2008).

At the microeconomic level, savings produce a significant lever effect on economic development through the provision of investment funds in developing nations given that investments and economic growth positively but significantly depend on savings levels (Attanasio and Banks 2001). However, diverse drawbacks including low and indecent revenues and limited access to finance remain sources of poor savings in sub-Saharan African (SSA) countries (Chowa et al. 2012). Obayelu (2012) adds that households' low capacity to save is directly linked to the low rates and sustainability levels of capital formation, as well as the economic performance of poor nations. Hence, it is very important for policymakers to account for individual and households' savings or savings accounts as all these provide opportunities for most people to gain increasing access to financial services (Consultative Group to Assist the Poor 2010).

The factors that influence households' decisions to opt for savings provide evidence for policymakers to come up with appropriate strategies to promote private savings and boost domestic investments in the country (Muradoglu and Taskin 1996). Policymakers and researchers' interest in savings and assets is motivated by their importance for consumers, producers, entrepreneurs, financial institutions, government institutions, and the economy as a whole. For individuals, financial stability alongside their life spans is intrinsically influenced by both their income and their access to productive and valuable assets. Since savings and assets are kept permanently by economic agents while incomes fluctuate over time, the former are considered economically more important than the latter (Chowa et al. 2012). Households with limited access to productive assets in sub-Saharan Africa face serious and sudden economic events and/or environmental catastrophes and consequently their life conditions are adversely affected in the long run (Hoddinott 2006). The accumulative returns from these productive and valuable assets increase long-term consumption and thus improve the welfare of household members since they enable them to survive in hard periods and surmount emergency situations (Chowa et al. 2012).

Individual savings along with salient financial plans are considered an important factor for sustaining consumption and resilience to income deficits and this results in poverty reduction, especially in the long run (Collins et al. 2009; Dupas and Robinson 2013; Hulme et al. 2015; Rutherford and Arora 2009). Savings play a catalyst for growth in economic growth and development through capital formation; this has been underlined in literature (Shawa 2016) because savings, either domestic or foreign, are among the primary drivers of investments (Harjes and Ricci 2005). These authors report that investment funds using external sources can be an important factor for internal investments in the form of foreign direct investments. In contrast, a country can build its long-term economic development not only on foreign investment sources but also on internal funding sources, mainly households' savings.

Knowing that a household is a basic economic entity in economic development (Larionova et al. 2014), and savings are the main influential factor of investments and economic growth (McKinnon 1973; Shaw 1973), the Government of Rwanda recently put in place diverse initiatives to boost savings in the country such as the national savings mobilization strategy), the Umurenge Saving and Credit Cooperative (Umurenge SACCO) program that is a grassroots savings scheme, the Umwalimu SACCO program launched in 2008, the Zigama Credit and Savings Society (Zigama CSS) created in 1997, and the Rwanda Stock Market which started in 2011.

There are very few studies on the determinants of savings in Rwanda and most of them focus on macroeconomic aspects (see, for example, Iragena 2015 and Murindahabi 2010) because of which documentation of household savings is still very rare. This study uses household level data to identify the factors driving private savings in Rwanda with special focus on the rural poor. This is important because literature can comply with a specific situation, or cannot comply with it, or can apply it in a different way. The results of this study enable a comparison of existing literature with Rwanda's context. Whereas previous studies use the age and the education level of the household head, this study also considers the ratio of household members who have completed different levels of education as well as the ratio of household members in different age groups.

This study identified the factors determining the savings of poor households using EICV5 data. The two-stage least squares (2SLS) method was used for estimating an instrumental variables (IV) regression model to account for endogeneity and simultaneity bias. The results show where more efforts are needed to promote private savings among poor households to enhance rural socioeconomic development and for improving the welfare conditions of the poor households. The most influential factors of private savings among rural poor households are farm income, the rent paid, access to other formal forms of savings, and the bank balance which have a positive effect; shares of household members with secondary and higher education levels have a negative effect. After this introduction, the paper does a literature review. This is followed by a discussion of the Materials and methods used, the results of the study and a discussion. The last section gives the conclusion and policy implications of the study's findings.

2 Literature Review

Savings have played a primary role in economic analyses so far. Keynes (1936) defined it as the part of income that is not allocated to consumption during the period it is produced. According to Attanasio and Rohwedder (2003), "Saving is measured as the residual between disposable household income and total household expenditure" which means that it is obtained by subtracting consumption from income. A household's decision to save is influenced by both economic (wealth, consumption expenditure, insurance, labor force participation, and income) and demographic (home ownership, household size or dependents, age, gender, social status, geographical location, and income sources) factors (Tandoh 2016).

The earlier theory of savings maintains that there is a positive relationship between savings and investments. It is also important to note that higher savings result in higher investments, and higher investments induce higher economic growth (Odhiambo 2009), which implies that savings are the cornerstone of the development process (McKinnon 1973) particularly in developing countries that have excess demand for loanable funds, which is the main barrier to investments (Shaw 1973). This implies that investments and economic growth increase with an increase in savings and ultimately all this comes back to an increase in savings. In such a way, economic growth keeps on increasing as the savings go on increasing, until the equilibrium between savings and investments is achieved. According to Odhiambo (2009), a sustained increase in investments as a result of an increase in savings leads to a higher economic growth rate.

A macroeconomic analysis indicates that savings and investments are two primary sustainable factors contributing to economic growth related to its microeconomic roots of keeping prices stable and promoting job creation (Mishra et al. 2010). Savings are also considered a main source of capital supply for investments. This implies that the relationship between income and savings is recognized as the root in economic theory. Aryeetey (2004) differentiated the various forms of household savings, namely, physical assets (land, stored harvest) and financial assets including cash, which is more liquid than all the other assets. According to Zeller (1994) and Zeller et al. (1997), savings in the form of cash may be mainly kept as physical cash, interest bearing assets, and cash in a current or savings account in a bank. This study considers households in a similar way.

Different theoretical and empirical economic analyses describe the determinants of savings. Keynes (1936) defined savings as excess income over consumption, that is, the income that is not spent in the right period is gained. This implies that income is a primary determinant of both consumption and income. Keynes also explained the reasons why people prefer cash or opt for savings, or transaction motives, precautionary motives, and speculative motives. Davidson (2000) highlights the way in which savers may choose to use saved income between the products of industry and savings, and consequently allocate savings among alternative assets (i.e., stores of value).

The same way as Keynes (1936) identified absolute disposable income as the main factor of savings, Friedman (1957) and Modigliani and Miller (1963) identified additional variables that affect households' savings: permanent income, transitory income, and human and non-human wealth. Modigliani (1944) pointed out that the real income and interest rate are the main determinants of savings. To these factors, Schultz (2005) added that household size and/or the number of dependents also influence the level of household savings. He said, "smaller family sizes might be expected to boost parent savings rates out of lifetime income and increase the demands of parents for public and private pensions."

Different researchers have empirically analyzed the factors affecting household savings. Beverly and Sherraden (1999) focused on institutional drivers that can stimulate savings; they pointed out that the income level, financial education, saving incentives, and saving facilitation were the primary influential factors that determined household savings. Crossley et al. (2012) extended this list and added tax and a household's benefit policy. For Athukorala and Sen (2004), the real remuneration rates on deposits in banks and the rate of the level of disposable income positively and significantly affected savings rates.

In his macroeconomic analysis, Gupta (1970) found that the marginal propensity to consume was positively influenced by an increase in per capita income. He added that an increasing concentration of income among rural households resulted in greater aggregate household savings.

Analyzing socioeconomic factors, Lusardi (2007) showed that household savings were positively affected by education levels and income status of the household, while marital status and the race group affected a household's savings negatively. Kibet et al. (2009) found that household savings were influenced by the main livelihood activity, income, age, and sex of the household head; the level of education; the number of dependents; a household's service expenditure; transport charges; and access to finance.

Among the researchers who concentrate on a microeconomic analysis, Swasdpeera and Pandey (2012) assessed the connection of the life cycle hypothesis and neoclassical theories of saving with real life. They found that a drop in the dependency ratio was linked to increasing private savings rates, which means that the households that reduced the number of children during the working age increased their savings. They support neoclassical scholars and underline that households with more children will increase their savings when their children leave home. Hence, they maintained that the high dependency ratio was negatively related to household savings. They show from their research finding that both the level and the rate of growth of a household's disposable income were among the main influential drivers of a household's saving behavior. Some recent studies have shown that the impact magnitude of the real deposit rate on savings is significantly positive even though it was very low (Athukorala and Tsai 2003).

Household savings are also determined by housing capital gains (Engelhardt 1996), household income (Ahmad and Asghar 2004; Gedela 2012; Kraay 2000; Syed et al. 2017), and demographic factors like gender, age, education, household size, and the number of dependents (Ahmad and Asghar 2004; Rha et al. 2006; Seguino and Floro 2003; Syed et al. 2017). Rha et al. (2006) reported that household savings were positively predicted by expectations from savings, planned household expenditure, saving rules, a household's access to financial and real assets, a household's perceptions about savings, household income, expected future income, expected interest rate, and a household's behavior toward a risk. This was negatively explained by age, education, marital status, and consumer loans that a household had. Seguino and Floro (2003) analyzed the relationship between gender and savings and showed that an increase in women's relative and real incomes made the gross domestic saving rate increase. At the level of individual factors, Rurangwa et al. (2018) reported that marital status, the number of members in a household, education level of the household head, the size of cultivated land, extensionist assistance, distance to coffee washing stations, and a producer's perceptions affected the saving decisions of small-scale coffee growers positively, while age, saving experience, farming experience, and a farmer's awareness affected it negatively. These researchers showed that farmers' experience of saving, the size of the cultivated land, the distance from home to coffee washing stations, and the farmers' perceptions were the only significant determinants of small-scale coffee growers.

Kibet et al. (2009) found that among low-income individuals in rural areas, households with low incomes saved mainly as precautionary measure, meaning that the savings deferred from consumption expenditure, and this scarcely served as a source of investment funds. Another finding from the study of Kibet et al. (2009) is that the barriers to credit encouraged people to save, whereas easy access to finance led to low savings and thus a low investment growth rate especially in the short run.

Gedela (2012) identified the influential factors in saving decisions in rural areas and found that a household's savings increased with an increase in the age of the household head but declined as the household head grew older. He adds that the high dependency ratio or the number of household members negatively affected a household's savings and stated that income influenced a household's saving decisions significantly. Keeping in mind that rural areas are dominated by farmers especially in developing countries, Meier zu Selhausen and Musinguzi (2011) point out that famers' savings are negatively limited by their low incomes because they have too little revenue that does not enable them to save part of it. This supports Athukorala and Sen's (2001) finding that there was a positive relationship between a household's saving growth rate and the level of disposable income.

Dirschmid and Glatzer (2004) focused their analysis on the role of financial incentives in enhancing household savings. They report that high interest rates stimulated households to limit their consumption today and thus save more for future consumption, which contrasts with the lasting mindset that only high-income earners are the winners in the future.

3 Data and Methods

3.1 Sources of Data

This study uses the EICV5 cross-section survey data collected during a period of 12 months from October 2016 to October 2017 using a random cross-section sample of 14,580 households, 2,526 from rural area and 12,054 from the urban area sampled from 245 villages and 1,015 villages. This is a nationwide survey covering rural and urban areas of the whole country. It contains 10 cycles to account for seasonality of household revenues and expenditure. Even though data was collected at the household level, the survey enabled the aggregation of key indicators at the provincial and district levels. Part of EICV5's purpose was collecting the required statistics to enable an assessment of the anti-poverty initiatives taken by the Government of Rwanda (NISR 2018). The pairwise correlations of the variables and sample distribution by welfare categories and by regions are described in Tables 1 and 2.

3.2 Model Formulation and Definitions of the Study's Variables

The model used in this study is backed by existing literature describing the potential factors that can influence household savings. Since it is not always possible for an OLS estimator to give consistent coefficients, the most common approach is using the instrumental variables (IV) model (Angrist and Pischke 2009; Cameron and Trivedi 2005, 2010; Gujarati 2009; Wooldridge 2013), a simultaneous equations model is specified as follows:

$$Y_{1i} = \alpha_0 + \sum \alpha_{ki} X_{ki} + \varepsilon_{1i} \qquad (1)$$

$$X_{yi} = \phi_0 + \sum \phi_{\ell i} X_{\ell i} + v_{1i} \qquad (2)$$

where Y_{1i} is the saving of household i, X_{ki} the vector of the predictors of the saving, X_{yi} is the agricultural income of the household i, $X_{\ell i}$ the vector of the predictors of the household's agricultural income, α_i and $\phi_{\ell i}$, are the constants, while ε_1 and v_1 are the error terms. The study's variables are defined in Table 3.

Table 1 Pairwise correlations of the key variables in the study

Variables	(1)	(2)	(3)	(4)	(5)	(6)	(7)	(8)	(9)	(10)
(1) Savings	1									
(2) Farm income	0.02	1								
	0.61									
(3) Salary	−0.02	−0.02	1							
	0.59	0.56								
(4) Age	−0.03	0.04	−0.05	1						
	0.4	0.26	0.13							
(5) HH size	0.12	0.13	0.14	0.1	1					
	0	0	0	0						
(6) Loan	0.52	0.07	−0.04	−0.07	0.19	1				
	0	0.04	0.25	0.03	0					
(7) Balance	0.49	0.004	−0.02	0	0.11	0.33	1			
	0	0.9	0.56	0.99	0	0				
(8) Remittances	0.03	0.03	−0.002	0.1	0.1	0.07	0.04	1		
	0.4	0.36	0.96	0	0	0.03	0.17			
(9) Rent	0.16	0.02	0.04	−0.004	0.17	0.17	0.12	0.15	1	
	0	0.47	0.23	0.89	0	0	0	0		
(10) Consumption	0.18	0.17	0.1	0.09	0.74	0.21	0.19	0.12	0.22	1
	0	0	0	0.01	0	0	0	0	0	

Source Authors' calculations

Table 2 Sample distribution by welfare categories and regions

Region	Welfare categories		
	Severely poor	Moderately poor	Total
Southern rural	110	248	358
Western rural	119	207	326
Northern rural	65	145	210
Eastern rural	40	93	133
Total	334	693	1027

Source Authors' calculations

3.2.1 Method of Data Analysis

Traditional Keynesian models imply that consumption and savings depend on the level of current income (see Keynes 1936). Tandoh (2016) specifies that household savings are influenced by economic and demographic characteristics. On the other hand, household income depends on production, which in turn depends on a combination of different inputs. If production is used as a proxy for income, this is explained by the quantity and quality of inputs combined by the households, that is, from human activities for creating goods and services or wealth through input combinations (see Dieden 2004, 2005 for example). In this study, household income is one of the predictors of household savings, while income is determined by the factors that influence production (that is, land size, livestock, consolidation, and crops maize and potatoes). There may be some missing variables in the model's specifications, or some covariates that are correlated with the error term (Wooldridge 2013). This situation justifies the use of an instrumental variables (IV) model instead of a linear regression (Gujarati 2009; Wooldridge 2013) for estimating the specified Models (1) and (2) and to account for endogeneity. It is important to note that the econometric estimates include robust standard errors to deal with the common issue of heteroskedasticity in cross-sectional data (Wooldridge 2013). The Durbin–Wu–Hausman specification test (Durbin 1954; Wu 1973; Hausman 1978) showed that the IV-2SLS estimates were systematically different from those of OLS (Chi2 = 334.92; Prob > Chi2 = 0.00), which is the reason why the former model was preferred. But for the sake of comparison, we used both 2SLS and OLS estimators to estimate the specified model (see Table 7).

Besides the econometric approach, we also used a T-test, a parametric approach, to test for the significance of the savings (whether it was statistically different from zero). A one-sample t-statistic was computed using Eq. (3) (see results in Table 5):

$$t = \frac{M - M_0}{SE} \quad (3)$$

Table 3 Descriptive statistics and definitions of the variables used

Variable	Obs	Mean	Std. Dev.	Min	Max	Definition
Savings	1080	6755.45	14089.55	0	180,000	Total amount of money deposited in the account in the last 12 months
Balance	1080	6238.85	26082.51	0	421,000	Total amount of money held by household members in their savings accounts in Rwandan francs
Age	1080	47.47	12.745	22	92	Age of the household head in years
Sex	1080	0.21	0.408	0	1	Sex of the household head (equals 1 if female, and 0 otherwise)
Household size	1080	5.72	1.856	1	14	Number of the household members
Ratio less 6	1080	0.17	0.16	0	0.667	Ratio of household members aged less than 6 years
Ratio btn 7 ~ 18	1080	0.37	0.197	0	0.833	Ratio of household members aged between 7 and 18 years
Ratio btn 19 ~ 60	1080	0.41	0.163	0	1	Ratio of household members aged between 19 and 60 years
Ratio more 60	1080	0.05	0.122	0	1	Ratio of household members aged more than 60 years
Share no education	1080	0.34	0.23	0	1	Ratio of HH members with no formal education

(continued)

Table 3 (continued)

Variable	Obs	Mean	Std. Dev.	Min	Max	Definition
Share primary	1080	0.59	0.225	0	1	Ratio of HH members who have completed primary education
Share secondary	1080	0.01	0.045	0	0.4	Ratio of HH members who have completed secondary education
Share higher	1080	0.06	0.113	0	0.667	Ratio of HH members who have completed higher education
Share other	1080	0.001	0.013	0	0.2	Ratio of HH members who have completed other levels of education (technical and professional training)
Marital status	1080	0.95	0.224	0	1	Marital status of the household head (equals 1 if married)
Land size	1080	42.99	115.323	0.02	2715.31	Land surface held by the household in acres
Land tenure	1080	0.69	0.459	0	1	Land ownership (equals 1 if the household owns a certificate of for least one land plot, 0 otherwise)
Consolidation	1078	0.32	0.465	0	1	Land consolidation (equals 1 if some of the land plots are consolidated, 0 otherwise)
Occupancy	1080	0.95	0.222	0	1	House ownership (equals 1 if the owner is occupying the house, 0 otherwise)

(continued)

Table 3 (continued)

Variable	Obs	Mean	Std. Dev.	Min	Max	Definition
Rent	1061	3166.19	2304.086	300	30,000	Estimated monthly rent paid in Rwandan francs
Remittances	1080	6327.64	18199.24	0	291,000	Remittances received in 12 months in Rwandan francs
Consumption	1027	747,000	299,000	77,982	2,150,000	Annual consumption expenditure in Rwandan francs
Poverty	1080	1.66	0.47	1	2	Welfare category (1 = severely poor, 2 = moderately poor)
Salary	1080	49396.43	50452.61	0	884,000	Monthly salary of the household in Rwandan francs
Livestock	1080	3.26	3.53	0	32	Number of animals owned by the household
Loan	1080	63080.04	165,000	100	2,550,000	Current amount of loans in Rwandan francs owed by a household
Other income	1080	49943.23	160,000	0	3,450,000	Other income of a household in Rwandan francs
Farm income	1080	2831.25	13149.03	0	200,000	Annual agricultural income in Rwandan francs

Source Authors' calculations

where M is the mean, M_0 is the comparison value (M_0 is zero in this case), and SE is the standard error ($SE = \frac{S}{\sqrt{n}}$, S = standard deviation, and n the sample size).

The t-statistic was also used for comparing savings between male and female groups (Table 6) as well as between age groups (youth and elderly) (Table 7). This t was computed using Eq. 4:

$$t = \frac{M_1 - M_2}{\frac{S_1}{\sqrt{n_1}} + \frac{S_2}{\sqrt{n_2}}} \tag{4}$$

where $(M_1 - M_2)$ is the difference between the means of the two groups (sex group and age group), S_1 and n_1 are the standard deviations and the size of one group, respectively, S_2 and n_2 are the standard deviations and the size of another group, respectively.

4 Results

4.1 Level of Savings Among Rural Poor Households

We tested the significance of the savings of rural poor households. The results of the one-sample T-test (formula 3) show that the average saving was 6,755 Rwandan francs with $t = 15.16$ and a P-value of 0.00, which implies that it is positive and statistically different from zero. The detailed output of this test is summarized in Table 4.

A comparison of savings between female- and male-headed poor households
Average savings were compared between male-headed and female-headed households. The results of the independent samples' T-test (formula 4) show that the mean for male-headed households was 6,976 Rwandan francs while that for female-headed households was 5,925 Rwandan francs with a difference of 1,050 Rwandan francs with $t = 0.99$ and a P-value $= 0.32$. This implies that this difference is not significantly different from zero. The results are described in Table 5.

A comparison of savings between youth- and older headed poor households
This study compared the mean savings between the youth- and the older headed households (Table 6). The results of the T-test (formula 4) show that the average savings were 7,017 and 5,657 Rwandan francs for the youth- and older headed households, respectively. The difference was 1359.89 and the P-value was 0.21. This implies that the mean savings were statistically the same for the two groups.

Table 4 One-sample T-test for the savings

Variable	Obs	Mean	Std. err.	Std. dev.	[95% conf. interval]	
Savings	1,080	6,755.45	428.73	14,089.55	5,914.21	7,596.89
Mean = mean (savings)				$t = 15.16$		
Ho: mean = 0				Degrees of freedom = 1079		
Ha: mean < 0		Ha: mean ≠ 0			Ha: mean > 0	
Pr $(T < t) = 1.00$		Pr $(|T| < |t|) = 0.00$			Pr $(T > t) = 0.00$	

Source Authors' estimations

Table 5 Two-sample T-test with equal variance of savings by sex

Group	Obs	Mean	Std. err.	Std. dev.	[95% conf. interval]	
Male (0)	853	6,976.28	503.48	14,704.6	5,988.08	7,964.48
Female (1)	227	5,925.65	761.85	11,478.4	4,424.41	7,426.88
Combined	1,080	6,755.45	428.73	14,089.55	5,914.21	7,596.69
Diff.		1,050.63	1,052.26		−1,014.07	3,115.34
Diff. = mean (0) − mean (1)				$t = 0.99$		
Ho: Diff. = 0				Degrees of freedom = 1078		
Ha: Diff. < 0		Ha: Diff. ≠ 0			Ha: Diff. > 0	
Pr $(T < t) = 0.84$		Pr $(|T| > |t|) = 0.32$			Pr $(T > t) = 0.16$	

Source Authors' estimations

Table 6 Two-sample T-test with equal variance of savings by age group

Group	Obs	Mean	Std. err.	Std. dev.	[95% conf. interval]	
Elder (0)	872	7017.36	496.91	14673.67	6042.07	7992.64
Youth (1)	208	5657.47	782.25	11281.81	4115.26	7199.67
Combined	1080	6755.45	428.73	14089.55	5914.21	7596.67
Diff.		1359.891				
Diff. = mean (0) − mean (1)				$t = 1.25$		
Ho: Diff. = 0				Degrees of freedom = 1078		
Ha: Diff. < 0		Ha: Diff. ≠ 0			Ha: Diff. > 0	
Pr $(T < t) = 0.89$		Pr $(|T| > |t|) = 0.21$			Pr $(T > t) = 0.11$	

Source Authors' estimations

4.2 Determinants of Savings Among Rural Poor Households

We estimated the IV-2SLS model to identify the determinants of savings among rural poor households (Table 7). The results show that the sex (being female) of the household head, education level, the ratio of household members aged between 19 and 60 years, the current amount in the bank account, access to formal forms of savings, the rent paid, the loan amount, and consumption positively influenced savings. The factors which had a significant positive effect were sex, account balance, access to other savings, rent paid and consumption; the other factors with a positive influence were age, education level of the household head, share of household members with no formal education, share of household members with secondary education, and the share of household members with other levels of education (vocational and professional training). On the other hand, the results reported no factors with significant but negative influence on the savings of rural poor households.

Table 7 The 2SLS regression estimates. Factors affecting savings among rural poor households

Saving	Coef.	St. err.	t-val.	p-val.	[95% conf. interval]		Sig
Farm income	−0.05	0.16	−0.29	0.77	−0.36	0.27	
Age	3.63	36.56	0.10	0.92	−68.03	75.29	
Sex	1769.59	1055.52	1.68	0.09	−299.18	3838.36	*
Education	1193.230	967.94	1.23	0.22	−703.89	3090.36	
Marital status	−12.55	1142.82	−0.01	0.99	−2252.44	2227.34	
Household size	−208.91	350.29	−0.60	0.55	−895.46	477.64	
Ratio less 6	−4599.59	5664.62	−0.81	0.42	−15700.00	6502.86	
Ratio btn 7–18	−2998.45	3980.59	−0.75	0.45	−10800.00	4803.37	
Ratio btn 19–60	2636.92	5001.77	0.53	0.59	−7166.37	12440.21	
Ratio more 60	0.00						
Share no education	6262.33	4574.01	1.37	0.17	−2702.56	15227.23	
Share secondary	3018.39	10115.43	0.30	0.77	−16800.00	22844.27	
Share higher education	−4794.00	3667.89	−1.31	0.19	−12000.00	2394.93	
Share other education	−23800.0	25409.63	−0.94	0.35	−73600.00	26042.15	
Balance	0.18	0.04	5.04	0.00	0.11	0.25	***
Savings other	2439.28	1031.84	2.36	0.02	416.91	4461.65	**
Occupancy	−2715.88	1830.79	−1.48	0.14	−6304.18	872.42	
Salary	−0.003	0.01	−0.49	0.63	−0.02	0.01	
Other income	0.00	0.002	−0.18	0.86	−0.005	0.004	
Rent	0.34	0.17	1.97	0.05	0.002	0.68	**
Loan	0.03	0.01	3.27	0.001	0.01	0.05	***
Remittances	−0.03	0.02	−1.60	0.11	−0.06	0.01	
Consumption	0.01	0.002	2.53	0.01	0.001	0.01	**
Southern province	0.00						
Western province	2717.74	938.37	2.90	0.004	878.57	4556.91	***
Northern province	1524.92	895.92	1.70	0.09	−231.06	3280.89	*

(continued)

Table 7 (continued)

Eastern province	759.07	886.47	0.86	0.39	−978.38	2496.53
Constant	−1274.03	5980.90	−0.21	0.83	−13000.00	10448.32
Mean dependent var	6823.73			SD dependent var		14359.38
R-squared	0.42			Number of obs		1012
Chi-square	128.84			Prob > chi2		0.00

Note *** $p < 0.01$, ** $p < 0.05$, and * $p < 0.1$ Farm income was instrumented with land size, land tenure, land use consolidation, livestock labor, chemical fertilizers, organic fertilizers, pesticides, traditional seeds, improved seeds, irrigation (use of water), bean (1 = yes), coffee (1 = yes), maize (1 = yes), potatoes (1 = yes), rice (1 = yes), soybean (1 = yes), and wheat (1 = yes). The variables "Ratio more 60" and "Southern province" were removed because of collinearity

As farm income has been instrumented, the most influential instruments were land tenure and access to loans. The other instruments had a positive effect on farm incomes but were not statistically significant (land size and land consolidation).

5 Discussion

The results of the one-sample T-test show that the mean savings among rural poor households were statistically different from zero. This follows the efforts of the Government of Rwanda to pull citizens out of poverty and promoting savings. These results are similar to study of Karlan et al. (2014) that the poor can and do save no matter the efforts and the costs involved.

A comparison of mean savings between male-headed and female-headed households (Table 5) and between the youth- and the older headed households (Table 6) shows that there was no significant difference between the mean savings for the two group pairs that were compared. The lack of difference in mean savings between male- and female-headed households on the one hand, and between youth- and older headed households on the other hand contrasts Tandoh's (2016) findings that gender and age are among the primary factors that influence private savings. This could imply that the socioeconomic development programs and savings promotion schemes benefit youth and older household head categories equally.

The econometric (IV-2SLS) estimates (Table 7) identified the most influential factors of private savings among rural poor households. The results show that the most influential determinants of savings for the rural poor in Rwanda were sex, account balance, loan amount, rent paid, and consumption.

Farm incomes and all other forms of income were not among the significant drivers of private savings, while consumption was among the significant drivers of savings for the rural poor in Rwanda. This supports existing literature which states that consumption is among the key indicators of wealth among households in the context of developing countries (Dercon et al. 2009; Islam and Maitra 2012).

The current situation in Rwanda shows the positive effects of diverse anti-poverty programs initiated by the Government of Rwanda. One example is VUP public works that provide money to the poor, which is spent on consumption or for savings as contributions to savings groups (Murphy-McGreevey et al. 2017). These authors suggest that the VUP public works scheme should be expanded to include non-poor households for it to provide more valuable contributions to socioeconomic development. The rent paid by a household positively impacts its savings. This implies that a household that rents a house is also willing to own one. This could be due to the culture and mindset of Rwandans that possessing one's own house is a sign of security, stability, and nobility.

Access to other formal forms of savings is another factor that positively and significantly influences a household's savings. This is in line with Kelly and Mavrotas' (2008) findings that a well-organized financial sector encourages individual savings in most African economies. In the Rwandan context, this is a result of developing the financial sector, mainly the recent proliferation of microfinance institutions and Umurenge SACCOs (AFR 2017), which have enabled different categories of people to access finance including smallholder poor farmers.

The education level of the household head positively but not significantly influenced a household's savings. This is in line with most previous research (Ahmad and Asghar 2004; Lusardi 2007; Kibet et al. 2009; Syed et al. 2017). However, the share of household members with secondary and higher education levels had a negative influence on rural poor households' savings. Consumption expenditure affected a household's savings positively and significantly, which supports previous literature that consumption is among the key indicators of wealth among households in the context of developing countries (Dercon et al. 2009; Islam and Maitra 2012). Besides, the results of the correlational analysis (Table 1) show that savings were positively correlated with household size, the amount of loan taken, the balance in the account, and the rent paid.

6 Conclusion and Policy Implications

This study analyzed the factors affecting savings among rural poor households. Economic theory states that income is a primary driver of savings. We tested whether this relationship between income and savings is also valid in Rwanda's context. We specified a simultaneous equations model and applied a 2SLS estimator to estimate the coefficients. For the sake of comparison, the OLS option was also used to estimate the model.

The econometric estimates showed that in contrast with existing literature, income (like all other forms of wealth) was not among the primary factors pushing households to save. The most influential factors that stimulated rural poor people to save were the sex of the household head, balance in the account, rent paid, loan amount, and consumption (these with positive effects), while no factors with negative and significant influence on savings were reported.

Based on these findings we recommend that socioeconomic development programs, projects, and/or policies that take into account the identified drivers of savings among rural poor households should be enhanced. The government and development partners should focus on initiatives that help people move out of poverty; schemes that increase poor individual and households' incomes; and creating an environment that enables people to save and have access to different financial services, which will help them access productive assets.

References

AFR (2017). *Access to finance Rwanda. Annual Report 2017 Summary.* Kigali: Access to Finance Rwanda (AFR).
Ahmad, M., & Asghar, T. (2004). Estimation of saving behavior in Pakistan using micro data. *Lahore Journal of Economics, 9,* 73–92.
Angrist, J. D., & Pischke, J. S. (2009). *Mostly harmless econometrics.* Princeton: Princeton University Press.
Aryeetey, E. (2004). *Household asset choice among the rural poor in Ghana.* Institute of Statistical: Social and Economic Research, University of Ghana.
Athukorala, P. C., & Sen, K. (2001). *Liberalization and business investment in India.* United Kingdom.
Athukorala, P. C., & Sen, K. (2004). The determinants of private saving in India. *World Development, 32*(3), 491–503.
Athukorala, P. C., & Tsai, P. L. (2003). Determinants of household saving in Taiwan: growth, demography and public policy. *The Journal of Development Studies, 39*(5), 65–88.
Attanasio, O. P., & Banks, K. (2001). The assessment: Household saving—Issues in theory and policy. *Oxford Review of Economic Policy, 17,* 1–19.
Attanasio, O. P., & Rohwedder, S. (2003). Pension wealth and household saving: Evidence from pension reforms in the United Kingdom. *American Economic Review, 93*(5), 1499–1521.
Attanasio, O. P., & Szekely, M. (2000). Household saving in developing countries: Inequality, demographics and all that. In *Paper for World Bank April 2000 ABCDE Conference in Development Economics.*
Beverly, S. G., & Sherraden, M. (1999). Institutional determinants of saving: Implications for low-income households and public policy. *The Journal of Socio-Economics, 28*(4), 457–473.
Brata, A. G. (1999). Household saving behavior: The case of rural industry in Bantul. *Analysis CSIS, 28*(1), 75–86.
Cameron, A. C., & Trivedi, P. K. (2005). *Microeconometrics: methods and applications.* New York: Cambridge University Press.
Cameron, A. C., & Trivedi, P. K. (2010). *Microeconometrics using stata* (Vol. 2). College Station, TX: Stata press.
Chowa, G. A., Masa, R. D., & Ansong, D. (2012). Determinants of saving among low-income individuals in rural Uganda: Evidence from assets Africa. *Advances in Applied Sociology, 2*(4), 280.
Ciftcioglu, S., & Begovic, N. (2010). Are domestic savings and economic growth correlated? Evidence from a sample of Central and East European countries. *Problems and Perspectives in Management, 8*(3), 30–35.
Collins, D., Morduch, J., Rutherford, S., & Ruthven, O. (2009). *Portfolios of the poor: How the world's poor live on $2 a day.* Princeton, New Jersey: Princeton University Press.

Consultative Group to Assist the Poor (CGAP). (2010). *Financial access 2010 report*. Washington DC: Consultative Group to Assist the Poor.

Crossley, T. F., Emmerson, C., & Leicester, A. (2012). *Raising household saving*. London: British Academy Policy Centre, Institute for Policy Studies.

Davidson, P. (2000). There are major differences between Kalecki's theory of employment and Keynes's general theory of employment interest and money. *Journal of Post Keynesian Economics, 23*(1), 3–25.

Dercon, S., Gilligan, D. O., Hoddinott, J., & Woldehanna, T. (2009). The impact of agricultural extension and roads on poverty and consumption growth in fifteen Ethiopian villages. *American Journal of Agricultural Economics, 91*(4), 1007–1021.

Dieden, S. (2004). *Homing in on the core-households incomes, income sources and geography in South Africa*. University of Cape Town.

Dieden, S. (2005). Income generation in the African and coloured population: Three essays on the origins of household incomes in South Africa. Economic Studies No. 143. Doctoral thesis, School of Business, Economics and Law, Göteborg University.

Dirschmid, W., & Glatzer, E. (2004). Determinants of the household saving rate in Austria. *Monetary Policy & The Economy Q, 4*, 25–38.

Dupas, P., & Robinson, J. (2013). Savings constraints and microenterprise development: Evidence from a field experiment in Kenya. *American Economic Journal of Applied Economics, 5*(1), 163–192.

Durbin, J. (1954). Errors in variables. *Revue de l'institut International de Statistique*, 23–32.

Engelhardt, G. V. (1996). House prices and homeowner saving behavior. *Regional Science and Urban Economics, 26*(3–4), 313–336.

Friedman, M. (1957). *A Theory of the Consumption function*. Princeton: Princeton University Press.

Gedela, S. P. R. (2012). Determinants of saving behaviour in rural and tribal households (An empirical analysis of Visakhapatnam District). *International Journal of Research in Social Sciences, 2*(3), 108–128.

Gujarati, D. N. (2009). *Basic econometrics*. New Delhi: Tata McGraw-Hill Education.

Gupta, K. L. (1970). On some determinants of rural and urban household saving behaviour. *Economic Record, 46*(4), 578–583.

Harjes, T., & Ricci, L. A. (2005). What drives saving in South Africa? *Post-Apartheid South Africa: The First Ten Years, 48*.

Hausman, J. A. (1978). Specification tests in econometrics. *Econometrica: Journal of the Econometric Society*, 1251–1271.

Hoddinott, J. (2006). Shocks and their consequences across and within households in rural Zimbabwe. *Journal of Development Studies, 42*, 301–321.

Hulme, D., Moore, K., & Barrientos, A. (2015). Assessing the insurance role of microsavings. In R. Vos, N. Islam, & M. Koparanova (Eds.), *Financing for overcoming economic insecurity*. Bloomsbury Publishing.

Iragena, J. (2015). Determinants of savings in Rwanda (1978–2012)—An empirical analysis, Master's dissertation, The Open University of Tanzania.

Islam, A., & Maitra, P. (2012). Health shocks and consumption smoothing in rural households: Does microcredit have a role to play? *Journal of Development Economics, 97*(2), 232–243.

Karlan, D., Ratan, A. L., & Zinman, J. (2014). Savings by and for the poor: A research review and agenda. *Review of Income and Wealth, 60*(1), 36–78.

Kasongo, A., & Ocran, M. K. (2017). Determinants of household saving in South Africa. In *Biennial Conference of the Economic Society of South Africa, Rhodes University*, Grahamstown, South Africa (Vol. 30).

Kelly, R., & Mavrotas, G. (2008). Savings and financial sector development: Panel cointegration evidence from Africa. *The European Journal of Finance, 14*(7), 563–581.

Keynes, J. M. (1936). *The general theory of employment, interest and money*. New York: Har-court, Brace and Co.

Kibet, L. K., Mutai, B. K., Ouma, D. E., Ouma, S. A., & Owuor, G. (2009). Determinants of household saving: Case study of smallholder farmers, entrepreneurs and teachers in rural areas of Kenya. *Journal of Development and Agricultural Economics, 1*(7), 137–143.

Kraay, A. (2000). Household saving in China. *The World Bank Economic Review, 14*(3), 545–570.

Larionova, N., Varlamova, J., & Singatullina, G. (2014). The trends on household economic behavior in emerging countries of Europe. *Procedia Economics and Finance, 15,* 421–429.

Loayza, N., Schmidt-Hebbel, K., & Servén, L. (2000a). What drives private saving across the world? *Review of Economics and Statistics, 82*(2), 165–181.

Loayza, N., Schmidt-Hebbel, K., & Servén, L. (2000b). Saving in developing countries: An overview. *The World Bank Economic Review, 14*(3), 393–414.

Lusardi, A. (2007). *Household saving behavior: The role of literacy, information and financial education programs* (No. 2007/28). CFS Working Paper.

McKinnon, R. I. (1973). *Money and capital in economic development.* Washington, DC: Brookings Institution.

Meier zu Selhausen, F., & Musinguzi, J. (2011). The current performance of business and operations of rural microfinance institutions (MFIs) in the Rwenzori region. *Rwenzori Journal, 1*(1), 77–99.

Melese, N., & Ejigu, F. (2016). Determinants of saving behaviours of households in the case of Robe, Ginir and Dellomena: South East Ethiopia. *EPRA International Journal of Economic and Business Review, 6*(4), 105–111.

Mishra, P. K., Das, J. R., & Mishra, S. K. (2010). The dynamics of savings and investment relationship in India. *European Journal of Economics, Finance, and Administrative Sciences, 18,* 163–172.

Modigliani, F. (1944). Liquidity preference and the theory of interest and money. *Econometrica, Journal of the Econometric Society,* 45–88.

Modigliani, F., & Miller, M. H. (1963). Corporate income taxes and the cost of capital: A correction. *The American Economic Review, 53*(3), 433–443.

Muradoglu, G., & Taskin, F. (1996). Differences in household savings behavior: Evidence from industrial and developing countries. *The Developing Economies, 34*(2), 138–153.

Murindahabi, E. (2010). *Financial liberalisation and saving: Empirical evidence from Rwanda.* Master's dissertation, University of Nairobi.

Murphy-McGreevey, M., Roelen, K., & Nyamulinda, B. (2017). *Making Rwanda's vision 2020 Umurenge programme public works care-responsive. Programmatic notes for women's economic empowerment policy and programming.* IDS Policy Brief, Brighton: Institute of Development Studies (IDS).

National Institute of Statistics of Rwanda (NISR). (2018). *EICV5 main indicators report.* Kigali, Rwanda: National Institute of Statistics of Rwanda.

Obayelu, O. (2012). Saving behavior of rural households in Kwara state, Nigeria. *African Journal of Basic & Applied Sciences, 4*(4), 115–123.

Odhiambo, N. M. (2009). Savings and economic growth in South Africa: A multivariate causality test. *Journal of Policy Modeling, 31*(5), 708–718.

Rha, J. Y., Montalto, C. P., & Hanna, S. D. (2006). The effect of self-control mechanisms on household saving behavior. *Journal of Financial Counseling and Planning, 17*(2).

Rurangwa, E., Mburu, D. M., Mulyungi, P., Ntaganira, E., & Nsengiyumva, E. (2018). Factors affecting savings of small-scale coffee farmers in Rwanda. *International Journal of Innovative Research in Science, Engineering and Technology, 7*(2), 1285–1290.

Rutherford, S., & Arora, S. (2009). *The poor and their money.* New Delhi: Oxford University Press.

Schultz, T. P. (2005). Demographic determinants of savings: Estimating and interpreting the aggregate association in Asia. IZA Discussion Papers, No. 1479, Institute for the Study of Labor (IZA), Bonn.

Seguino, S., & Floro, M. S. (2003). Does gender have any effect on aggregate saving? An empirical analysis. *International Review of Applied Economics, 17*(2), 147–166.

Shaw, E. S. (1973). *Financial deepening in economic development.* Rome: Food and Agriculture Organization.

Shawa, K. C. (2016). Drivers of private saving in Sub-Saharan African countries. *Journal of Economic Development, 41*(2), 77–110.

Swasdpeera, P., & Pandey, I. M. (2012). Determinants of personal saving: a study of salaried individuals in Thailand. *Afro-Asian Journal of Finance and Accounting, 3*(1), 34–68.

Syed, H., Nigar, S., & Ullah, S. (2017). An analysis of household saving and investment behavior among different income groups in urban area of district Peshawar. *iBusiness, 9*(04), 188–202.

Tandoh, A. (2016). A micro-econometric analysis of household savings in Ghana. Master's dissertation, University Kwame Nkrumah University of Science and Technology, Ghana.

Wooldridge, J. M. (2013). *Introductory econometrics: A modern approach* (5th ed.). South-Western: Cengage Learning.

Wu, D. M. (1973). Alternative tests of independence between stochastic regressors and disturbances. *Econometrica (pre-1986), 41*(4), 733.

Zeller, M. (1994). Determinants of credit rationing: A study of informal lenders and formal credit groups in Madagascar. *World Development, 22*(12), 1895-1907.

Zeller, M., Schrieder, G., Von Braun, J., & Heidhues, F. (1997). *Rural finance for food security for the poor: Implications for research and policy* (Vol. 4). Washington, DC: International Food Policy Research Institute.

Chapter 3
Economic Modeling of Capital Markets and Sustainable Investments in Rwanda

Fidèle Mutemberezi and Christian N. Mbabazi

Abstract Rwanda needs investments to uplift the level of its economy. This study tests the significance of the capital market for investments in Rwanda. It uses a regression model for the analysis and gives a graphical presentation of the variables used in the model. The study shows that investments, number of shares, turnover, and market capitalization have a trend and intercept. In addition, the test of stationarity shows that investments, number of shares, and turnover are stationary at level, that is, I(0). Market capitalization too is stationary at first difference, that is, I(1). These variables are cointegrated at a 95% confidence interval. In the error correction method, 4.34 quarters or approximately a year and one month are needed to recover from investment downturn in the short run. The long-run relationship between capital market and investments shows that the model fits at 81% using the R^2 interpretation. It also tests the impulse-response function for observing how shocks affect one another (variables). The capital market needs important support from both the public and private sectors to raise investments in Rwanda because this will have a positive impact on sustainable investments in the country.

Keywords Capital markets · Investments · Economy · Growth

Classification Codes E22 · E27 · E44

1 Introduction

Investments are an addition to the stock of capital goods in the public or private sector over a given time period. Gross investments include both net investments and replacement investments for keeping the stock intact. Theories of the determination

---

F. Mutemberezi (✉)
School of Economics, University of Rwanda College of Business, Kigali, Rwanda
e-mail: f.mutemberezi@yahoo.com

C. N. Mbabazi
World Bank Research Group, Kigali, Rwanda
e-mail: mbabazinc@gmail.com

© Springer Nature Singapore Pte Ltd. 2020
G. G. Das and R. B. Johnson (eds.), *Rwandan Economy at the Crossroads of Development*, Frontiers in African Business Research,
https://doi.org/10.1007/978-981-15-5046-1_3

of the volume of investments include the accelerator principle and marginal efficiency of capital approaches (Rutherford 2013). Investments can also be expressed as the purchase of a financial asset (Junanker 1972). In an economic sense, an investment is the purchase of goods that are not consumed today but are used in the future for creating wealth. The Rwanda Development Board (RDB) registered investments worth USD 1.675 billion in 2017. In comparison, in 2016, foreign investments were worth USD 650.4 million while the local investments were worth USD 479 million.[1] Based on these figures, we find a difference of USD 171.4 million between foreign and domestic investments in 2016. Hence, domestic investments need to be taken seriously and increased. Awareness and profitability should be explored and explained to the people so that they are open to competing on the international level. This study econometrically tests the capital markets and the stock exchange to verify if they can promote investments in Rwanda. The tests significance using data for 2011–18 helps us understand investments in the Rwandan economy.

Investments are key factors in an economy in both developed and developing countries. In Rwanda, investments remain low because of several reasons, for instance, the cost of transport due to its geographical location. Moreover, the effects of the 1994 genocide against the Tutsi have meant that the least qualified labor comes to the country. The country's vision is increasing domestic production and contributing to its budget rather than waiting for foreign investments. However, this means enforcing increased domestic taxes. It also means that a large market either domestic or foreign is needed for the economy to grow. This issue of investments must be solved systematically and planned for in the short and long term to reach sustainable investments and development. Diversification and innovations play an important role in improving investments. The level of taxes can sometimes influence investments (Schumpeter 1982; Waygood 2014). Rwanda still has a small market and administrative processes can also delay investments.

This study tests the role of the capital market in investments in Rwanda where positive results indicate the right direction for Rwanda to take for strengthening its sustainable investments and the capital market so that it becomes an international market listed on the stock exchanges. This will help improve the financial balance both in the short and long runs. The main objective of this study is demonstrating the role of capital markets in sustainable investments in Rwanda. For this, it tests the significance of the capital market for sustainable investments in Rwanda and checks the extent to which the capital market influences investment in the country. Investments are one part of income which are not consumed immediately. Investments are the sum of purchases using newly produced capital (Opreana 2010). Higher interest rates can decrease the quantity of investments, while will lower interest in increasing investments.

A variation in the investments changes upcoming production capacity. Therefore, plans to change the capital stock depend on expectations. A firm considers likely prospects for trade (Amir et al. 2012). Firms need capital for goods and services. A growth in the level of production is likely to increase demand for capital and thus lead

---

[1] Rwanda Development Board annual report.

to better investments. Therefore, GDP growth is likely to shift the investment demand curve to the right. The size of capital already in use touches the level of investments in two ways. First, because most stock substitutes capital that has depreciated, a bigger capital stock is likely to lead to extra investments and there will be more capital to replace. Second, a larger capital stock can reduce investments. The capacity utilization of capital is about to count the percentage of the capital store in usage. Because capital generally necessitates downtime for preservation and repairs, the measured capacity operation rate typically falls below 100%. The demand curve for investments displays the quantity of investments at each interest rate, all other things being unaffected. Businesses have several choices for producing specific products. A factory, for instance, might use more capital and moderately few workers, or it might use extra workers and fairly a smaller amount of capital. The application of original skills in technology frequently involves new investments. Variations in technology can thus raise demand for capital. Advances in computer technology have led to massive investments in computers. The development of fiber-optic technology for transmitting signals has stimulated enormous investments by telephone and cable television corporates.

Private investments as an influential progress enabler where if delivered in the right way private investments can generate self-employment or other employment, build talent, spur improvements, be responsible for essential infrastructure and services, enhance economies, and set stronger standards in public and corporate governance. Both domestic and foreign investments need to be scaled up meaningfully in the coming years to contribute to the post-2015 agenda in Rwanda or generally. More investments are, however, not enough. They must also be of decent quality. Even though private finance accounts for a lion's share of capital inflows to developing countries, its influence on improvements is still to completely materialize. The Sustainable Development Goals (SDGs) clearly call for investments to sustain change. Tapping the sustainable improvement potential of investments will lead to increasing the capacity of domestic economies and the public sector, restructuring frameworks to mark countries as good investment destinations, and supporting accountable business conduct along the length of universal supply chains.

1.1 Capital markets in Africa

Auditing firm Price Waterhouse Coopers (PWC 2015), *Africa Capital Markets Watch report* says: "This report surveys all new primary market equity Initial Public Offerings (IPOs) and Further Offers (FOs) by listed companies, as well as High-Yield (HY) and Investment-Grade (IG) debt capital markets activity, in which capital was upraised on Africa's principal stock markets and market segments (including exchanges in Algeria, Botswana, Cameroon, Cape Verde, Côte d'Ivoire, Egypt, Libya, Gabon, Ghana, Kenya, Malawi, Mauritius, Mozambique, Namibia, Nigeria, Morocco, Rwanda, Seychelles, Somalia, South Africa, Sudan, Swaziland, Tanzania, Tunisia, Uganda, Zambia and Zimbabwe)."

In 2015, both local and intercontinental capital markets featured sustainability as a primary funding source for growth in conjunction with private equity, investments, and mergers and acquisitions (M&A), reflecting a continued appetite among investors with key portfolio allocations targeted toward emerging and frontier markets. On December 31, 2015, African exchanges had a market capitalization of nearly $1 trillion, with 23% of this value residing in exchanges outside South Africa (PWC Report 2015). Over the last few years, there have been 105 IPOs by African companies on both African and international exchanges and non-African businesses on African exchanges, raising $6.1 billion. Despite the volatility in global equity markets, companies continue to be attracted to African markets as seen in the stable progress in first-time listings in 2011 as compared to 2014. There was an overall increase of 12% in terms of the number of IPOs and 17% in terms of capital raised in 2014–2015 (Fig. 1). In 2015, the top four IPOs by proceeds involved firms or exchanges in North Africa. Each of these listings was oversubscribed, showing healthy investor demand in the region in the first half of 2015 (PWC Report 2015).

According to Vera Songwe (2016), African nations toned to have tougher capital market admissions to improve their levels of investments. In the short to medium term, this involved discovering new ways of shielding market access and improving admissibility to capital markets for sub-Saharan African countries in an economically viable way. The universal community has an essential role to play in this. On a continent where admission to markets is a novel phenomenon and where it is still challenging to draw investors due to inherited problems of macroeconomic mismanagement and fiscal correction as well as persistent corruption and fragile institutions, trying to raise capital from the markets is a creditable goal. However, this needs discipline as this has facilitated countries who have been positive in identifying the importance of market observations and the need for better macro-fiscal discipline.

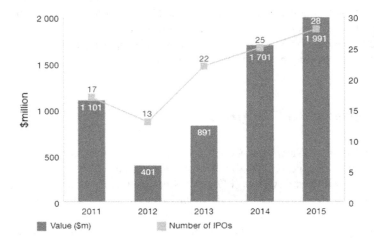

Fig. 1 Trends in African IPOs (2011–15). *Source* Africa Capital Markets Watch (2015)

1.2 Capital Markets in the East African Community

According to PWC's 2015 Africa Capital Markets Watch report, management of East African exchanges and planned collaborations between the exchanges (such as the London and Nigerian Stock Exchanges) have permitted these markets to become liquid and active leading to an improvement in their turnover ratios. The East African Community's (EAC) countries have been enlarging their capital markets through regional amalgamations. Considering well-operational home-grown capital markets is important for these countries because they need enormous sponsorship for constructing infrastructure for continuous growth. Capital markets are desirable as a substitute funding source, complementing commercial banks, which govern the EAC's financial sector with low attractiveness (Gaertner et al. 2011). Studying the payback from capital markets and the boundaries of individual country approaches, the EAC member states are devoted to instituting a common market which will include free drive of capital under the treaty that established the community. Further, incorporating financial markets in government deficit markets is indispensable for a monetary union to have a successful common monetary strategy across the region to realize the benefits of the monetary union (Yabara 2011). According to PWC's (2016) Africa Capital Markets Watch report, East Africa remained a brighter spot in terms of growth with a number of countries in the region such as Ethiopia, Kenya, and Tanzania still having healthy GDP growth rates of 5.5% or higher while other oil-importing countries too continued to be strong. Côte d'Ivoire, for example, was forecast to be the fastest growing economy in SSA in 2017, with its GDP growth expected to top 8% (PWC 2016).

1.3 Capital Markets in Rwanda

The Capital Market Authority (CMA) is a public institution established by Law No. 23/2017 of 31/05/2017 responsible for developing and regulating capital markets, the commodities exchange and related contracts, collective investment schemes, and the warehouse receipts system in Rwanda. The Rwanda Stock Exchange Limited was incorporated on October 7, 2005 with the objective of carrying out stock market operations. The stock exchange was demutualized from the start as it was registered as a company limited by shares. The company was officially launched on January 31, 2011 (RSE 2013). The recorded performance positively impacted RSE's financial performance during the year. RSE's internal income increased by 30% from Rwf 301.5 million in 2016 to Rwf 392.1 million in 2017.

2 Data and Method

This research used econometric modeling with secondary data collected from the National Institute of Statistics of Rwanda (NISR), the Capital Market Authority (CMA), and the Rwanda Stock Exchange (RSE). There were eight companies listed on RSE, half of which were of foreign origin and the remaining were domestic (Bank of Kigali) BK, BRALIRWA (BLR), Nation Media Group (NMG), Kenya Commercial Bank (KCB), Uchumi Super Market Ltd. (USL), Equity Bank Group Ltd. (EQTY), Crystal Telecom (CTL), and I&M Bank Rwanda in 2016–17. The study used the software EViews to estimate econometrically the long-run regression model.

This study tested the hypothesis of zero influence of the independent variables on the dependent variable. It found out whether the independent variables had any significant influence on the dependent variable or not, which is significantly equal to zero or not. Mathematically, this hypothesis can be written as follows:

$$H_0 = 0 \text{ and } H_1 \neq 0$$

where:

H_0: The capital market has a significant impact on promoting investment sustainability in Rwanda.
H_1: The capital market does not impact promoting investment sustainability in Rwanda significantly.

2.1 Model Specification

A regression model, $Y = f(X_1, X_2, X_3)$ is used where investment is the dependent variable and the independent variables are share index, turnover, and market capitalization. The model is expressed as an implicit function as follows:

$$Y = \beta_0 + \beta_1 X_1 + \beta_2 X_2 + \beta_3 X_3 + \varepsilon_i \tag{1}$$

where Y is investment, X_1 is the share index, X_2 is the turnover ratio, and X_3 is market capitalization. β_0 is an intercept, β_1 measures the coefficient of the share index, β_2 is the coefficient of the turnover ratio, β_3 is the coefficient measure of market capitalization, and ε_i is the stochastic error term.

This study focuses on the economic modeling of capital markets and investment sustainability.

The variables need to be illustrated graphically to verify if the following step of stationarity test uses either intercept or intercept and trend. Moreover, the stationarity test was also done to check if the means and variance of the variables were constant over time for all the variables (dependent and independent). After testing the stationarity, the next step was cointegration testing where we say that the two variables are cointegrated. Economically speaking, two variables are cointegrated if they have a long-term, or equilibrium, relationship between them (Anghel 2014; Gujarati and Porter 2004). The Engle–Granger (EG) method was useful in this test. Once the variables are cointegrated, it implies that the model is statistically significant, and it can be used for formulating policy. Otherwise, other alternatives need to be found. The long-run model was regressed after the cointegration was successfully computed. Moreover, to check whether the series was integrated or not, the study relied on the Augmented Dickey Fuller tests (Anghel 2014; Amir et al. 2012); of course, in the short run there may be a disequilibrium (Gujarati and Porter 2004). The study had to find a mechanism to resolve this situation for which it used the error correction method (ECM) which had to have a negative sign to adjust rather than increasing the errors. We also had to generate residuals because they were used in the regression model. The vector autoregression (VAR) was tested as well. So, for each variable from each equation, a unit shock was applied to the error separately, and its effects on the VAR system were noted over time (Brooks 2019).

3 Results and Discussion

Figures 2, 3, 4 and 5 in the Appendix show whether we get an intercept, or, an intercept and trend. The graphical illustration in Fig. 2 shows how investments in Rwanda changed in 2011–18. They first increased but then fell in 2014 in the third quarter and increased in the following quarter. The graphical illustration in Fig. 3 also shows how the number of shares increased to the market, where we see a significant

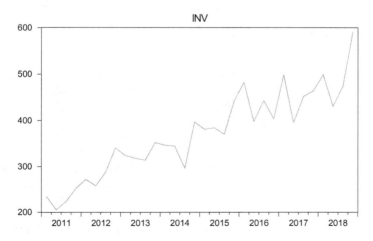

Fig. 2 Graphical illustration of investments

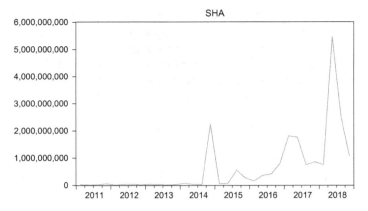

Fig. 3 Graphical illustration of the number of shares

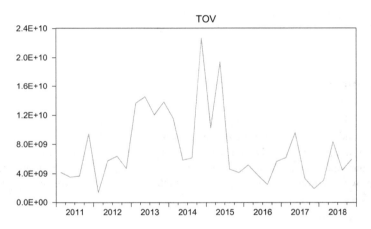

Fig. 4 Graphical illustration of turnover

impact in 2014 due to new listed companies. Figure 4 illustrates how turnover varied over time, and it also relates to the number of shares in the market. Figure 5 for market capitalization shows how this grew between 2011 and 2018 with a big boom in 2014, due to the expansion of the market to almost double its existing level.

Stationarity test's results are explained as: Investments are I(0), investments are stationary because ADF calculated |−4.693089| is greater than ADF critical |−3.595026| at the 5% significance level, at level, and the P-value is 0.0047 which is less than 5%. Number of shares are I(0), volume (number of shares) traded is stationary because ADF calculated |−4.823396| is greater than ADF critical |−3.562882| at the 5% significance level, at level, and the P-value is 0.0027 which is less than 5%. Turnover is I(0) and it is stationary because ADF calculated |−3.977368| is greater than ADF critical |−3.562882| at the 5% significance level, at level, and the P-value

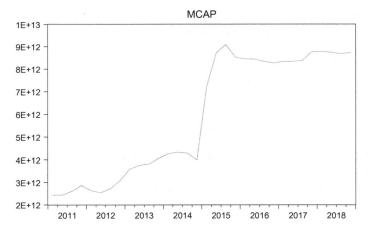

Fig. 5 Graphical illustration of market capitalization

is 0.0203 which is less than 5%. Market capitalization in Rwandan Francs (at the end of the period) is not stationary because ADF calculated |−2.314242| is less than ADF critical |−3.568379|, |−3.568379|, and |−3.218382| at the 1%, 5%, and 10% significance levels, respectively, at level, and the *P*-value is 0.4141 which is greater than 1%, 5%, and 10%, respectively. Market capitalization is I(1) which in Rwandan Francs (at the end of the period) is stationary because ADF calculated |−3.952924| is greater than ADF critical |−3.568379| at the 5% significance level, at first difference, and the *P*-value is 0.0219 which is less than 5%.

Investments, shares, turnover, and market capitalization are cointegrated, that is, these variables have a long-run relationship because the *P*-values of the Engle–Granger Tau-statistic and Z-statistic are 8% and 3%, respectively, with 10% and 5% significance intervals which deal with 90% and 95% of the confidence intervals (Bulere 2015). See Table 1 in the Appendix for the summary of these discussions in a tabular format.

$$\textbf{Log(inv)} = -5.07557 + 0.03178\textbf{log(sha)} + 0.00141\textbf{log(tov)} \\ + 0.35287\textbf{log(mcap)} - 0.22994\textbf{e}(-1) + \varepsilon$$

In addition to this estimated model, we found that the errors will be corrected within 4.34 quarters or in approximatively a year and one month.

	Log(inv) =	−606997 +	0.02729**log(sha)** +	0.01827**log(tov)** +	0.37656**log(mcap)** + ε
se		(1.93981)	(0.01856)	(0.03245)	(0.06785)
t-test		(−3.12915)	(1.46996)	(0.56316)	(5.54963)
prob		0.0041	0.1527	0.5778	0.0000

The probability of MCAP shows how much it is significant and how it affects investments. Value of R^2 is equal to 0.81 which shows higher regression coefficient. The lag selection is at lag 1 selected by the criterion in the computed results. The test of normal distribution is very important to check if the variables are normally distributed. Based on the joint probabilities' values, we observe that this is significant at the 10% level here. Another test of autocorrelation deals with how the values of the predictor variables are correlated. Based on the results, we found a P-value of 0.0060 which leads to the significance of market capitalization in the model. This is explained in the long-run relationship. Homoskedasticity mentions a circumstance in which the variance of the residual, or error term in a regression model is constant, that is, the error term does not change many times as the values of the independent variables vary. The homoskedasticity test is one assumption of linear regression modeling and we found that the P-value was 30% which is not bad.

4 Summary and Conclusion

The number of shares and bonds and turnover is not significant because of their P-values of 15% and 57%, respectively. Moreover, market capitalization is significant because it has percent P-value of 0%. The coefficient of determination fits the regression due to 81% R^2. In the short run, ECM's results show that the errors will be corrected in 4.34 quarters. Rwandans should be aware that the capital market is very important and join the market so that their level of investments can be lifted up.

The government's participation in capital markets to encourage the private sector also to invest and save more for the future will lead to sustainable investments. Further, non-financial businesses like individuals, small enterprises, and corporates should be sensitized and encouraged to invest in capital markets that can help in the future. Lastly, an adequate reporting system of trading on the stock exchanges which helps stakeholders should be in place.

Appendix

See Table 1.

3 Economic Modeling of Capital Markets ...

Table 1 Results of the vector autoregression estimates

	LOGINV	LOGSHA	LOGTOV	LOGMCAP
LOGINV(-1)	0.169834	−1.176437	1.914350	0.418578
	(0.21015)	(1.92837)	(1.20093)	(0.18138)
	[0.80815]	[−0.61007]	[1.59406]	[2.30775]
LOGINV(-2)	0.211422	1.878889	1.112724	−0.210817
	(0.22707)	(2.08364)	(1.29762)	(0.19598)
	[0.93107]	[0.90173]	[0.85751]	[−1.07569]
LOGSHA(-1)	0.029348	0.044630	−0.117866	0.054442
	(0.02604)	(0.23895)	(0.14881)	(0.02248)
	[1.12700]	[0.18677]	[−0.79205]	[2.42229]
LOGSHA(-2)	0.015333	0.076580	−0.009865	−0.015727
	(0.02740)	(0.25142)	(0.15658)	(0.02365)
	[0.55962]	[0.30459]	[−0.06301]	[−0.66502]
LOGTOV(-1)	0.009855	−0.197952	0.160082	0.023322
	(0.04677)	(0.42920)	(0.26729)	(0.04037)
	[0.21068]	[−0.46121]	[0.59890]	[0.57771]
LOGTOV(-2)	0.018646	−0.612043	0.027839	0.017897
	(0.03822)	(0.35068)	(0.21839)	(0.03298)
	[0.48791]	[−1.74530]	[0.12747]	[0.54258]
LOGMCAP(-1)	−0.031099	0.642368	−0.022919	1.119819
	(0.24912)	(2.28593)	(1.42360)	(0.21501)
	[−0.12484]	[0.28101]	[−0.01610]	[5.20822]
LOGMCAP(-2)	0.141651	1.660161	−1.236744	−0.370300
	(0.24878)	(2.28280)	(1.42165)	(0.21472)
	[0.56939]	[0.72725]	[−0.86994]	[−1.72460]
C	−1.032796	−36.56010	39.79085	4.479610
	(2.88018)	(26.4288)	(16.4589)	(2.48584)
	[−0.35859]	[−1.38335]	[2.41759]	[1.80205]
R-squared	0.835994	0.782790	0.356588	0.972164
Adj. R-squared	0.773516	0.700044	0.111479	0.961560
Sum sq. resids	0.256019	21.55696	8.360591	0.190713
S.E. equation	0.110415	1.013174	0.630970	0.095297
F-statistic	13.38055	9.460104	1.454813	91.67705
Log likelihood	28.88736	−37.61068	−23.40313	33.30458
Akaike AIC	−1.325824	3.107379	2.160209	−1.620305
Schwarz SC	−0.905465	3.527738	2.580568	−1.199946
Mean dependent	5.917705	18.93510	22.55163	29.34181

(continued)

Table 1 (continued)

	LOGINV	LOGSHA	LOGTOV	LOGMCAP
S.D. dependent	0.232011	1.849930	0.669383	0.486057
Determinant resid covariance (dof adj.)	2.60E−05			
Determinant resid covariance	6.23E−06			
Log likelihood	9.509573			
Akaike information criterion	1.766028			
Schwarz criterion	3.447465			
Number of coefficients	36			

Source Author's estimations

References

Amir, Z. B., Zaman, T., & Ali, M. (2012). The macroeconomic determinants of investment: Empirical evidence from Bangladesh. *International Journal of Scientific & Engineering Research, 3*(9), 1–13.

Anghel, M. G. (2014). Econometric model used in the capital market analysis. *Theoretical & Applied Economics, 21*(10).

Brooks, C. (2019). *Introductory econometrics for finance*. London: Cambridge University Press.

Bulere, T. (2015). Stock market development and economic growth in Uganda: A time series analysis for the period (1998Q1–2012Q4), (Uganda), International Institute of Social Studies of Erasmus University Rotterdam (ISS), The Hague.

Gujarati, D. N., & Porter, D. C. (Eds.). (2004). *Basic econometrics*. McGraw-Hill. *Irwin, a business*.

Gaertner, M., Sanya, S., & Yabara, M. (2011). *Assessing banking competition within the Eastern African community*. Unpublished Manuscript. Washington: International Monetary Fund.

Junankar, P. N. (1972). *Investment: Theories and evidence*. London: Macmillan.

Opreana, A. (2010). The long-run determinants of investment: A dynamic approach for the future economic policies. *Studies in Business and Economics, 5*(3), 227–237.

Price Waterhouse Coopers. (2015). *Africa capital markets watch annual report*.

Price Waterhouse Coopers. (2016). *Africa capital markets watch annual report*.

RSE-Rwanda Stock Exchange

Rutherford, D. (2013). *Routledge dictionary of economics*. London: Routledge.

Schumpeter, J. A. (1982). The theory of economic development: An inquiry into profits, capital, credit, interest, and the business cycle (1912/1934). *Transaction Publishers, 1,* 244.

Songwe, V. (2016). *Africa's capital market appetite: Challenges and prospects for financing rapid and sustained growth (Africa Growth Initiative)*.

Waygood, S. (2014). A roadmap for sustainable capital markets: How can the UN sustainable development goals harness the global capital markets. Aviva White Paper.

Yabara, A. B. (2011). International mechanisms for ensuring the transparency of African elections. *Afrique Contemporaine, 3,* 143–143.

Chapter 4
The Working of Monetary Policy Transmission Mechanisms in Rwanda: An Econometric Analysis Using the Equilibrium Model

Ferdinand Nkikabahizi, Veneranda Hategekimana, and Edouard Musabanganji

Abstract This paper focuses on the impact of monetary policy transmission mechanisms (selected channels of monetary transmission) on Rwanda's nominal gross domestic product (NGDP). Using a documentary review and by applying an econometric analysis technique on a set of data collected from 1999 to March 2013, the paper finds a relationship between the two. The study shows that the growth in money supply and the nominal exchange rate greatly affect the Rwandan economy's NGDP; various unknown factors also affect its NGDP. Growth in money supply has a huge impact on NGDP. The paper explores the effects of stochastic shocks of each of the endogenous variables using the error correction model (ECM). The study shows that a long-run relationship exists among the variables. Also, the core findings of the study show that the exchange rate and broad money are statistically significant monetary policy instruments that drive economic growth in Rwanda.

Keywords Monetary policy · Transmission mechanisms · Economic growth · Cointegration · Error correction model

JEL Classification E4 · E5 · E6

1 Introduction

Classical and Keynesians economists did not have an understanding of the impact of monetary policy on an economy's real variables like economic growth. This was supported by the use of economic models by theorists in these schools who used real evidence and some economic models to come up with their own theories. Various

---

F. Nkikabahizi (✉) · E. Musabanganji
School of Economics, College of Business and Economics, University of Rwanda, Kigali, Rwanda
e-mail: fnkikabahizi@yahoo.fr

V. Hategekimana
Faculty of Commerce, Catholic University of Rwanda, Huye, Rwanda

researchers such as Freedman et al. (2009) have shown that globally there is a multiplier effect of an expansionary fiscal policy when combined with an accommodative monetary policy on the world economy. Cheng's (2006) study in Kenya showed that any change in the monetary policy effectively affected prices and exchange rates through the interest rate channel but had no effect on output. Therefore, the monetary policy's effects on prices and real economic activities were closely linked to the core of macroeconomic theory and were at the heart of the monetary policy.

It is generally agreed that monetary policy, specifically unanticipated monetary shocks, has a significant effect on an economy, even if it is only in the short run because money as the most accepted medium of exchange has become the most important commodity in modern economies. Therefore, policymakers must appreciate the timing and effect of their policies on the economy for coming up with successful monetary policies. A monetary policy is all about manipulating a central bank's instruments to control the level of inflation. This is one of the key aspects of the work that many central banks do with the aim of maintaining price stability (that is, keeping inflation low and stable). There are different ways through which a central bank can achieve this objective, which are called monetary policy transmission mechanisms (Friedman 2010). Monetary policy transmission mechanisms refer to the processes through which changes in monetary policy instruments (such as monetary aggregates or short-term policy interest rates) affect the rest of the economy and output and inflation in particular. Monetary policy impulses transmit through various channels, affecting different variables and different markets at various speeds and intensities (Loaza and Schmidt 2002).

Monetary policy as a technique of economic management helps bring about sustainable economic growth and development and hence has been followed by many nations along with a formal articulation of how money affects economic aggregates. This thinking dates back to the time of Adams Smith and was later championed by monetary economists. Since the exposition of the role of monetary policy in influencing macroeconomic objectives like economic growth, price stability, equilibrium in the balance of payments, and a host of other objectives, monetary authorities are saddled with the responsibility of using monetary policies to grow their economies (Onyeiwu 2012). Monetary policy is one of the least understood economic processes, but its successful conduct requires a clear understanding of the process by which changes in this policy affect the economy.

This study is important from both theoretical and empirical points of view. It pays special attention to monetary policy that needs to be based on a forecast of the future evolution of the economy and estimates how the forecast's outcomes are likely to be affected by possible policy changes. It also evaluates the capacity of the monetary policy (channels of monetary transmission) to impact production and price in the context of Rwanda, that is, how a monetary policy's outcomes affect growth. It identifies and underlines the interdependence that exists between monetary policy and economic growth from the point of view of the influence that the effects of a monetary policy and its instruments have on the evolution and achievements of expected values of macroeconomic variables such as output, interest rate (Homer and Sylla 1996), exchange rate (O'Sullivan and Sheffrin 2003), and money supply

(Friedman 1987). Specifically, this study focuses on the channels selected and mostly operating in Rwanda (the bank lending channel, the exchange rate channel, and the interest rate channel).

The rest of the study is structured as follows. Section 2 presents a literature review. Section 3 gives the data and the methods used and Sect. 4 presents the results which are followed by a summary and conclusion in Sect. 5.

2 Literature Review

Monetary policy is also known as the monetary authority's discretionary control of money supply (the central bank and the central government) for achieving stated or desired economic goals. Monetary policy is not only an action taken for controlling and regulating money supply, but it also mandates regulating the flow of credit with a view to achieving predetermined macroeconomic goals (Dwivedi 2005). According to Hameed and Ume (2011), monetary policy is defined as the process under three categories by which the government, the central bank, or the monetary authority of a country control (i) the supply of money, (ii) the availability of money, and (iii) cost of money or rate of interest for attaining a set of objectives oriented toward the growth and stability of the economy.

A monetary policy's main objectives are economic growth and stability in the economy. (Shamshad 2006) proved these objectives in the case of Pakistan's monetary policy where has the dual objective of promoting economic growth and price stability helping it achieve its goal by targeting monetary aggregates (growth in broad money supply as an intermediate target and reserve money as an operational target) in accordance with real GDP growth and inflation targets set by the government. In addition, economic growth has also been considered an important goal of economic policy with a substantial body of research dedicated to explaining how this goal can be achieved (Fadare 2010).

Real macroeconomic variables such as output, price, and employment levels are affected by changes made in the nominal money supply and the nominal interest rate, and hence the traditional monetary transmission mechanism (MTM) is helpful in explaining the working of the three basic channels: the money channel, other asset price channels (exchange rate and equity price channels), and credit channels. The traditional interest rate channel is based on the standard IS-LM model, also known as the money channel; this is the origin of the other channels. This channel is based on two assets, money and bonds (Birgül and Güneş 2011). The structural features of the economy and financial markets influence the effectiveness of various channels of monetary policy transmission. Monetary policy works mostly through its influence on aggregate demand with a somewhat limited direct impact on the supply side depending on the degree of interest rate pass-through and the extent of price rigidities. There are several channels of monetary policy transmission, but the functioning and effectiveness of these channels vary across countries due to differences in the extent of financial intermediation, the development of domestic capital markets, and structural economic conditions (Cevik and Teksoz 2012).

The interest rate channel operates through the impact of monetary shocks on liquidity conditions and real interest rates, which in turn affect interest rate sensitive components of aggregate demand such as consumption and investments. Although the interest rate channel is a long-established mechanism of monetary transmission, it may not account for the full extent of output fluctuations, particularly in a small open economy (Mishkin 1996; Taylor 1995). Transmission channels (money channel, the bank lending (or credit) channel, the exchange rate channel, and the interest rate channel) impact differently and show their linkages with growth (Bernanke and Blinder 1992; Bernanke and Gertler 1995; Kamin and Klau 1998; Mishkin 1995; Taylor 1995).

In a small open economy with a flexible exchange rate regime, the exchange rate channel is typically an important transmission mechanism for monetary policy's actions. Money supply plays a dominant role in the economy and shows its possible effects on the price level, inflation, and business cycle (Majid 2007). The relationship between money supply and economic growth has been receiving increasing attention in the field of monetary economics in recent years (Emenuga 2003). Consequently, both developed and developing economies, particularly some African countries have failed in growing and developing their economies due to the low level of money supply, in general, money stocks, and also due to poor implementation and weaknesses of the policy executors on behalf of the government and its agencies.

Ogunmuyiwa and Ekone (2010) evaluated the effect of money supply within the institutional framework and the basic theoretical model of economic growth. Their findings showed that both aggregate money supply and economic growth and development were positively related, even if implementation of the monetary policy may lead to other problems (inflationary or deflationary). A country's economic condition and its specific purpose during any period might be helpful in making the best choices about the actions to be taken for managing the economy and achieving the targeted goals, for instance, contractionary and expansionary policies are adopted by a government to squeeze down the money supply, to curb inflation, and to stimulate economic activity to combat unemployment in the time of a recession.

The working of monetary policy transmission mechanisms is quite different among countries and depends on various factors; even the effects of changes on other macroeconomic variables (that is, output) are not similar and do not have the same extent. Montiel (1995) and Emenuga (2003) report that a possible effect of financial depth (money in circulation) on economic growth can manifest itself through three channels: (1) improved efficiency of financial intermediation, (2) improved efficiency of capital stock, and (3) an increased national savings rate.

Importantly, the working of MPTM is closely linked to interest rates and economic growth as has been recognized in literature on growth using the neoclassical growth framework and the McKinnon–Shaw hypothesis. For example, Molho (1986) argues that the real growth rate is reduced by interest rates in conjunction with existing financial repressions. To support the basic arguments of the McKinnon–Shaw model, we look at the inverse relationship between investment rates and the real loan rate of interest which is positively related to the growth rate. Conversely, poorly managed exchange rates can be disastrous for economic growth. Due to proven reasons and macroeconomic disturbances, economists have recommended that overvaluation of a currency may be avoided as one of the most robust imperatives that can be gleaned from the diverse experiences with economic growth around the world (for evidence and strong support through cross-country statistical results see Johnson et al. 2007; Rajan and Subramanian 2009; Razin and Collins 1997). Devaluation of a currency has been used as a tool for economic stabilization which led to reforms in the trade policy (Edwards 1986). This leads to a reallocation of resources resulting in increased production in import competing sectors. Devaluations are also believed to contribute to the enhancement of external competitiveness stimulating production in the export sector. On the other hand, the import prices go up as a direct consequence of nominal devaluations which are likely to depress the demand for imports in the domestic economy. Increased exports and reduced imports are expected to improve the external trade balance, and many developing countries have relied on devaluations to correct the fundamental disequilibria in their balance of payments. It is argued that by expanding the production of the traded sector, in general, and of exports, in particular, devaluation should have an expansionary effect on the overall economy.

MPTM effects economic growth in the short term and has an indirect effect on long-term growth. Éva (2012) reports this by introducing the concept of the long-run neutrality of money which is known and widely supported by experience. His introduction states that in the short term, monetary policy influences economic growth through stimulating or dampening demand but it has no influence on real variables such as employment and growth in the longer term because only movements in supply determine the long-run equilibrium levels of those variables together with the use of available technology, demographic factors, and economic agents' preferences. There is a maximum attainable level of production in an economy which is achieved by full utilization of all available factors of production. Growth in potential output or long-term potential growth is determined by improvements in supply-side factors (technological progress, capital accumulation, and an increase in the pool of labor available for work). However, it is important to note that a monetary policy can greatly contribute to the development of a predictable and certain environment, a precondition for the economy to realize its longer term growth potential by maintaining price stability, and this can have a positive indirect effect on long-term growth.

3 Data and Methods

This study used quarterly secondary data obtained from the National Bank of Rwanda, the Ministry of Finance, and the National Institute of Statistics of Rwanda as a time series from 1999 quarter 1 to 2013 quarter 1 which gives 57 observations. The data is made up of four variables: GDP, money supply (M3), bank lending rate, and the nominal exchange rate.

It uses a methodology in four steps: test of the lags, an analysis of the stationarity of the series (Augmented Dickey–Fuller (ADF) or the unit root test, the Johansen cointegration test, the Granger Causality test, the short-run relationship test, and the correlational test) between the variables.

The Augmented Dickey–Fuller unit root test was used to check the stationary of the variables while the Johansen cointegration test was used to confirm the existence of the long-run relationships (Bourbonnais 2007) between four variables, as mentioned above The following models were estimated using OLS for assessing the long-run and short-run relationship, respectively:

$$Y_t = \hat{a}_0 + \hat{a}_1 X_{1t} + \hat{a}_2 X_{2t} + \cdots + \hat{a}_k X_{kt} + e_t \qquad (1)$$

$$\Delta Y_t = \alpha_1 \Delta X_{1t} + \alpha_2 \Delta X_{2t} + \cdots + \alpha_k \Delta X_{kt} + \gamma_1 e_{t-1} + u_t, \gamma_1 < 0 \qquad (2)$$

The coefficient γ_1 which constitutes the strength of the convergence toward the balance must be significantly negative. Should the opposite occur, it is advisable to reject the ECM specification (Engle and Granger 1987, as cited in Bourbonnais 2007). Note that, Eq. (1) of the long-term relationship will be valid if the residuals are stationary (or do not have a unit root).

OLS was used for calculating the residuals as follows:

$$e_t = Y_t - \hat{a}_0 - \hat{a}_1 X_{1t} - \hat{a}_2 X_{2t} - \cdots - \hat{a}_k X_{kt} \qquad (3)$$

The study used a quantitative method for the analysis. It adopted an econometric approach for examining how the monetary policy influenced economic growth.

4 Empirical Results

4.1 Model Specification and Estimation

The concept of causality in Hameed et al. (2012) is appropriate and used by most existing studies for testing the relationship between economic growth and monetary policy.

As monetary policy actions are transmitted to the rest of the economy through changes in financial prices (for example, interest rates, exchange rates, yields, asset prices, and equity prices) and financial quantities (money supply, credit aggregates, supply of government bonds, and foreign denominated assets), the model is given as follows:

$$Y_t = \beta_0 + \beta_1 X_{1t} + \beta_2 X_{2t} + \beta_3 X_{3t} + \beta_4 X_{4t} + U_t \qquad (4)$$

where Y_t is the output of the rest of the economy, X_{1t} is inflation, X_{2t} is money supply, X_{3t} is the exchange rate, X_{4t} is the interest rate, and U_t is the error term or control variables.

Monetary policy transmission mostly in developing countries like Rwanda is done via the following instruments (channels): money supply (M_3), the lending interest rate, and the nominal exchange rate. Thus, for assessing the effect of the monetary policy on economic growth in Rwanda, this study selected the following variables: output of the rest of the economy (NGDP) as the dependent variable, and money supply (broad money), the exchange rate, and the lending interest rate as the independent variables.

Both inflation and exchange rate were used for measuring economic stability in Rwanda. They are the outcomes of monetary policy, so they cannot be used in the same model; inflation is not considered a monetary channel and depending on the nature of broad money, the credit channel cannot be taken into account for avoiding duplication in the model.

Among the macroeconomic correlations, the interest rate–investments–GDP growth relationship plays a fundamental role. As general rule, we can see that the GDP growth rate is higher for smaller values of the interest rate and for higher values of the investment ratio. In contrast, a smaller growth rate corresponds with higher values of the interest rate and smaller values of the investment rate (Lucian 2010).

As in most developing countries, the transmission mechanisms for monetary policy in Rwanda are found through monetary aggregates and the exchange rate. No significant effect is found through the interest rate channel. Shocks to the monetary aggregates and to the exchange rate have significant effects on prices, but not on real activity. In the case of Rwanda, the aggregate demand reacts slightly to variations in the lending interest rate (Kigabo et al. 2008).

Therefore, for the case of Rwanda after describing all the variables, the following statistical model is considered for the analysis and an interpretation of the results:

$$Y = f(money\,supply, exchange\,rate, bank\,lending\,rate) \qquad (5)$$

Note that the variables money supply, exchange rate, and NGDP have been transformed in their logarithms and this leads us to scale reducing and allows interpreting the results in terms of elasticity. This leads us to writing Eq. (2) in a log-linear format and we obtain the following long-run equation of the variation in NGDP:

$$Log Y_t = \beta_0 + \beta_1 Log M3_t + \beta_2 Log ER_t + \beta_3 BLR t + U_t \qquad (6)$$

where $Log Y$ = NGDP, $Log M3$ = log of money supply, $Log ER$ = log of exchange rate, and BLR is bank lending rate.

The coefficients $\beta_i (i = 0, 1, 2, 3)$ in Eq. (6) are parameters associated with the values of the variables in the model and are to be estimated.

This multivariate analysis is articulated around an analysis of the possible existence of one or several cointegrating relations (long-run relationships) and the existence of possible short-run relations between the variables to be studied using the vector error correction model.

4.2 Lag Selection and Tests for the Stationarity of the Series

The results of the lag tests for all the series show that we have to select the value of p equal to 3 according to AIC and HQC. For the purposes of our macroeconomic modeling, it is important that all the core variables used in the empirical analysis have been tested for stationarity. The null hypothesis is that a series does contain a unit root (that is, it is non-stationary). The results are given in Table 1 which show that for most of the variables, the null hypothesis is rejected under the ADF test when applied to their first differences, but this provides no evidence with which to reject the unit root hypothesis when the tests are applied to their levels.

The ADF test's statistic for NGDP (-5.428775) is less than the critical value at 5% (-3.4952). Then NGDP is stationary around the trend at first difference. We fail to reject H_0 and we conclude that NGDP is stationary around the trend at first difference, that is, the variable is integrated of order 1.

For the variable Log M3, the results show that at 5% its critical value of -3.5025 is greater than the ADF test statistic which is -3.579650 which means that Log M3 in the second difference has no unit root. It is integrated of order 2. Regarding variable LogER, the results in Table 1 show that the value of the ADF test statistic of -5.139252 is less than the critical value of -3.4969 at the 5% significance level,

Table 1 Stationary tests—the augmented Dickey–Fuller (ADF) unit root tests

ADF test statistic for NGDP	-5.4288	1% critical value*	-4.1383
		5% critical value	-3.4952
		10% critical value	-3.1762
ADF test statistic for LogM3	-3.5797	1% critical value*	-4.154
		5% critical value	-3.5025
		10% critical value	-3.1804
ADF test statistic for LogER	-5.1393	1% critical value*	-4.142
		5% Critical Value	-3.4969
		10% critical value	-3.1772
ADF test statistic for BLR	-10.772	1% critical value*	-4.1314
		5% critical value	-3.4919
		10% critical value	-3.1744

Source Author's estimations

Note *MacKinnon critical values for rejection of hypothesis of a unit root

Table 2 Stationarity tests—the augmented Dickey–Fuller (ADF) unit root tests

Variables	At level	Critical value (5%)	At first difference	Critical value (5%)	At second difference	Critical value (5%)	Conclusion
LogNGDP	−1.118786	−3.4935	−5.428775**	−3.4952	–	–	I(1)
LogM3	−0.254271	−3.4987	−3.000128	−3.5005	−3.579650***	−3.5025	I(2)
LogER	−3.295315	−3.4935	−3.373047	−3.4952	−5.139252***	−3.4969	I(2)
BLR	−3.932280	−3.4904	−10.77159**	−3.4919	–	–	I(1)

Source Author's estimations
Note ** and *** indicate the rejection of the null hypothesis of the presence of the unit root

which means that NER in the second difference is stationary. This also means that LogER is integrated of order 2 while BLR is stationary after the first difference. Table 2 reports the summary results for the stationarity tests in our model.

The null hypothesis is that the series has a unit root. The results of the ADF test are based on the MacKinnon critical values. The models with trends and intercepts indicate that the null hypothesis is rejected for all the variables as the values of the ADF T-statistics are well below the 5% critical value. Thus, we conclude that the LogNGDP series is stationary after the first difference and the other series are stationary after the second difference (LogM3 and LogER).

4.3 Testing for Cointegration

Since our time series was non-stationary, we followed the Box–Jenkins approach to purge the non-stationarity by differencing and estimating model, using only the differenced variables. But this would mean that valuable information from economic theory concerning the long-run equilibrium properties of the data would be lost, as has been stressed by those who developed the error correction model (ECM) approach (Kennedy 2008).

Econometricians have discovered a way out of this dilemma by testing whether the variables are cointegrated: although individually they are integrated of order 1, I(1), a particular linear combination is integrated of order 0, I(0). In other words, if a set of I(1) variables are cointegrated, then regressing one on the others should produce residuals that are I(0). EViews implements VAR-based cointegration tests using the methodology developed by Johansen (1988, 1991).

4.3.1 Results of the Johansen Cointegration Test and the Long-Run Relationship

The Johansen cointegration test and the estimation of the long-run relationship are done according to the methodology presented in Sect. 3 of this study.

First Step: Estimation of the Long-Run Equation
The long-run relationship or the cointegration equation is given by the relationship below. The *P*-values associated with the coefficients estimated by the model are given in parenthesis:

$$Log\,NGDP_t = -1.86 + 0.88 Log M3_t + 0.59 Log ER_t - 0.053 BLR_{t(-4)} + U_t$$
$$(0.0175) \quad (0.0000) \quad\quad (0.0000) \quad\quad (0.0166) \quad\quad\quad (7)$$

The coefficient of determination R^2 is equal to 0.990570 and shows that the LogNDGP is explained by the variables we used in the model at 99%. R^2 is used to test the goodness of fit from the regression results, and the value is 0.99 which implies that in the long run, 99% of the variations in LogNGDP are explained by the independent variables LogM3, LogER, and BLR. Before drawing any conclusions regarding the estimated coefficients, we have to check for the stationarity of the residuals (U_t). The next section gives the details of the ADF test for the residuals based on information summarized in Table 3.

Second Step: ADF Test for the Residuals
The augmented Dickey–Fuller test for Model 1 gives a test statistic equal to -2.60218 which is less than the critical value of 0.00898 at 5%. It gives -2.56724 which is less than 0.09988 for Model 2. It also gives -0.790325 and 0.9652 for Model 3. The results of the ADF test done for the residuals of the cointegrating relation for all cases are presented in Table 3. These show that these residuals do not have a unit root because the null hypothesis is rejected at a significance level of 5%.

The residuals are stationary at level, and we conclude that they are integrated of order 0. This leads us to confirm the presence of a cointegration relationship or the existence of a long-run relationship between LogNGDP and the independent variables LogM3 and LogER.

Table 3 ADF test on the residuals of the cointegrating model

Variable name	Model	Test statistic	*p*-value
Residuals (U_t)	Model 1 (without constant)	-2.60218	0.00898
	Model 2 (with constant)	-2.56724	0.09988
	Model 3 (with constant and trend)	-0.790325	0.9652

Source Author's estimations

4.3.2 Economic Interpretation of the Long-Run Relationship

These results allow us to interpret the coefficients of the cointegration model. By analyzing the *P*-values associated with Model (7), we conclude that all estimated coefficients are statistically different from 0 at the 5% level of significance.

For the nominal exchange rate, an increase of 1% will increase the nominal gross domestic product by 0.59%, and with regard to the money supply, an increase of 1% will increase the nominal gross domestic product by 0.88%. Their coefficients are statistically different from zero (0.0000), and consequently there is a significant long-run relationship between them. The value of -1.86 for the constant of the model means that in the absence of money supply, the nominal exchange rate, and the bank lending rate, the nominal gross domestic product has a value of -1.86. This means that there are other economic factors which are not taken into account in the model that influence the nominal gross domestic product increasingly or decreasingly.

The probability of BLR_t (0.0166) is less than 5% which means that the coefficient of BLR_t is significantly different from zero, which further means that after four quarters, there is a significant long-run relationship between $NGDP_t$ and BLR_t. An increase of 1% in BLR_t reduces $NGDP_t$ by -0.053%. This may depend on the structure of our economy where the financial sector is not yet developed, and people do not have alternative ways for borrowing. The demand for credit does not depend on LR but mainly on income. The shock of the lending interest rate does not impact NGDP directly; it requires a lapse of a period to have a significant impact on NGDP.

4.3.3 Estimation of the Short-Run Relationship

The results of the cointegration test show that more than a long-run relationship exists among the variables. This means that we can estimate the error correction model. An error correction model is designed for use with non-stationary series that are known to be cointegrated. ECM has cointegration relations built into its specifications so that it restricts the long-run behavior of the endogenous variables to converge to their cointegrating relationships while allowing for short-run adjustment dynamics. The use of cointegration and ECM adds more quality, flexibility, and versatility to the econometric modeling of dynamic systems and the integration of short-run dynamics with the long-run equilibrium. We evaluated ECMs using the conventional diagnostic tests and adopted the Akaike Information Criterion (AIC) for choosing the appropriate lag length. The model with the lowest AIC was adopted. The results give a cointegrating relationship among the variables within the ECM framework and are now presented.

The short-run relationship or ECM is given by the relation presented as follows:

$$DLog\,NDGP_t = 0.47D\log M3_t + 0.58D\log ER_t + 0.011DBLR_t - 0.216284U_{t-1}$$
$$(0.0000)\quad\quad (0.0189)\quad\quad (0.3589)\quad\quad (0.0112) \tag{8}$$

4.3.4 Interpretation of the Short-Run Equation

As the coefficient of the error term U_{t-1} is significantly negative, the short-run relationship model is valid and worthy of being interpreted. In this regard, the probability of DLM3$_t$ (0.0000) is less than 5%, meaning that DLM3's coefficient is significantly different from zero, meaning that there is a significant short-run relationship between NGDP and DLM3. An increase of 1% in M3 will increase NGDP by 0.47%. The probability of DLNER$_t$ (0.0189) is less than 5%, meaning that DLNER's coefficient is significantly different from zero, further meaning that there is a significant short-run relationship between NGDP and DLNER$_t$. An increase of 1% in NER will increase NGDP by 0.58%. The probability of DBLR$_t$ (0.3598) is greater than 5%, meaning that DBLR$_t$'s coefficient is not significantly different from zero, further meaning that there is no significant short-run relationship between NGDP and LR. For this ECM model, the lending rate is not significant which is normal because even in the long-run equation it was significant after four quarters.

As residuals have a probability of 0.0112 which is less than 5%, their coefficient is significantly different from zero. The coefficient (-0.216284) means that the effect of the shock will reduce by 21% in each quarter, meaning that it will end at 4.7–5 quarter.

It is important to state that it is necessary to do global tests of the reduced model to verify its specifications. The results related to this test show that the reduced model is well specified. The statistics of the test (Fisher $(3, 53) = 16.15343$ with a P-value of $1.98e-07$ leads us to reject the null hypothesis of simultaneous nullity of the reduced model's coefficients. In the next step, we test if there is structural stability of the coefficients over the period of the study and if all the parameters of the variables deleted when reducing the model are statistically non-significant. The answers to these two questions are presented in the following sections.

4.3.5 Chow Test for Structural Break in ECM

To test a structural break (stability) for time series data, we applied the Chow test. This led us to conclude that no structural break was observed. Based on the Fisher statistic ($F(4, 49) = 2.06564$) of the Chow test equals 2.06564 with a P-value of 0.0996698 ($P(F(4; 49) < 2.06564) = 0.0996698$), so we do not reject the null hypothesis of the absence of a structural break.

We thus conclude that the parameters of the model are stable over the period of the study: $P(F(4, 49) < 2.06564) = 0.0996698$.

4.3.6 The Granger Causality Test

The Granger approach (see Granger 1969) for answering the question whether a variable X causes Y is to see if the current Y can be explained by P-values of Y and then to see whether adding lagged values of X can improve the explanation. Y is said to be Granger caused by X if X helps in the prediction of X, or equivalently if the coefficients on the lagged X are statistically significant.

It is important to note that the statement "X Granger causes X" does not imply that Y is the effect or the result of X. Granger causality measures precedence and information but does not by itself indicate the causality in the more common use of the term. The results of the test show the pairwise Granger causality tests with a lag 4 preferred as it is important to use more rather than fewer lags.

The results of the first null hypothesis "nominal exchange rate does not Granger cause the nominal gross domestic product (NGDP$_t$)" indicate a P-value of 0.55750 which is greater than the 5% critical value. Hence, we accept the null hypothesis. On the other hand, the second null hypothesis "nominal gross domestic product does not Granger cause nominal exchange rate" indicates a P-value of 0.34677 which is greater than the 5% critical value, meaning that we fail to reject the null hypothesis, further meaning that NGDP does not lead to a nominal exchange rate.

The third null hypothesis "M3 does not Granger cause NGDP" gives a P-value of 0.00999 which is less than the 5% critical value, which means that we reject the hypothesis and accept that M3 causes NGDP. The fourth hypothesis "NGDP does not Granger cause M3" has a P-value of 0.10254 which is greater than the 5% critical value, so we accept the null hypothesis, meaning that NGDP does not cause M3. The fifth hypothesis "BLR does not Granger cause NGDP" has a P-value of 0.31302 which is greater than the 5% critical value, so we accept the hypothesis which means that BLR does not cause NGDP. The sixth hypothesis "NGDP does not Granger cause BLR" has a P-value of 0.21946 which is also greater than the 5% critical value, which gives the same results and hence we accept the null hypothesis that NGDP does not cause BLR. As an outcome of the Granger causality tests, there is a one-direction causality between M3 and NGDP but in the case of NGDP and other variables there is no causality.

4.3.7 Correlation Tests

The results of the correlational analysis are given in Table 4.

Table 4 Summary of correlation coefficients

Variables	Correlation coefficient (r)	Sign	Conclusion
M3 and NGDP	0.99	+	Very high correlation
NER and NGDP	0.74	+	Strong correlation
BLR and NGDP	0.52	+	Modest or moderate correlation

Source Author's estimations

4.4 Expected Signs and Findings

4.4.1 M3 and NGDP

This study evaluated the effect of monetary policy within the institutional framework and basic theoretical model of economic growth. Our findings support the fact that aggregate money supply is positively related to economic growth and development (Ogunmuyiwa and Ekone 2010).

4.4.2 Nominal Exchange Rate and NGDP

According to Mishkin (1996), the lower value of the domestic currency makes domestic goods cheaper than foreign goods, thereby leading to an increase in net exports (NXe↑) and hence in aggregate output.

4.4.3 Bank Lending Rate and NGDP

Bank lending rate, as shown in the estimated equations, is significant after the lapse of a period, i.e., four quarters in our model. In the short run, the coefficient of the lending rate is positive because it does not affect NGDP which continues to increase till when the shock starts and has a significant impact on NGDP (after four quarters as this study found). The expected signs of the independent variables in our model are summarized in Table 5.

Table 5 Summary of the expected signs

Variable	Definition	Expected sign
$NGDP_t$	The nominal gross domestic product (the value of final goods and services calculated at current year's prices) for each year, $NDGP_t = Q_t * P_t$	Dependent variable
$M3_t$	Money supply (M3), is the broadest measure of money, it is used by economists to estimate the entire supply of money in an economy M3 = M2 + all other CDs (certifications of deposits)	(+)
NER_t	The nominal exchange rate is the price of one currency in terms of the number of units of some other currency, $NER_t = \frac{E*P_i}{P}$ where E is real exchange rate, Pi is the foreign price, and P is domestic price	(+)
BLR_t	The rate of interest to be paid when repaying a loan	(−)

Source Author's predictions

Table 6 Findings and prior signs

Variables	Expected	Obtained	Conclusion
$NGDP_t$			
$M3_t$	Positive	Positive	Confirmed
NER_t	Positive	Positive	Confirmed
BLR_t	Negative	(−) (+)	Confirmed

Source Author's estimations

4.4.4 Summary of the Link Between Our Findings and Prior Signs

From the results obtained in the regression, the results are expected to follow a prior expectation of magnitude and signs. Table 6 analyzes the outcomes of the parameters.

In terms of the signs and the magnitude of the coefficients which highlight the effects of the monetary policy transmission mechanisms on economic growth, it was observed that M3 and ER had their expected signs. The relation between NGDP and both M3 and ER is positive, which means that as one goes up the other also goes up. In addition, we also examined the coefficients of individual variables to determine the nature of the relationship between channels of monetary transmission and other macroeconomic variables. The coefficients of M3 and ER were positive and significant while BLR had both negative and positive coefficients in the long-run and short-run estimated models, respectively, due to the nature of the economy and financial intermediation. Therefore, all theoretically expected signs were empirically obtained.

5 Summary and Conclusion

This study established that the channels of monetary policy transmission in Rwanda influence the growth of its economy. This study evaluated the impacts of the monetary policy's variables within the institutional framework and the basic theoretical model of economic growth. It concludes that a significant relationship between M3, the nominal exchange rate, the bank lending rate, and NGDP reflects the potency of the variables as being important in transmitting monetary policy's impulses to the aggregate economy. Overall, the study found evidence that innovations in monetary policy have both real and nominal effects on economic parameters depending on the policy variables selected for this study.

The findings of this study also suggest that the existence of a cointegration vector indicates a valid long-run relationship among the nominal gross domestic product and other macroeconomic variables. Rwanda's long-run nominal gross domestic product appears to be influenced by the nominal exchange rate. The exchange rate affects foreign financial flows, net exports, and thus aggregate demand. The study found that overall, NBR's monetary policies play a crucial role in influencing the level of productivity in the country. This result gives weight to the place of the central bank in the national development process in a nation.

The conclusions of this study can be summarized as follows: M3 positively affects NGDP, the nominal exchange rate (NER) positively affects NGDP, BLR negatively and positively affects NGDP, and an increase in M3 and NER has a similar effect of increasing NGDP. From our econometric analysis, we conclude that money supply, the nominal exchange rate, and the bank lending rates had a significant effect on changes in NGDP in Rwanda in 1999–2013.

References

Bernanke, B. S., & Blinder, A. S. (1992). The federal funds rate and the channels of monetary transmission. *American Economic Review, 82*(4), 901–921.

Bernanke, B., & Gertler, M. (1995). Inside the black box: The credit channel of monetary transmission. *Journal of Economic Perspectives, 9*(4), 27–48.

Birgül, C., & Günes, S. (2011). Monetary transmission mechanism in Turkey and Argentina. *International Journal of Economics and Finance Studies, 3*(2), 23–33.

Bourbonnais, R. (2007). *Econométrie, 6ème édition*. Paris: Dunod.

Cevik, S., & Teksoz, K. (2012). The effectiveness of monetary policy transmission channels in the GCC countries. IMF working paper, No. 12/191, Middle East and Central Asia Department (pp. 1–34).

Cheng, K. C. (2006). A VAR analysis of Kenya's monetary policy transmission mechanism: How does the Central Bank's REPO rate affect the economy? IMF Working Paper, No. 06/300, African Department (pp. 1–26).

Dwivedi, D. N. (2005). *Managerial economics* (6th ed.). New Delhi: Vikas Publishing House Pvt. Ltd.

Edwards, S. (1986). Are devaluations contractionary? *Review of Economics and Statistics, 68*(3), 501–508.

Emenuga, C. (2003). The outcome of financial sector reforms in West Africa. In *African voices on structural adjustment: A companion to our continent, our future* (p. 471). Africa World Press.

Engle, R. F., & Granger, C. W. J. (1987). Co-integration and error correction: Representation, estimation and testing. *Econometrica, 55*(2), 251–276.

Éva, K. (2012). *Monetary policy in hungary*. Budapest: The Magyar Nemzeti Bank.

Fadare, S. O. (2010). Recent banking sector reforms and economic growth in Nigeria. *Middle Eastern Finance and Economics, 8,* 1450–2889.

Freedman, C., Kumhof, M., Laxton, D., & Lee, J. (2009). The case for global fiscal stimulus. IMF Staff Position Note. SPN/09/03, Washington: International Monetary Fund.

Friedman, B. M. (2010). DSGE models for monetary policy analysis. *Handbook of Monetary Economics, 3A,* 3–1520.

Friedman, M. (1987). Quantity theory of money. *The New Palgrave: A dictionary of economics* (Vol. 4, pp. 15–19). New York: Stockton Press.

Granger, C. W. J. (1969). Investigating causal relations by econometric model and cross-spectral method. *Econometrica, 37*(3), 424–438.

Hameed, G., Mughal, K., & Rahim, S. (2012). Linkage between monetary instruments and economic growth. *Universal Journal of Management and Social Sciences, 2*(5), 69–76.

Hameed, I., & Ume, A. (2011). Impact of monetary policy on gross domestic product (GDP). *Interdisciplinary Journal of Contemporary Research in Business, 3*(1), 1348–1361.

Homer, S., & Sylla, R. (1996). *A history of interest rates* (3rd ed.). New Brunswick, NJ: Rutgers University Press.

Johansen, S. (1988). Statistical analysis of cointegrating vectors. *Journal of Economic Dynamics and Control, 12*(2–3), 231–254.

Johansen, S. (1991). Estimation and hypothesis testing of cointegration vectors in Gaussian vector autoregressive model. *Econometrica, 59*(6), 1551–1580.

Johnson, S. H., Ostry, J., & Subramanian, A. (2007). The prospects for sustained growth in Africa: Benchmarking the constraints. IMF Working Paper, No, 07/52.

Kamin, S. B., & Klau, M. (1998). Some multi-country evidence on the effects of real exchange rates on output. FRB International Finance Discussion Papers, No, 611; BIS Working Paper No. 48.

Kennedy, P. (2008). *A guide to econometrics* (6th ed.). Cambridge, MA: Wiley-Blackwell.

Kigabo, T. R., Pascal, M., & Adha, A. (2008). Monetary transmission mechanisms in Rwanda. *National Bank of Rwanda, Economic Review, 002,* 34–66.

Loaza, N., & Schmidt, K. H. (2002). *Monetary policy functions and transmission mechanisms: An overview* (pp. 1–20). Santiago, Chile: Central Bank of Chile.

Lucian, L. A. (2010). Scenarios for post-crisis period based on a set of presumed changes in the interest rate—investment—GDP growth relationship. In Institute for Economic Forecasting, Romanian Academy, *Paper Prepared for the EEFS 2010 Conference* (pp. 1–9), Athens, 3–6 June 2010.

Majid, M. Z. A. (2007). Causality link between money, output and prices in Malaysia: An empirical re-examination. *Applied Econometrics and International Development, 7*(1), 221–230.

Mishkin, F. S. (1995). Symposium on the monetary transmission mechanism. *Journal of Economic Perspectives, 9*(4), 3–10.

Mishkin, F. S. (1996). The channels of monetary transmission: Lessons for monetary policy. Working Paper, No. 5464. National Bureau for Economic Research, Cambridge (pp. 1–27).

Molho, L. E. (1986). Interest rates, saving, and investment in developing countries: A re-examination of the McKinnon-Shaw hypotheses. *Staff Papers, 33*(1), 90–116.

Montiel, P. J. (1995). Financial policies and economic growth: Theory, evidence and country specific experience, from Sub-Saharan Africa. *AERC Special Paper* 18. African Economic Research Consortium, Nairobi (pp. 1–33).

Ogunmuyiwa, M. S., & Ekone, A. F. (2007, 2010). Money supply—Economic growth nexus in Nigeria. *Journal of Social Science, 22*(3), 199–204.

Onyeiwu, C. (2012). Monetary policy and economic growth of Nigeria. *Journal of Economics and Sustainable Development, 3*(7), 62–70.

O'Sullivan, A., & Sheffrin, S. M. (2003). *Economics: Principles in action.* New Jersey: Pearson Prentice Hall.

Rajan, R. G., & Subramanian, A. (2009). Aid, Dutch disease, and manufacturing growth. Unpublished paper, International Monetary Fund.

Razin, O., & Collins, S. M. (1997). Real exchange rate misalignments and growth. Working Paper 6174, NBER, 1050 Massachusetts Avenue, Cambridge, MA (pp. 1–21).

Shamshad, A. (2006). Perspectives on Pakistan's monetary policy developments. *BIS Review, 55,* 1–6.

Taylor, J. (1995). The monetary transmission mechanism: An empirical framework. *Journal of Economic Perspectives, 9*(4), 11–26.

Chapter 5
Population Growth's Effect on Economic Development in Rwanda

Daniel Ruturwa Sebikabu, Eric Ruvuna, and Martin Ruzima

Abstract Population growth plays a crucial role in every country's development process. Thus, both demographers and development economists emphasize on the population growth–economic development nexus. This study explores the effects of population growth on economic development in Rwanda over the period of 1974–2013. The study uses data from the World Development Indicators (WDI) and uses economic growth as a proxy for economic development and the neoclassical growth model to capture the effects of population growth on economic development. It also uses the ARDL technique for a time series analysis. In the long run, ARDL results show that the population growth has a positive and statistically significant impact on economic development. In the short run, population growth does not have any significant impact on economic development in Rwanda. Based on the findings, the study recommends that policymakers should keep controlling the population growth rate for economic development.

Keywords Population growth · Economic development · ARDL · Rwanda

JEL Classification Codes A10 · J11 · J13 · O11

D. R. Sebikabu (✉)
Department of Applied Statistics, School of Economics, University of Rwanda, Kigali, Rwanda
e-mail: danielruturwa@gmail.com

E. Ruvuna
Department of Economics and Management, Business and Development Studies Faculty, Kibogora Polytechnic, Nyamasheke, Rwanda
e-mail: kajavieux@gmail.com

M. Ruzima
Institute of Policy Analysis and Research - Rwanda (IPAR-Rwanda), Kigali, Rwanda
e-mail: ruzimam@gmail.com

© Springer Nature Singapore Pte Ltd. 2020
G. G. Das and R. B. Johnson (eds.), *Rwandan Economy at the Crossroads of Development*, Frontiers in African Business Research,
https://doi.org/10.1007/978-981-15-5046-1_5

1 Introduction

The connection between population growth and growing economic output has been studied widely (Heady and Hodge 2009). Numerous analysts believe that economic growth in high-income nations is likely to be comparatively slow in the approaching years since population growth in these nations is forecasted to become significantly sluggish (Baker et al. 2005). Others argue that the population growth has been and will continue to be difficult as more people use more finite resources available on earth, thus decreasing long-term possible evolution (Linden 2017). Klasen and Lawson (2007) offer theoretical arguments and empirical evidence to show that robust population growth enhances economic growth, while others have found evidence to come to the opposite conclusion (Malthus 1970). Still others find that the effects of population growth vary with the level of a country's development, the source or nature of the population growth, and other factors that lead to non-uniform impacts of population growth. Numerous authors have classified, listed, and measured the special effects of demographic modifications particularly on progressive financial prudence to complete their special effects on fiscal sustainability of retirement pension systems (Bouzahzah 2000; De la Croix et al. 2012; Rotehr et al. 2003), reserves (Heijdra and Romp 2008), output (Skirbekk 2008), and fiscal growth (Bloom and Canning 2008; Kelley and Schmidt 2005; Song 2013).

Population growth affects many aspects, such as age in building of a nation's population, movement of human resources, economic disparities, and the dimensions of a nation's work power (Linden 2017). These influence population growth and human development and are exaggerated by overall economic growth (Peterson and Wesley 2017). This study uses long-term data along with an evaluation of theoretical and observed work on the relationship between population growth, total output and capital formation output, agriculture development, foreign direct investments, and the consumption price index to measure their impact on economic growth, and generally on economic development. Piketty (2014) found that the fiscal growth contained only a demographic module and had a purely economic constituent. It is the economic constituent that helps achieve perfection in achieving normal living standard. In addition to the potential effects of population growth on economic development, literature also studies the relationships between them to evaluate the inferences of their probable relationships for growing economics (Peterson and Wesley 2017). Statistical proof of the long-term evolution of the population and total economic production in various regions and selected countries is laid out in World Economics (2016) and Maddison (2001).

Several years ago, agriculture was seen as a major source of livelihood for most developing countries. High fertility rates led to an increase in the number of employees, enhanced productivity, and facilitated economic activities (Latimer and Kulkarni 2008). Furthermore, findings of the impact of population growth on economic growth based on empirical studies are varied. A number of studies such as Adewole (2012), Shaari et al. (2013), and Tartiyus et al. (2015) found that population growth had a positive effect on fiscal growth. According to McWhinney and Angela (2007) human population puts a great strain on the environment. It also has a socioeconomic and environmental impact on social well-being and on the sustainability of global life care systems.

According to Darrat and Al-Yousif (1999), there are three schools of thought on the association between population growth and economic progress. First, is the conventional (Malthusian) school, which states that fast population growth leads to inferior economic growth and poverty. The second takes the opposite view and argues that a higher population growth rate raises the stock of human capital, leading to economic growth. Finally, the change theory maintains that population growth is in part due to changes in incomes. In developing countries where the association between population growth and economic progress can be seen as positive, the demographic situation leads to economic development which in turn leads to an improvement in living standards. Simon (1996) emphasizes the positive side of population growth when he says that a human being is a vigorous indispensable element and 'the ultimate resource' that contributes to economic growth.

Impacts of demographic changes on economic growth matched with the emergence of the 'technology gap' or 'convergence' model in economic progress literature (Barro and Sala-i-Martin 1991). The positive benefits of population size on agriculture have been debated the most in the literature. Higher population concentrations can lower per unit costs and increase the competencies of transport, irrigation, addition services, markets, and communication (Glover and Simon 1975). Possibly the most quoted work is that by Boserup (1965, 1985), who observes that increasingly productive agricultural tools are made economically beneficial with efficiency improvements in response to developed land densities. Osipian (2009), in his study on the hypothetical and empirical examination of the influence of human capital on economic growth in Ukraine, finds a positive impact on economic growth.

Ahlburg (1996) argues that if human capital per capita is satisfactorily large, the economy will move to a stable state of growth, where on the steady-state growth path consumption per capita will increase at a slower rate than human capital if the population is growing and if the production of consumer goods does not keep pace with it. Even though this is the reality, the positive links between population growth and economic growth leading to economic development are discussed more. A large number of educationists have found evidence that an educated population is a key factor for economic growth (Lucas 1988; Hanushek and Kimko 2000). However, other researchers have questioned these findings and hence the role of human capital as an important determinant of economic growth (Levine and Renelt 1992) has emerged. Trade openness has been used extensively in empirical literature as a major element of economic growth in the long run. A large body of empirical literature gives credence to the view that trade openness has a positive impact on economic growth. However, despite these positive perceptions about the effects of trade openness on economic growth, some researchers have questioned the robustness of the outcomes of these studies (Acemoglu and Robinson 2008).

Any discussion on the effects of population variations on economic development should address some specific questions: (1) Will a relaxed population growth increase the growth proportion of per capita revenue through increasing per capita accessibility of exhaustible resources? (2) Will a slower population growth rate increase the growth degree of per capita income increasing per capita availability of renewable capital? (3) Will a decreasing population growth rate alleviate pollution and the degradation of the natural environment? (4) Will an increase in leisure among the population lead to more wealth per worker, there by increasing per worker output and consumption? (5) Do lower population densities lead to lower per capita revenues via a condensed stimulus to technological inventions and reduced exploitation of economies of scale in production; (6) Will a slower population growth rate increase per capita training and well-being?

An analysis of the links between demographic changes and economic growth (David et al. 1999) in Asia during 1965–1990 showed that the overall rate of population growth had little effect on economic growth.

The progress made by many present-day developed nations clearly shows an expansion of opportunities as their economies grew (Hughes and Cain 2003). Studies have found that the simple aspect that is common to these countries is the percentage of city residents in a region and GDP per capita which is about 85% (Henderson 2002), which shows development is a part of current society. There is vast literature on the role of urbanization in promoting economic growth (Davis and Henderson 2003).

The impact of population growth on economic growth (Tartiyus et al. 2015) has been a subject of divergence among economists. The rate of population growth in Rwanda is high, and thus evaluating its impact on economic growth is necessary. Human capital accumulation (Strulik 2005), with a focus on R&D in a variety and quality of intermediate goods and information spillovers are important for economic growth. Economic growth is no longer individually tied to population growth as earlier growth models without scale effects suggest. The macroeconomic growth models maintain that economic growth be determined by its positive impact on the rate of social capital in addition to seeing whether population growth positively or negatively impacts economic growth. The purpose of this study is to find the impact of population growth on economic progress and examine the causality between population growth and economic progress. This study discusses the relationship between population growth and economic development in the context of Rwanda as population growth could deter or enhance economic growth.

2 Literature Review

Various researchers including demographers and economists have studied the interrelationships between population growth and economic progress (Menike 2018). They have studied the effects of population advancements on development and basically follow a pessimistic and optimistic view. The optimistic view of this relationship adopts attitudes that are in favor of population growth. These scholars think that it is not necessary to limit the population of a country, but the pessimists' view is that if a country is to reach a proper state of development it has to reduce its population.

2.1 Why Population Matters?

How big a problem is population growth for developing economies? How does each aspect of population growth including fertility and family size, the percentage of children relative to working-age members of a family, human density, and changes in collective economic demand affect the way societies manage productive assets and allocate goods and services derived from them? Economists maintain that changes in population influence economic growth, employment, poverty, and the organization of assets, including physical (infrastructure), natural (natural resources), and human (health and education status) assets.

2.2 On Economic Growth

Economists Kelley and Schmidt (1994) showed that population growth affected economic growth negatively as measured by the growth degree of per capita gross domestic product (GDP). GDP growth can be forced by a high needs' ratio, which happens when quick population growth uses more children and youth relative to the workforce. Because administrations and households spend far more than what the children can rapidly refund in economic production, especially as modern schooling and healthcare services replace child labor, economists anticipate that consumption related to children will delay household investments, increase government expenditure, and eventually impact GDP growth.

Thirlwall (1993) emphasizes the relationship between population growth and economic development, which he calls a complex topic with regard to reason and effect. He adds that many people consider rapid population growth to be a major obstacle to development.

Afzal (2009) and Boadu (1994) show that population growth affects economic growth negatively. However, others including Kelley (1988) and Thuku et al. (2013) show that population growth has a positive effect on economic growth in the long run due to an increase in productivity. Wang and Mason (2007) worked on the impact of demographic dividend on China's economic growth. They point out that during the last 25 years the People's Republic of China has experienced demographic as well as economic changes in significant proportions. In the last two decades, China has become one of the most active and fastest growing economies in the world. In particular, the first demographic dividend was responsible for this rapid development (mainly due to an increase in the working age population). The first dividend refers to a steady increase in the growth rate of per capita income. This occurs when the productive population grows at a rate faster than the rate of growth of the total population. However, this period with its growth trend has to ultimately end. As the demographic transition happens, growth of the working age population gradually becomes slower than the growth of the total population as the proportion of the aging population increases. This has an effect of reducing the growth of per capita output and per capita consumption. Overall, Wang and Mason note that demographic factors proved to be very favorable for China's economic growth over the last quarter century.

2.3 Population Progress and Economic Development

The relationship between population growth and economic development has been, and still, a main concern of today's development process (Chowdhury and Hossain 2019). Malthus (1970) argues that population growth would depress living standards in the end. Excessive population growth could decrease per head land availability, which creates pressure on the fixed amount of land.

2.4 Theoretical Framework

Some economists consider overpopulation as an opportunity to increase economic growth while others see it as a problem (Rohan 1999). Two theories are widely used in the literature. One states that population increases growth and growth helps a nation's economy by augmenting the rate of economic growth and also through development. This theory was developed by Solow while the second was developed by Thomas Malthus.

2.5 The Robert Solow Theory

Solow's theory of growth describes how increased capital stock produces greater per capita output. Solow starts with the hypothesis that society saves a constant proportion of its income; population and employment grow at a constant rate; capital intensity (or capital per employee) can be controlled; and capital intensity is determined by the prices of the production factors. Due to diminishing returns, additional capital increases (or increasing capital strength) make smaller contributions to production.

In this model, in the long term and under the condition of absence technological progress, a steady-state growth path is reached when output, capital, and employment grow at the same rate. Therefore, output per worker and capital per worker are constant, and the economy comes up with methods of equal growth rates for capital, labor, and total production. An increase in the proportion of saved income cannot lead to an enduring increase in the rate of growth. Moreover, in the absence of technological advancements, the rate of growth will stay the same (irrespective of the share of savings) and will rely on an increased supply of labor.

Solow (1956) criticized the Harrod-Domar long-term growth model for its assumption that production takes place in fixed proportions. Consequently, these conditions question the potential dysfunctional aspects of economic growth (e.g., increased joblessness or long-term inflation). Hence, Solow proposed a model of long-run growth 'which admits all the Harrod-Domar assumptions except that of fixed proportion in production'. It considers labor–capital substitution, that is, a change in manufacturing techniques as a result of changes in relative prices of inputs including labor and capital. This implies that there is the neoclassical aggregate production function at the center of Solow's growth model. The factors of production, capital K and labor L, change because of investments and population growth, respectively. Moreover, markets are in a perfect relationship (Aghion and Howitt 2003). The model can be represented as: First, there is an aggregate production function to control technological likelihoods. Y is output (net output after depreciation of capital) while K and L are capital and labor inputs, respectively. Then,

$$Y = F(K, L) \tag{1}$$

Equation (1) represents the cumulative production function, which is expected to satisfy a series of technical conditions:

- Cumulative in both arguments
- Displaying decreasing peripheral returns to each factor
- Displaying constant returns to scale
- Cobb-Douglas is a production function satisfying these properties. It assumes that F exhibits constant returns to scale in K and L (i.e., it is linearly homogeneous or homogeneous of degree 1 in these two variables).

A law of motion for the stock of capital also characterizes the Solow model. The stock of capital $K(t)$ takes the form of an accumulation of the composite commodity. Net investment $I(t)$ is the rate of increase of this capital stock dK/dt. Therefore, we have the basic identity at every instant of time:

$$dK/dt \equiv \Delta K = I(t) \tag{2}$$

The third important equation of the Solow model is the savings/investments function. Savings and investments (in a closed economy) are a constant fraction(s) of total income:

$$Y(t) : S(t) = I(t) = sY(t) \tag{3}$$

Inserting Eq. (1) in Eq. (3) gives us:

$$K = sF(K, L) \qquad (4)$$

Solow ends his model following Harrod.

2.6 The Thomas Malthus Theory

The Malthusian theory of population is a well-known theory of the relationship between population growth and economic development. It states that human population grows geometrically while food production grows following an arithmetic progression. This theory has been used by many developmental economists, demographers, and policymakers who have found that rapid population growth affects economic development negatively by limiting jobs, generating underemployment, and discouraging labor.

Malthus stated that if measures were not put in place to check a rapidly growing population, then the population would check itself through what he called positive checks. According to him the earth and its entire resources are fixed in supply and if population growth surpasses food production, there will be famines, wars, and other natural disasters as a check on population growth. He proposed that since population growth is detrimental to a country's economic growth stringent measures should be put in place to control population increase among including moral persuasion, education, delay in marriages, spacing of children, and the use of contraceptives.

2.7 Empirical Framework

Abdul and Deyuan (2018) investigated the linkage between economic growth, electricity access, energy use, and population growth in Pakistan during the period 1990–2016. They used an autoregressive distributed lag (ARDL) bounds testing approach for cointegration to study the causality between the variables. Their results showed that in the longrun the connections between the variables, access to electricity by the population, access to electricity by the urban population, and energy usage had a positive impact on economic growth, while electricity access to the rural population had a negative impact on economic growth.

Ali and Amin (2013) worked on the impact of population growth on economic development in Pakistan. They used the ARDL approach to investigate the relationship between population and economic development and their results showed that population had a positive and significant effect on economic development. The study reported that the only problem associated with a high population growth rate was the failure to employ the newly created workforce, its management, and even providing for its basic needs which became a big challenge for the Government of

Pakistan. To critically analyze this problem, they included unemployment rate and expenditure on health and education in the model to assess the impact of population growth directly and indirectly on economic growth. Their results showed that population growth impacted economic development positively and significantly whereas the unemployment rate influenced economic growth negatively. Based on their findings, the authors advised the Government of Pakistan to use the additional workforce efficiently as a policy for achieving a high level of growth.

Anudjo (2015) studied the relationship between population and financial growth in Ghana. His study analyzed the short-run and long-run relationships between population and economic growth as well as the direction of causation between them. The study used the autoregressive distributed lag bounds (ARDL) model. It also used the Granger causality test to determine the direction of causality between population growth and economic growth. The results showed a negative relationship between population growth and economic growth in the shortrun and unidirectional causality in the longrun between the two. The error correction model's (-1) results showed a high speed of 83.6% of long-run equilibrium adjustment every year after a long-run shock in the model. The study recommended that the government should continue its campaign on family planning and policies that encouraged the creation of jobs in Ghana.

Eli et al. (2015) assessed the impact of population growth on economic progress in Nigeria. They found that the rate of population growth was high in Nigeria and there was a need to assess its impact on economic growth. To assess this effect, they used secondary data obtained from the World Development Indicators in 1980–2010. The data was analyzed using descriptive and inferential statistics. The results of their study showed that there was a positive relationship between economic growth measured by GDP and population. The authors recommended that the average population growth rate of Nigeria had to be maintained since it was impacting economic growth positively.

Furuoka (2010) studied the association between population and economic growth in the Philippines. To analyze the data, the study used unit root (ADF), the Johansen cointegration, and the Granger causality tests. The results of the analysis showed that there was a cointegration relationship between population and economic growth in the Philippines implying that these variables had a long-run equilibrium. The study used the Granger causality test to examine the causality between population and economic growth and the findings showed that an increase in population did not Granger cause the country's GDP. This also means that the Philippines's economic growth Granger caused population growth. He concluded that there was an economic development-induced population growth meaning that population growth was driven by economic growth.

Koduru and Tatavarthi (2016) studied the effects of population growth on economic development in India. The data for the study was obtained from the Reserve Bank of India and the National Sample Survey Organization. To estimate the coefficients, the author used a regression analysis and the results showed that for every unit increase in population, the GDP grew by 3.383 units indicating that population growth had a positive impact on economic development in India.

Nwosu et al. (2014) studied the effects of population growth on economic growth in Nigeria. Their study used time series data for the period 1960–2008 by employing a linear model to analyze variations in economic growth vis-à-vis population growth. Based on the results of the augmented Dickey-Fuller (ADF) test combined with Granger causality and cointegration tests, the study proved that population growth had a significant impact on economic growth. The study also showed that there was a long-run equilibrium relationship between economic growth and population growth and that there was also evidence of unidirectional causality between population growth and economic growth.

Thuku et al. (2013) investigated the relationship between population and economic growth in Kenya. They used time series data for the period 1963–2009. To analyze the data, they used the stationarity test, the vector autoregressive technique, causality test, impulse-response, and variance decomposition. Their findings showed that population and economic growth were positively correlated showing that an increase in population will affect economic growth in Kenya positively. They concluded that in Kenya, population growth increased economic growth.

Yao et al. (2013) investigated the relationship between economic development and population growth in China. They used time series data on China to find out the existing relationship between the two. The results of their cointegration analysis showed that population growth had a negative impact on GDP per capita income, whereby the savings rate, total factor productivity, and the degree of industrialization had a positive impact on per capita GDP.

3 Methodology

3.1 Data and Proxy Measures

This study used time series data sourced from the World Development Indicators database (2015). To capture population growth's effect on economic growth, we used data from 1974 to 2013. The variable Y measures economic development and is proxied by real per capita GDP; it is measured by the real GDP growth rate. The variable L is total labor force; however, in this study L is used as a proxy for population growth and measured by Rwanda's total population. In this study population is abbreviated as POP. We used gross domestic investment (K), denoted by CFN to capture the effect of the investments on economic growth. Investments were proxied by the gross fixed capital formation, measured as a percentage of GDP. Agriculture development (AGD) was measured by agriculture production; we used this variable to capture the effect of agriculture on economic development. The variable FDI represents foreign direct investments measured by FDI inflows. CPI represents inflation and is measured by the annual percentage change in the consumer price index. We used the variable CPI to capture the impact of macroeconomic instability on economic development. The statistical package EViews version 9.5 (Demo version) was used for the econometrics analysis.

3.2 Model Specification

An aggregate production function is a crucial point for empirically examining the drivers of economic growth for any country:

$$Y = f(A, K, L) \tag{5}$$

where A represents technological progress. It is noteworthy to mention that A captures the growth in output, which cannot be captured by an increase in labor and capital. The endogenous growth theory put forward by Romer (1986) allows economies to be endogenously influenced by other factors such as foreign direct investments, inflation, and agricultural development. Therefore, the level and adjustment in technological progress for the Rwandan economy is given as:

$$A = h(FDI, AGD, CPI) \tag{6}$$

As stated above, K is denoted by CFN and L is represented by POP. Substituting Eq. (5) in Eq. (6), we get:

$$Y = F(POP, CFN, FDI, AGD, CPI) \tag{7}$$

In the final model, Y is replaced by GDP and the operational model of this study is specified as:

$$Y = F(POP, CFN, FDI, AGD, CPI) + \varepsilon \tag{8}$$

where ε is the error term. The dependent variable is economic development proxied by real per capita growth and the explanatory variables include population growth as the main independent variable.

3.3 Time Series Approach

Before proceeding with the econometrics analysis, we did a stationary test to assess the stationarity property of the time series data. Time series data is non-stationary if the unit root test reports the existence of unit root in the data. This implies that the non-stationary data has a permanent shock while stationary data shocks have a temporary impact. We used the augmented Dickey-Fuller (ADF) unit root test to explore the stationarity property of the variables of interest.[1]

To explore the impact of population growth on economic development for the Rwandan economy, we adopted the autoregressive distributed lag (ARDL) approach for cointegration, developed by Pesaran et al. (2001). The ARDL method has a number of advantages, including an estimation of both the $I(1)$ and $I(0)$ variables and estimation of a small sample and gives good results besides addressing issues of endogeneity (Haug 2002; Pesaran et al. 2001). The ARDL model estimation has three steps: estimating the unrestricted error correction model (UECM) to test whether a long-run relationship exists, determining the-long run coefficients of the ARDL, and estimating the short-run error correction model (ECM).

In the first step, we estimated the unrestricted error correction model (UECM) to test for long-run equilibrium among the variables of interest as:

$$\ln \Delta GDP_t = \alpha_0 + \sum_{i=1}^{a} \alpha_1 \Delta \ln GDP_{tt-i} + \sum_{i=0}^{b} \alpha_2 \Delta \ln POP_{t-i} + \sum_{i=0}^{c} \alpha_3 \Delta \ln CFN_{t-i}$$
$$+ \sum_{i=0}^{d} \alpha_4 \Delta \ln FDI_{t-i} + \sum_{i=0}^{e} \alpha_5 \Delta \ln AGD_{t-i} + \sum_{i=0}^{f} \alpha_6 \Delta \ln CPI_{tt-i}$$
$$+ \beta_1 \ln GDP_{tt-1} + \beta_2 \ln POP_{tt-1} + \beta_3 \ln CFN_{tt-1} + \beta_4 \ln FDI_{tt-1}$$
$$+ \beta_5 \ln AGD_{tt-1} + \beta_6 \ln CPI_{tt-1} + \varepsilon_t \tag{9}$$

where α_0 is the intercept, ε_t is an error term, Δ is the first difference operator. $\alpha(s)$ stands for error correction dynamics while $\beta(s)$ represents the long-run multipliers. To test the existence of a long-run association between population growth and economic development, the critical values produced by Pesaran et al. (2001) were compared with the calculated F-statistics.

In the second step, we estimated the long-run coefficients ($a, b, c, d, e,$ and f) of the ARDL model as:

$$\ln GDP_t = \beta_0 + \sum_{i=1}^{a} \beta_1 \ln GDP_{tt-i} + \sum_{i=0}^{b} \beta_2 \ln POP_{tt-i} + \sum_{i=0}^{c} \beta_3 \ln CFN_{tt-i}$$
$$+ \sum_{i=0}^{d} \beta_4 \ln FDI_{tt-i} + \sum_{i=0}^{e} \beta_5 \ln AGD_{tt-i} + \sum_{i=0}^{f} \beta_6 \ln CPI_{tt-i} + \varepsilon_t \tag{10}$$

Finally, we estimated the short-run coefficients through the error correction model as:

---

[1] For more details of the unit root testing, see Gujarati (1995).

$$\ln \Delta GDP_t = \alpha_0 + \sum_{i=1}^{a} \alpha_1 \Delta \ln GDP_{tt-i} + \sum_{i=0}^{b} \alpha_2 \Delta \ln POP_{t-i}$$
$$+ \sum_{i=0}^{c} \alpha_3 \Delta \ln CFN_{t-i} + \sum_{i=0}^{d} \alpha_4 \Delta \ln FDI_{t-i}$$
$$+ \sum_{i=0}^{e} \alpha_5 \Delta \ln AGD_{t-i} + \sum_{i=0}^{f} \alpha_6 \Delta \ln CPI_{tt-i} + \phi ECT_{t-1} + \varepsilon_t \quad (11)$$

The ECM_{t-1} is lagged by a one-year period and ϕ is the speed of adjustment. The speed of adjustment indicates the rate at which the system can restore to the equilibrium due to a shock to the model.

4 Results and Discussion

4.1 Trend Analysis

Figures 1 and 2 show the trends of economic and population growth over time. In general, the trends show that economic and population growth were volatile during the period under study (1974–2013). In particular, population growth was stable between 1974 and 1983 and then increased between 1984 and 1987. Moreover, there was a remarkable decline in the population growth rate in 1994 because of the genocide against the Tutsi. Many people were killed, and others fled the country to different parts of the world. However, the population growth rate increased rapidly in 1996 to reach a peak of 10.26% in 1998. This was generally stimulated by a large number of citizens (refugees) returning home and others who came back after a long stay in foreign countries. Further, due to government policies and strategies

Fig. 1 Population growth

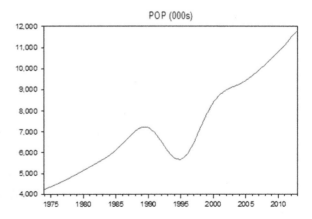

Fig. 2 Real GDP

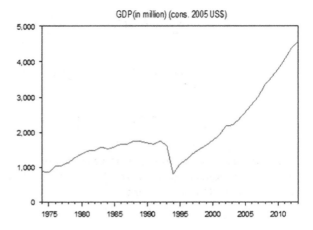

such as family planning the population growth rate stabilized at a reasonable rate. For instance, the period 1999–2004 was characterized by a steady decline in the population growth rate (2.74%) and then the trend was stable from 2005 up to 2013.

Figure 2 shows that the gross domestic product growth rate fluctuated in Rwanda during 1974–2013. This GDP trend had an upward and downward movement and there was a slower growth rate during 1974–1992. However, 1993–1994 was characterized by a steady decrease in GDP due to the genocide against the Tutsi which also collapsed the country's economy. In 1995, economic growth increased sharply because of the rebuilding of the country; foreignaid contributed a lot to this. Steady increase in economic growth was maintained till 2013 and the economic growth rate averaged at 9.8% over the 19-year period (Figs. 3 and 4).

Fig. 3 Population growth rate

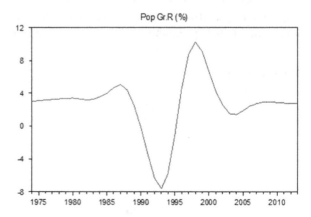

Fig. 4 Economic growth rate

4.2 Descriptive Statistics

Table 1 gives the descriptive statistics of the variables used. Data used in this study had 40 observations for economic growth (the dependent variable), the independent variables include population growth as the main independent variable and foreign direct investments, investments, inflation, and agriculture as control variables. Thus, 40 observations were used for the analysis. The data show that the average economic growth rate was 7.485 and the standard deviation was 0.449 for the period 1974–2013. This result of the standard deviation indicates that during the period under study the economic growth was less volatile. The average population growth rate was 8.858% and its standard deviation was 0.296. In addition, the volatility in population growth was very low at 0.296 in Rwanda during 1974–2013.

Table 1 Summary statistics

Variables	LAGD	LCFN	LCPI	LFDI	LGDP	LPOP
Mean	8.280	5.514	3.161	6.936	7.485	8.858
Median	8.254	5.487	3.097	6.788	7.418	8.833
Maximum	8.685	7.046	4.763	9.177	8.427	9.376
Minimum	8.074	3.738	1.281	5.043	6.688	8.341
Std. dev.	0.150	0.767	1.047	1.130	0.449	0.296
Observations	40	40	40	40	40	40

Source Authors' calculation

4.3 Units Root Test

The unit root test was done to assess the time series property before doing an analysis. The results are given in Table 2. The findings show that except CPI and inflation, which was stationary at the 5% level of significance in both the trend and constant at level (I0) other variables (economic growth (LGDP), population growth (LPOP), agriculture (LAGD), capital formation (LCFN), and foreign direct investments (LFDI) were not stationary. However, after differencing the data (I1) all the variables were found to be stationary at the 1% level of significance. This shows that no variable was integrated of order 2 (I2) which allows us to use the ARDL model for estimation.

4.4 ARDL's Estimation

Generally, the ARDL model starts with the bound test to investigate whether a long-run relationship among the variable of interests exists. We conducted the bound test (Table 3). The results show that there was no long-run relationship or null hypothesis

Table 2 ADF units root test's results

Variable	Level		Difference	
	Constant (ADF)	Trends and constant (ADF)	Constant (ADF)	Trends and constant (ADF)
LGDP	0.445017	1.527126	6.541286***	6.475584***
LPOP	0.804342	2.477724	5.364209***	5.283512***
LAGD	3.12445**	3.520464	–	7.410651***
LFDI	1.41047	1.667923	8.283915***	8.258962***
LCFN	1.215051	2.201428	8.578926***	8.523779***
LCPI	4.082335**	4.082335**	–	–

Note **Denotes significance at the 5% level. ***Denotes significance at the 1% level
Source Authors' calculation

Table 3 ARDL bound test's results

Bounds test				
90%		95%		F-statistic [13.323***]
Lower bound	upper bound	Lower bound	Upper bound	
2.483	3.708	2.962	4.338	
Model: LGDP = F(LPOP, LAGD, LFDI, LCFN, LCPI); K = 5				

Note ***Denotes significance at the 1% level
Source Authors' calculation

among economic growth and control variables; population growth was rejected at the 95% level of significance in favor of the alternative hypothesis. The reason for this is that the calculated F-statistics (13.323) is higher than the upper bound (4.338). Thus, a long-run correlation exists among the selected indicators (GDP, POP, AGD, FDI, CFN, and CPI).

4.5 Long Run Results

Hence, a long-run relationship was detected, and we proceeded with the long-run and short-run estimates, the results of which are presented in Tables 4 and 5.

Table 4 ARDL long-run findings (GDP as the dependent variable)

Variable	Coefficient	Std. error	t-statistic
LPOP	0.355	0.159	2.235**
LFDI	0.245	0.145	1.688
LCPI	13.79	10.371	1.321
LCFN	−0.423	1.657	−0.255
LAGD	0.429	0.308	1.393
C	57.703	53.766	1.072

Note **Denotes significance at the 5% level
Source Authors' calculation

Table 5 ARDL (2, 2, 2, 2, 2) short-run findings, ΔGDP as the dependent variable

Variable	Coefficient	Std. error	t-statistic
LΔGDP(−1)	−0.514	0.171	−3.002****
LΔ POP	0.185	0.117	1.578
LΔPOP(−1)	−0.372	0.177	−2.109**
D(FDI)	0.040	0.011	3.493***
LΔFDI(−1)	−0.018	0.009	−2.008*
LD(CPI)	−13.559	8.438	−1.607
LΔCPI(−1)	−10.339	8.793	−1.176
LΔCFN	0.124	0.316	0.392
LΔCFN(−1)	0.008	0.298	0.025
LΔAGD	0.089	0.041	2.168**
LΔAGD(−1)	−0.001	0.032	−0.307
ecm(−1)	−0.343	0.073	−4.687***

Note *Denotes significance at the 10% level. **Denotes significance at the 5% level. ***Denotes significance at the 1% level
Source Authors' calculation

Table 4 shows that population growth positively impacted economic development proxied by economic growth. The coefficient of population growth is 0.355 and is statistically significant at the 5% level of significance. In particular, a 1% increase in population growth increased economic growth by 0.355%. This positive correlation between economic growth and population growth can be explained by the government's achievements in terms of increase in life expectancy, that is, increase in the working age population and an increase in per capital income. Theoretically, this result agrees with Solow (1956) while disagreeing with Malthus' theory of population. Empirically, the findings corroborate those reported earlier (Ali and Amin 2013; Eli et al. 2015; Koduru and Tatavarthi 2016; Thuku et al. 2013; Wang and Mason 2007) while disagreeing with Afzal (2009), Boadu (1994), and Yao et al.'s (2013) results. Further, other independents variables including foreign direct investments (FDI), consumer price index (inflation) (CPI), capital formation (CFN), and agriculture (AGD) did not have a significant effect on economic growth in Rwanda.

4.6 Short-Run Results

The ARDL estimates for the short-run coefficients are given in Table 5.

As can be seen from the results in Table 5, the coefficients of population growth are positive but statistically insignificant. The reason for this is that it takes time for a newborn to reach the working age. The FDI coefficient is positive and statistically significant at the 1% level. In particular, a 1% increase in foreign direct investments increased economic growth by 0.40%. Thus, FDI can be used for boosting economic growth in the short run. Agriculture positively impacted economic growth and it is statistically significant at the 5% level. This is theoretically correct because agriculture has increasing returns in the short run, while it has decreasing returns in the long run. Moreover, the findings show that the error correction model had the right sign and was statistically significant at the 1% level of significance. Specifically, its coefficient was −0.343, which implies that about 34.3% of the disequilibrium due to a shock to the system was corrected toward the long-run correlation equilibrium within a year.

4.7 Diagnostic Statistics

The diagnostic statistics test's results show that the model is well specified as it did not face problems of function form and heteroscedasticity, and autocorrelation and the residuals were normally distributed (Table 6).

Additionally, the model has a good fit as shown by the findings of the cumulative sum (CUSUM) and the cumulative sum of squares (CUSUM squares). The residuals were bounded within the 5% bound of significance. The CUSUM and CUSUM squares are given in Figs. 5 and 6.

Table 6 Diagnostic statistics test's results

Auto correlation[a]	Functional form[b]	Normality[c]	Heteroscedasticity[d]
1.735	0.052	1.9	1.63
[0.202]	[0.823]	[0.387]	[0.162]

[a]Lagrange multiplier test of residual serial correlation
[b]Ramsey's RESET test using the square of the fitted values
[c]Based on a test of skewness and kurtosis of residuals
[d]Based on the regression of squared residuals on squared fitted values
Note Probability in parentheses
Source Authors' calculation

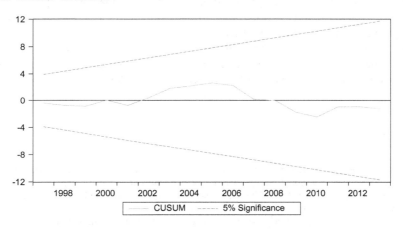

Fig. 5 CUSUM

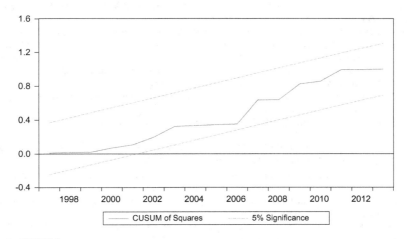

Fig. 6 CUSUM square

5 Conclusion

This study investigated the population–economic development nexus in Rwanda. It used time series data sourced from WDI for the period 1974–2013. It used the ARDL technique for analyzing the data. Regarding the theoretical framework, this study adopted the Solow growth model. ARDL's results showed that population growth had a positive impact and was statistically significant for economic development in the long run while in the short run, population growth did not have a significant effect on economic development. Further, other control variables (physical capital formation, agricultural development, FDI, and the consumer price index) did not have a significant effect on economic development in the long run. Additionally, foreign direct investments and agricultural development had a positive significant effect on economic development in the short run. Based on the study's findings we recommend that the Government of Rwanda should maintain a stable population growth rate as it contributes positively to economic development ceteris paribus.

References

Abdul, R., & Deyuan, Z. (2018). Investigating the linkage between economic growth, electricity access, energy use, and population growth in Pakistan. *Journal of Applied Sciences, 8,* 2442.

Acemoglu, D., & Robinson, J. A. (2008). Persistence of power, elites, and institutions. *American Economic Review, 98*(1), 267–293.

Adewole, A. O. (2012). Effect of population on economic development in Nigeria: A quantitative assessment. *International Journal of Physical and Social Sciences, 2*(5), 11–17.

Afzal, M. (2009). Population growth and economic development in Pakistan. *The Open Demography Journal, 2*(1).

Aghion, P., & Howitt, P. (2003). *Endogenous growth theory.* Cambridge (MA): MIT Press.

Ahlburg, D. A. (1996). Population and poverty. In D. A. Ahlburg, A. C. Kelley, & K. O. Mason (Eds.), *The impact of population growth on wellbeing in developing countries.* Berlin: Springer.

Ali, S., & Amin, A. (2013). The impact of population growth on economic development in Pakistan. *Middle East Journal of scientific Research, 18*(4), 483–491.

Baker, D., Delong, J. B., & Krugman, P. R. (2005). Asset returns and economic growth. *Brookings Papers on Economic Activity, 1,* 289–330.

Barro, R. J., & Sala-i-Martin, X. (1991). Convergence across states and regions. *Brookings Papers on Economic Activity, 1,* 107–182.

Bloom, D. E., & Canning, D. (2008). Global demographic change: Dimensions and economic significance. *Population and Development Review, 34,* 17–51.

Boadu, E. A. (1994). *Rapid population growth and development in Ghana.* Accra: Department of Geography and Resource Development, University of Ghana.

Boserup, E. (1965). *The conditions of agricultural growth: The economics of agrarian change under population pressure.* Chicago, IL: Aldine.

Boserup, E. (1985). Economic and demographic inter-relationships in sub-Saharan Africa. *Population and Development Review, 11*(3), 383–397. Or 81.

Bouzahzah, M. (2000). *Développements de la Modélisationen Equilibre Général Calculable* (p. 2). Thèse de doctorat: Université de Lille.

Chowdhury, M. N. M., & Hossain, M. M. (2019). Population growth and economic development in Bangladesh: Revisited Malthus. *American Economic & Social Review, 5*(2), 1–7.

Dao, M. Q. (2012). Population and economic growth in developing countries. *International Journal of Academic Research in Business and Social Sciences, 2*(1), 6–20.

Darrat, A. F., & Al-Yousif, Y. (1999). On the long-run relationship between population and economic growth: Some time series evidence for developing countries. *Eastern Economic Journal, 25*(3), 301–313.

David, C., Bloom David, E., & Malaney, P. N. (1999). *Demographic change and economic growth in Asia*. Center for International Development (CID) at Harvard University.

Davis, J. C., & Henderson, J. Vernon. (2003). Evidence on the political economy of the urbanization process. *Journal of Urban Economics, 53*(1), 98–125.

De la Croix, D., Pierrard, O., & Sneessens, H. R. (2012). Aging and pensions in general equilibrium: Labor market imperfections matter. *Journal of Economic Dynamics and Control, 37*(1), 104–124.

Eli, H. T., Dauda, M. I., & Peter, A. (2015). Impact of population growth on economic growth in Nigeria (1980–2010). *Journal of Humanities and Social Sciences, 20*(4), 115–123.

Furuoka, F. (2010). Population growth and economic development: Empirical evidence from the Philippines. *Philippine Journal of Development, 37*(1), 81–93.

Furuoka, F. (2013). Population growth and economic development in Indonesia: A revisit with new data and methods. *Acta Oeconomica, 63*(4), 451–467.

Glover, D. R., & Simon, J. L. (1975). The effect of population density on infrastructure: The case of road building. *Economic Development and Cultural Change, 23*(3), 453–468.

Gujarati, D. N. (1995). *Basic econometrics*. New York: McGraw-Hill.

Hanushek, E. A., & Kimko, D. D. (2000). Schooling, labor-force quality, and the growth of nations. *American Economic Review, 90*(5), 1184–1208.

Haug, A. A. (2002). Temporal aggregation and the power of cointegration tests: A Monte Carlo study. *Oxford Bulletin of Economics and Statistics, 64*(4), 399–412.

Heady, D. D., & Hodge, A. (2009). The effect of population growth on economic growth: A meta-regression analysis of the macroeconomic literature. *Population and Development Review, 35*, 221–248.

Heijdra, B. J., & Romp, W. E. (2008). Retirement, pensions, and ageing. *Journal of Public Economics, 93*, 586–604.

Henderson, J. V. (2002). Urbanization in developing countries. *World Bank Research Observer, 17*(1), 89–112.

Hughes, J., & Cain, L. P. (2003). *American economic history* (6th ed.). Boston: Addison Wesley.

Kelley, A. C. (1988). *Population matters: Demographic change, economic growth, and poverty in the developing world*. New York: Oxford University Press.

Kelley, A. C., & Schmidt, R. M. (1994). Population and income change: Recent evidence. In *World Bank Discussion Papers* (No. 249).

Kelley, A. C., & Schmidt, R. M. (2005). Evolution of recent economic-demographic modeling: A synthesis. *Journal of Population Economics, 18*(2), 275–300.

Klasen, S., & Lawson, D. (2007). The impact of population growth on economic growth and poverty reduction in Uganda. Diskussionsbeiträgeausdem Volkswirtschaftlichen Seminar der Universität Göttingen.

Koduru, B. P. K., & Tatavarthi, A. (2016). Effect of population growth on economic development in India.

Latimer, A., & Kulkarni, K. (2008). Population and economic development: A comparative study. *Journal of Population and Social Studies, 14*, 47–66.

Levine, R., & Renelt, D. (1992). A sensitivity analysis of cross-country growth regressions. *American Economic Review, 82*, 942–963.

Linden, E. (2017). *Remember the population bomb? It's still ticking* (p. 4). New York Times: Baker Sunday Review.

Lucas, R. E., Jr. (1988). On the mechanics of economic development. *Journal of Monetary Economics, 22*(1), 3–42.

Maddison, A. (2001). *The world economy. A millennial perspective*. OECD Development Centre.

Malthus, T. (1970). *An essay on the principle of population and a summary view of the principles of population.* London: Pickering.

McWhinney, E., & Angela, S. M. (2007). Human population dynamics in protected areas. Innovations in a conservation series. Parks in Peril Program. Arlington, VA, USA. *The Nature Conservancy.*

Menike, H. R. A. (2018). A literature review on population growth and economic development. *International Journal of Humanities Social Sciences and Education, 5*(5), 67–74.

Mora, C., & Engelman, R. (2017). The interaction of human population, food production, and biodiversity protection. *Science, 356*(6335), 260–264.

Osipian, A. (2009). *The impact of human capital on economic growth: A case study in Post-Soviet Ukraine.* New York: Palgrave Macmillan.

Pesaran, M. H., Shin, Y., & Smith, R. J. (2001). Bounds testing approaches to the analysis of level relationships. *Journal of Applied Econometrics, 16,* 289-326.

Peterson, E., & Wesley, F. (2017). The role of population in economic growth. *SAGE Open, 7*(4), 2158244017736094.

Piketty, T. (2014). *Capital in the twenty-first century.* Cambridge, MA: Belknap Press of Harvard University Press.

Rohan, K. (1999). Does India's population growth has a positive effect on economic growth? *Social Science,* 410.

Romer, P. M. (1986). Increasing returns and long-run growth. *Journal of Political Economics, 94*(5), 1002–1037.

Rotehr, P. C., Catenaro, M., & Shwab, G. (2003). Ageing and pensions in the Euro area survey and projection results. Social Protection Discussion Paper Series No 0307, The World Bank.

Shaari, M. S., Rahim, H. A., & Rashid, I. M. (2013). Relationship among population, energy consumption and economic growth in Malaysia. *The International Journal of Significance. Population and Development Review, 34,* 17–51.

Simon, J. L. (1981). *The ultimate resource.* Princeton, NJ: Princeton University Press.

Simon, J. (1996). *The economics of population growth.* The University of Chicago journals.

Skirbekk, V. (2008). Age and productivity capacity: descriptions, causes and policy. *Ageing Horizons, 8,* 4–12.

Solow, R. (1956). A contribution to the theory of economic growth. *The Quarterly Journal of Economics, 70*(1), 65–94.

Song, S. (2013). *Demographic changes and economic growth: Empirical evidence from Asia* (p. 121). Paper: Honors Projects.

Strulik, H. (2005). The role of human capital and population growth in R&D-based models of economic growth. *Review of International Economics, 13*(1), 129–145.

Tartiyus, E. H., Dauda, T. M., & Peter, A. (2015). Impact of population growth on economic growth in Nigeria. *IOSR Journal of Humanities and Social Science (IOSR-JHSS), 20*(4), 115–123.

Thirlwall, A. P. (1993). *Growth and development with special reference to developing economies* (pp. 143–155). University of Kent at Canterbury.

Thuku, G. K., Gachanja, P. M., & Obere, A. (2013). The impact of population change on economic growth in Kenya University.

Wang, F., & Mason, A. (2007). Demographic dividend and prospects for economic development in China. In *United nations expert group meeting on social and economic implications of changing population age structures* (Vol. 141).

World Bank, & Anudjo, E. Y. (2015). *The population growth-economic growth Nexus: New evidence from Ghana*. Doctoral dissertation, University of Ghana.

Yao, W., Kinugasa, T., & Hamori, S. (2013). An empirical analysis of the relationship between economic development and population growth in China. *Applied Economics*, *45*(33), 4651–4661. Crist, E.

Part II
Firm's Performance, SMEs and Role of Entrepreneurship

Chapter 6
Innovation and Firms' Performance in the Rwandese Manufacturing Industry: A Firm-Level Empirical Analysis

Etienne Ndemezo and Charles Kayitana

Abstract The main objectives of this paper are: (i) determining the factors that support Rwandese manufacturing firms' engagement in innovative activities; (ii) assessing the effects of innovation decisions on innovation performance of Rwandese manufacturing firms; and (iii) evaluating the impact of innovations on the financial performance of Rwandese manufacturing firms. To address these objectives, the study uses a structural multi-stage framework as proposed by Crépon et al. (Econ Innov New Technol 7(2):115–158 1998). The study uses data from the 'World Bank Enterprise Survey: Rwanda 2006' and draws three main conclusions: (i) product innovations are positively linked to process innovations, that is, firms which engage in process innovations also introduce new or improved products in the market; (ii) for innovation output, the 'international quality recognition' is not linked to a firm's engagement with innovations; instead it is linked to the use of technology licensed from foreign firms; and (iii) 'international quality recognition' is the main determinant of a firm's financial performance.

Keywords Innovation · Manufacturing industry · International quality certification · Firm's performance

JEL Classification Codes L60 · O14 · O31 · O32

1 Introduction

Entrepreneurship and industrial development are essential for rapid economic growth in developing economies. While entrepreneurship is the mainstay of significant economic growth, an economy can only expect tangible results through innovations.

E. Ndemezo (✉)
Department of Economics, University of Rwanda, Kigali, Rwanda
e-mail: ndemo.etcroix@gmail.com

C. Kayitana
Department of Marketing and Human Resources, University of Rwanda, Kigali, Rwanda
e-mail: ckayitana@gmail.com

© Springer Nature Singapore Pte Ltd. 2020
G. G. Das and R. B. Johnson (eds.), *Rwandan Economy at the Crossroads of Development*, Frontiers in African Business Research,
https://doi.org/10.1007/978-981-15-5046-1_6

Innovations refer to all scientific, technological, organizational, financial, and commercial steps which actually lead to, or are intended to lead to, the implementation of technologically new or improved products or services (OECD 2005). OECD (2005) gives four types of innovations: product innovations, process innovations, organizational innovations, and marketing innovations.

A number of factors can affect innovation activities including economic factors such as production costs and demand; factors specific to an enterprise such as skilled personnel and knowledge; and legal factors such as competition regulations and tax rules (Crépon et al. 1998). Marques et al. (2011) stress that encouraging firms to innovate will lead to better economic performance in terms of their market and financial performance. Thus, policies that promote innovations may help in fostering growth and competitiveness among businesses, specific regions, and in the economy as a whole.

Based on Schumpeter's (1940) theory of creative destruction which proposes that non-innovative firms and products will be replaced by innovative ones, like many regional and African countries, Rwanda too has identified innovations to be a sustainable way of ensuring high economic growth and an enterprise's performance (MINECOFIN 2013). Although innovations are generally regarded as a means of improving firms' competitiveness and their performance locally or regionally, this has not been supported unambiguously by empirical work in Rwanda.

Empirical evidence shows the dynamic role of entrepreneurial activities in promoting innovations and technology, and economic growth and employment (Audretsch et al. 2006; Fritsch and Mueller 2004, 2008; Van Stel 2006). On the other hand, entrepreneurship development is based on innovative ideas and use of new technologies to support an enterprise's performance (Balachandran and Sakthivelan 2013; Tuan et al. 2016). According to Tuan et al. (2016) an enterprise's performance can be identified as a multi-dimensional concept that can be measured by three indicators: production, finance, and marketing.

Having accepted the importance of innovations and technology, it is disappointing to note that in the Rwandan context, no specific research has been done on measuring the impact of innovations and technology on enterprises' performance or even on the most direct and quantifiable outcomes of innovations and technology on entrepreneurship. In an attempt to bridge this gap, this study investigates the impact of innovations on entrepreneurship development in Rwanda as its main objective. It has three specific objectives: (i) determining the factors that support Rwandese manufacturing firms' engagement in innovative activities; (ii) assessing the effects of innovation decisions on innovation performance of Rwandese manufacturing firms; and (iii) evaluating the impact of innovation performance on Rwandese manufacturing firms' financial performance.

To address these three specific objectives, the study uses the structural multi-stage approach as suggested by Crépon et al. (1998). Crépon et al.'s (1998) modeling allows dealing with problems of selection bias and simultaneity. The study uses data from the World Bank Enterprise Survey for Rwanda in the year 2006. This study arrived at three main conclusions: (i) product innovations are linked to process innovations, that is, firms which are engaged in process innovations have also introduced new or improved products in the market; (ii) about innovation output, the 'international quality recognition' is not linked to a firm's engagement with innovations, it is instead linked to the use of technology licensed from foreign firms; and (iii) 'international quality recognition' is the main determinant of a firm's financial performance.

The rest of the study is organized as follows. After this introduction, it presents a brief literature review which is followed by a section on the methodology used and the empirical results. The study ends with a conclusion which summarizes the main findings and makes some recommendations.

2 Literature Review

As stressed by Fagerberg (2004), innovations are not a new phenomenon, but despite their importance they have not received enough attention by scholars. However, research on innovations and economic and social change has increased in recent years, particularly in social sciences. In particular, the relationship between innovations and productivity or firms' performance has been studied by Mairesse and Mohnen (2010), Hall (2011), and Mohnen and Hall (2013). Mairesse and Mohnen (2010) analyzed innovation surveys' characteristics and econometric problems raised by the data collected. Hall (2011) did a synthesis of the research on the relationship between innovations and productivity at the firm level, and Mohnen and Hall (2013) updated the literature reviews given in these two studies.

With the main aim of determining the relationship between innovations and productivity of European firms, Hall (2011) reviewed the ways in which economists have analyzed the relationship between productivity and innovations. He concluded that there were substantial positive impacts of product innovations on revenue productivity, but that the impact of process innovations was more ambiguous. He also observed that at the individual firm level, process innovations can increase real output while leaving revenue mostly unchanged. Further, one of the consequences of innovations is likely to be the entry of new innovating firms and the exit of some inefficient ones. Thus, he suggested directing attention to the extent to which entry and exit regulations impact the rationalization of industry structures in response to innovative activities.

Like Hall (2011), Mohnen and Hall (2013) also analyzed the effects of technological and non-technological innovations on firms' productivity by reviewing existing evidence in the literature. From their survey of empirical literature, they concluded that innovations led to a better productivity performance. They also observed that all types of innovations influenced productivity, but isolating individual effects remained difficult because of simultaneity of different types of innovations. Further, they observed that the effects of innovations were divided into two parts: one going to the real output, and another pertaining to the price at which the output is sold. However, they concluded that it was very difficult to dissociate the two because of measurement issues.

Individual studies give further insights about the relationship between innovations and performance and raise detailed econometric problems according to their specificities. They also provide a different understanding of the probability of firms engaging in innovative activities.

Crépon et al. (1998) used an econometric method which corrected for selectivity[1] found in their study, where some factors positively affected the probability of a firm engaging in innovation activities like its number of employees, sales share and distribution, market demand, and the technology used. However, they observed that a small proportion of firms is engaged in research activities and/or applied for patents. With regard to the effects of innovations on performance, taking into account both simultaneity and selectivity bias, they concluded that innovation output increased with innovation efforts (investments in R&D), and firms' productivity was correlated to innovation output, represented by the number of patents or innovative sales.

Considering different types of innovations, Mairesse et al. (2009) found that product innovations were the main driver of labor productivity in the French manufacturing and services industries. The impact of process innovations was either not significant or close to zero. Further, after studying the services sector, Morrar (2014) concluded that French manufacturing firms were more innovative in technological matters while innovations in service firms were more oriented toward marketing activities.

Legros and Galia (2012) analyzed the sources of knowledge and their effect on productivity in French manufacturing firms and found that market share and firm size had a positive impact on innovation decisions and the intensity of R&D. They concluded that size and workers' involvement mattered for ISO 9000[2] certification. However, the main result was amplified by the existence of competing products and patents. They suggested that firms must invest not only in R&D but also in different sources of internal and external knowledge such as workers' training and the ISO 9000 certification.

Previous results confirm Griffith et al.'s (2006) conclusions on a study of the role that innovation plays in firms' productivity in four European countries—France, Germany, Spain, and UK, using a structural multi-stage model (Crépon et al. 1998). Griffith et al. (2006) used data from the third wave of the internationally harmonized community innovation surveys. They found that firms that operated mainly in international markets and larger firms were engaged more in formal innovative activities (here R&D). They also found that process innovations were more positively influenced by suppliers' information, while product innovations were influenced more by demand information. Further, Griffith et al. (2006) concluded that process innovations were associated with productivity only in France, while product innovations were associated with productivity in France, Spain, and UK. These findings are supported by Zemplinerova and Hromadkova (2012) in their study on the determinants of

---

[1] This is known as the CDM method referring to the initials of the authors' names: Crepon, Duguet, and Mairesse.

[2] Series of standards defined and published by the International Organization of Standardization to maintain quality assurance by manufacturing and service firms.

firm innovation in Czechoslovakia. These authors found that the probability of a firm engaging in innovations was positively influenced by its size. Analyzing the relationship between innovations and productivity in the Mexican manufacturing industry, Brown and Guzman (2014) concluded that the largest firms had more propensity to innovate; these firms also had high technological intensity and market shares. Some of the other conclusions that these authors arrived at were that advertising, knowledge appropriability, foreign direct investments, information technologies, and access to credit had a positive effect on innovation efforts.

Beneki et al. (2012) investigated the relationship between innovativeness and firms' performance in Greece and concluded that the private sector was not willing to invest in R&D and that there was low productivity of innovations. Thus, they suggested leveraging private investments in innovations through public investments.

Using the structural multi-stage model which incorporates information on innovation success, an analysis of the impact of innovations on the productivity of small and medium enterprises (SMEs) in Italy, Bronwyn et al. (2009) found that international competition fostered R&D intensity, especially in high-tech firms. Determinants of engagement in both product and process innovations were firm size and investments in R&D and equipment. They also found that both product and process innovations influenced SMEs' productivity, especially process innovations. However, they observed that the productivity of larger and older firms among the SMEs was less influenced by their innovativeness.

However, in developing countries, findings about the impact of each type of innovation are somehow different. Analyzing the influence of product and process innovations on firms' productivity in Bangladesh and Pakistan, Waheed (2011) found that process innovations affected the productivity of firms more than product innovations. In Mexico, Brown and Guzman (2014) found that firms that had a higher propensity to innovate were larger in terms of intensity in high technology and market shares. They also found that firms which innovated had a level of labor productivity that was 1.3 times higher than firms that did not innovate. However, their study did not distinguish between process and product innovations.

In Vietnam, Tuan et al. (2016) found that process, organization, and marketing innovations had a significantly positive impact on innovative performance. However, they observed that product innovation activities had no statistical impact on firms' innovative performance. Further, they concluded that factors which influenced firms' innovative performance also had positive effects on their performance in production, market, and finance.

When it comes to methodological issues, Lööf and Heshmati (2006) analyzed the sensitivity of the estimated relationship between innovativeness and firms' performance. They found that the simultaneity between innovation activities and productivity or performance was of great importance and merited much more attention than the selectivity bias. They also found enough homogeneity in the relationship between innovations and productivity in both manufacturing and service firms.

Studies which link innovations to a firm's performance, or which analyze the determinants of firms' innovativeness are few in developing countries, especially in Rwanda. To the best of our knowledge, no other study has been done on innovations and firms' performance. Thus, this study fills this gap in the literature. The findings of this study will be useful for policymaking on the efficiency of innovativeness in the Rwandese manufacturing industry.

3 Methodological Framework

3.1 The Model

To address the objectives of this study, we used the CDM framework as detailed in Crépon et al. (1998). The theoretical foundation of this methodology is the Cobb-Douglas production function:

$$Q = AL^{\alpha} K^{\beta} \tag{1}$$

where Q is the total profit before taxes, A is the level of innovations, and L and K are labor and capital inputs. Parameters α and β are elasticity of production with respect to labor and capital inputs.

However, the CDM model has two econometric problems: selectivity bias and simultaneity bias. A selectivity bias arises from the fact that not all firms engage in innovations and some innovations are not successful. The simultaneity bias comes from various factors which can influence firms' decisions to innovate, their level of expenditure on innovations, and final performance.

To deal with these two problems, the CDM model is constructed in three steps. The first step accounts for the fact that a firm is engaged in innovative activities. Here, innovative activities are described by two equations: the first deals with the decision to innovate and the second deals with innovation inputs, for example, investments in R&D. The two equations are linked to their determinants in the first two stages of the innovation process.

In the third stage, a firm's innovation output (e.g., the number of patents) is related to its innovation intensity (spending on R&D). The last stage deals with the relationship between a firm's performance, innovation inputs, and innovation output.

We summarize the four equations used in the CDM modeling as:

$$g_i^* = x_{1i}\beta_1 + u_{1i} \tag{2}$$

where g_i^* a latent variable of innovation decision equals to 1 if a firm has undertaken innovative activities and 0 if it has not. Variable x_{1i} represents the vector of explanatory variables, and β_1 is the associated coefficient vector. Subscript i designates the firm unit, while u_{1i} is the term error:

$$k_i^* = x_{2i}\beta_2 + u_{2i} \tag{3}$$

where k_i^* represents the amount invested in innovations by firm i. Variables x_{2i} represent the vector of explanatory variables and β_2 is the associated coefficient vector. Subscript i designates the firm, while u_{2i} is the term error in Eq. (3). With regard to innovation literature, the first two stages of the systemic approach are estimated jointly by a generalized Tobit model using the maximum likelihood estimation method.

The second stage accounts for the impact of engagement and investments in innovations on innovation output. Here, we can consider innovation output as the number of new or improved products/services or the number of patents:

$$t_i^* = x_{3i}\beta_3 + u_{3i} \qquad (4)$$

The variable t_i^* is an innovation output. Other variables and parameters are defined as earlier.

Equation (5) accounts for the effects of innovation inputs and output on a firm's performance. Literature usually uses the Cobb-Douglas production function augmented to innovation variables:

$$q_i = x_{4i}\beta_4 + k_i^* + t_i^* + u_{4i} \qquad (5)$$

where q_i is the indicator of a firm's financial performance; k_i^* and t_i^* are variables representing innovation inputs and output, respectively; x_{4i} is the vector of explanatory variables; β_4 is the associated coefficient vector; and u_{4i} is the term error. All the variables in Eq. (5) are in log form except the dummy variables. Referring to literature on innovations, this last specification is estimated using the three-stage least squares (Lööf and Heshmati 2006) method where the inverse Mills ratio is introduced in Eq. (3) to deal with the selection bias.

3.2 Model Specification

In Eq. (2), the dependent variable is a firm's engagement in product innovations. Here, we consider that a firm engages in innovations if it introduces a new or significantly improved product in the market. Here, process innovations are considered as a prerequisite for reaching product innovations. The explanatory variables in Eq. (2) are process innovations, domestic competition, foreign ownership, and added value per worker.

Because of lack of appropriate data, Eq. (3), which deals with the relationship between the intensity of investments in innovations and appropriate explanatory variables, is not used in our modeling. Instead of Eq. (3), we use Eq. (4) which refers to innovation output. Thus, we determine the relationship between innovation decisions and innovation output, represented here by the fact that the firms have *international quality recognition*. The innovation output equation contains process innovations as defined earlier, the number of new competitors entering the market, use of websites and e-mails with clients and suppliers, use of licensed technology, company age in 2006, total fixed assets per worker, added value per worker, and number of employees in 2005 as explanatory variables. Equation (4) also includes the inverse Millsratio.

Equations (2) and (4) are estimated jointly using the generalized Tobit method. Equations (4) and (5) are also estimated jointly. All the variables in Eq. (5) are in log form except the dummy variables. With reference to literature on innovations, this last specification is estimated using the three-stage least squares method (Lööf and Heshmati 2006); but in our modeling, they are estimated using the two-stage least squares method because we do not use Eq. (3).

Equation (5) is a performance equation and has capacity utilization (representing the competitiveness of a firm), technology intensity represented by electricity expenditure, variables of market conditions (represented by the share of direct export sales and a share of the national market sales), use of information technology represented by use of e-mails and websites, company age, number of employees, total fixed assets (representing the physical capital), and international quality recognition (here representing the innovation output as mentioned earlier) as the explanatory variables.

3.3 Data

This study used data from the World Bank enterprise survey, Rwanda 2006. The World Bank collected data in Rwanda in 2006 under the theme '*Enquête sur le climat des investissements et la productivité*' and is referenced as RWA_2006_ES_v01_M_WB.

It would have been preferable to use 'the World Bank innovation follow-up module–enterprise survey Rwanda 2011' which focuses on the specific issue of innovations in manufacturing and service firms. However, this survey combined both manufacturing and service firms; and because of a lot of missing observations, the number of manufacturing firms was not enough for an appropriate analysis. Consequently, using the 2011 innovation survey did not allow determining the true relationship between innovations and a firm's performance in the manufacturing sector.

4 Empirical Findings

4.1 Overview of the Sample

We start this section with descriptive statistics on the age, size, capacity utilization, and the number of employees in the sample.

A. Employment and Size of Firms

The sample had 59 manufacturing companies located in Huye and Kigali cities. The categorization that we used is borrowed from the World Bank which defines company size as:

- A small company is defined as one which has between 5 and 19 full-time employees.
- A medium company has between 20 and 99 full-time employees.
- A large company has 100 or more employees.

According to Fig. 1, the sample is dominated by small and medium firms—23 and 25 firms respectively. Only 11 firms are categorized as large. With reference to the number of employees, about 41% of the firms are classified as small companies having less than 19 employees and about 81% of the companies studied fall in the category of SMEs as they have less than 100 employees. However, individually we observe that a large company has the highest number of full-time employees (on average about 305 employees per company). Small firms on average have only 10 employees (Fig. 2).

B. Age of Companies

Referring to a company's experience, young firms are also small while older firms are large. About 53% of the firms in the sample had been operating for less than eight years, meaning that most of the firms in Rwanda are very young. The oldest firm had completed 66 years of operations in 2006. On average, large firms had been

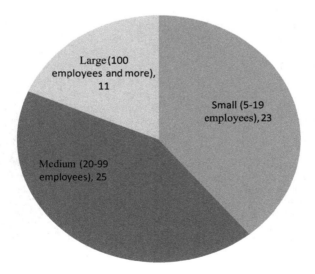

Fig. 1 Number of firms according to size. *Source* Authors' computations using the World Bank Enterprise Surveys: Rwanda 2006

Fig. 2 Average number of employees as per firm size. *Source* Authors' computations using the World Bank Enterprise Surveys: Rwanda 2006

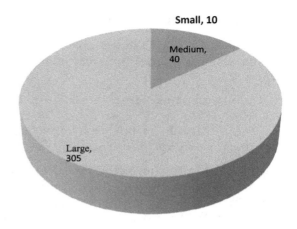

operating for 22 years, medium firms for 16 years, and small firms for seven years. A firm's age is positively correlated to its size (Fig. 3).

C. Capacity Utilization by Manufacturing Firms

Capacity utilization by firms also reflects their competitiveness. Consequently, according to their size, Fig. 4 shows that small firms were more competitive in Rwanda, as they used more than 76% of their potential capacity. Medium firms were less competitive because they used only 55.5% of their capacity. Further, large firms were also relatively more competitive as compared to medium firms.

Fig. 3 Age of firms according to size. *Source* Authors' computations using the World Bank Enterprise Surveys: Rwanda 2006

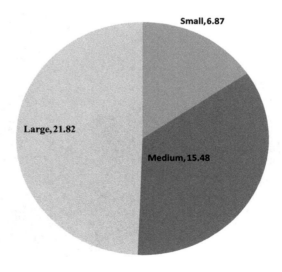

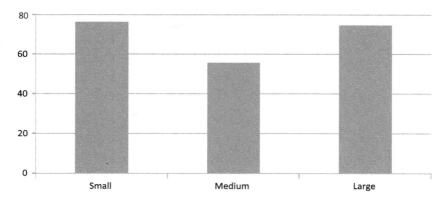

Fig. 4 Capacity utilization of firms as per size. *Source* Authors' computations using the World Bank Enterprise Surveys: Rwanda 2006

4.2 Effects of Innovations on Manufacturing Firms' Financial Performance

To analyze the effects of innovations on a firm's financial performance, we give the results in two stages. First, we analyzed the effects of innovation engagements on innovation output, or 'international quality recognition.' After this we analyzed the effects of 'international quality recognition' on firms' financial performance or the effects of innovation decisions on innovation performance.

According to Table 1, engagement with innovations was related to innovation output (international quality recognition) via the inverse Mills ratio. This ratio was not significantly relevant as we can observe from its P-value. This suggests that the selection bias was not enough; these results are similar to those in Lööf and Heshmati (2006). This allowed us to use the two-stage least squares method as the last stage without the inverse Millsratio. Product innovations represented here as firms' innovation decisions were positively linked to process innovations and negatively linked to value-added per worker. This shows that a firm engaged in process innovations have new or improved products. Also, a firm's financial performance was not the main determinant of innovation decisions. Firms engaged in innovative activities improve their finances and not the reverse. However, engagement with innovations had no significant effect on international quality recognition as this was influenced more by the use of technology licensed from foreign companies. As compared to the other variables, use of licensed technology had the highest coefficient and was statistically very significant. Against this, even if process innovations influenced product innovations significantly they had no effect on international quality recognition.

The number of full-time employees was one of the factors determining 'international quality recognition.' This shows that manufacturing companies' size influenced their international quality recognition. However, as the coefficient is low, the influence of a company's size on its innovation output was almost negligible. On the

Table 1 Effects of innovation engagements on innovation output: a generalized Tobit regression

International quality recognized	Coefficients	P-Values
Process innovations	0.238057	0.667
New competitor has entered the market	−0.059423	0.404
Use of website with clients or suppliers	0.055952	0.614
Use of licensed technology	0.723303	0.000
Use of e-mails with clients or suppliers	−0.212101	0.019
Company experience	0.0020135	0.483
Total fixed assets per worker	1.88E−09	0.664
Added value per worker	−8.82E−10	0.901
Employees	0.0015207	0.000
_cons	−0.183072	0.762
Product innovations		
Process innovations	2.376331	0.000
Domestic competitor or production costs	−0.010132	0.981
Foreign ownership	0.0061147	0.349
Added value per worker	−3.34E−08	0.096
_cons	−0.755568	0.059
Mills lambda	0.1361329	0.766
Rho	0.68301	
Sigma	0.1993147	
Number of observations	59	
Uncensored observations	35	
Wald chi2(9)	83.31	
Prob > chi2	0000	

Source Authors' estimations using the World Bank Enterprise Surveys: Rwanda 2006

contrary, the use of e-mails in relations with clients or suppliers impacted international quality recognition negatively. However, we think that in 2005 using e-mails was a new concept in the Rwandese manufacturing industry and was mainly adopted by a few small firms which were not innovative enough. Although the result seems difficult to interpret in terms of intuition, using e-mails in 2005 seems to be a new idea for business communication in the Rwandese manufacturing industry, and that communication channel was mainly adopted by less-innovative small firms.

A. Effects of Innovations on Financial Performance

In Table 2 we see that the main determinant of financial efficiency of manufacturing firms is 'international quality recognition.' Its coefficient is the highest and is also statistically significant. This variable is a proxy for innovation output and can be interpreted as having a positive impact on a firm's financial performance. Firms which had 'international quality recognition' were likely to be financially efficient as compared to firms without this recognition.

The second factor of performance is the use of websites in relations with clients or suppliers. However, its coefficient is negative and, as mentioned earlier, this shows that the use of information technology tools is still new and has been adopted more by small and less innovative firms. This is likely because, according to Table 2, a firm's size is also a positive determinant of financial performance. An increase in the number of employees by 10% leads to an improvement in financial performance by

Table 2 Effects of innovation output on financial performance: the two-stage least squares method

Log added value	Coefficients	P-Values
Log capacity utilization	0.5609422	0.055
Log electricity cost	0.2894754	0.000
Direct exports share	0.0170243	0.048
National sales share	0.0027956	0.700
Using e-mails with clients or suppliers	0.2029652	0.449
Using website with clients or suppliers	−0.8519364	0.004
Log company experience	0.1570394	0.226
Log employees	0.5086777	0.000
Log total fixed assets	0.1973117	0.001
International quality recognized	0.9073776	0.003
_cons	5.633773	0.000
Number of observations	51	
$F(9, 41)$	33.110	
Prob > F	0.000	
Total (centered) SS	189.7216	
Total (uncentered) SS	17600.32	
Residual SS	20.4518	
Centered R^2	0.88922	
Uncentered R^2	0.9988	
Root MSE	0.6333	
Sargan statistic (overidentification test of all instruments)	28.446	
Chi-sq(8) p-val	0.0002	

Source Authors' estimations using the World Bank Enterprise Surveys: Rwanda 2006

5%. Consequently, small firms on the basis of the number of full-time employees are handicapped by their size.

Competitiveness, technology intensity, and physical capital are the other determinants of a firm's performance. Competitiveness is represented by capacity utilization and the share of a firm's export sales. They are both positively linked to a firm's financial performance. Total electricity cost and total fixed assets are proxies for technology intensity and physical capital respectively. These two factors are correlated because they reflect that a firm has mastered its productive technology. Consequently, the results show that a combination of competitiveness and technology intensity was an important instrument of manufacturing firms' performance.

5 Conclusion and Recommendations

This study's specific objectives were: (i) determining the factors of innovation decisions; (ii) assessing the effects of innovation activities on the innovation performance of manufacturing firms; and (iii) evaluating the effects of innovation output on the financial performance of Rwandese manufacturing firms. To address these objectives, the structural multi-stage modeling method was used as suggested by Crépon et al. (1998). However, to conform with the available data, we used a two-stage technique, where in the first stage we determined the relationship between innovation decisions and innovation output and in the second stage, we established the relationship between innovation output and a firm's performance using data from the World Bank '2006—enterprise survey.'

This study came with three main conclusions: (i) product innovations are linked directly to process innovations, meaning that firms which engaged in process innovations introduced new or improved products in the market; (ii) 'international quality recognition' was not linked to a firm's engagement in innovations and was instead linked to the use of technology licensed from foreign firms; and (iii) 'international quality recognition' was the main determinant of a firm's financial performance. With respect to these empirical findings, we recommend public assistance to private manufacturing firms in R&D to boost their innovativeness. It is also recommended that manufacturing firms should apply for 'international quality recognition' because it is important for their financial sustainability. However, it is important to underline that the empirical findings of this study must be considered with caution. The data used is dated and did not allow us to consider all the variables of interest, particularly the gender and age of the owner. Consequently, we suggest undertaking deeper analyses which emphasize thematic studies (type of firms) and firms' ownership structures using more recent data.

References

Audretsch, D. B., Keilbach, M. C., & Lehmann, E. E. (2006). *Entrepreneurship and economic growth*. London: Oxford University Press.

Balachandran, V., & Sakthivelan, M. S. (2013). Impact of information technology on entrepreneurship (e-entrepreneurship). *Journal of Business Management and Social Sciences Research, 2*(2), 51–56.

Beneki, C., Giannias, D., & Moustakas, G. (2012). Innovation and economic performance: The case of Greek SMEs. *Regional and Sectoral Economic Studies, 12*(2), 31–42.

Bronwyn, H. H., Lotti, F., & Mairesse, J. (2009). Innovation and productivity in SMEs: Empirical evidence from Italy. *Small Business Economics, 33*(1), 13–33.

Brown, F., & Guzman, A. (2014). Innovation and productivity across Mexican manufacturing firms. *Journal of Technology Management and Innovation, 9*(4), 36–52.

Crépon, B., Duguet, E., & Mairesse, J. (1998). Research and development, innovation and econometric analysis at the firm level. *Economics of Innovation and New Technology, 7*(2), 115–158.

Fagerberg, J. (2004). Innovation: A guide to the literature. *Georgia Institute of Technology*.

Fritsch, M., & Mueller, P. (2004). Effect of new business formation on regional development over time. *Regional Studies, 38*, 961–975.

Fritsch, M., & Mueller, P. (2008). The effect of new business formation on regional development over time: The case of Germany. *Small Business Economics, 30*(1), 15–29.

Griffith, R., Huergo, E., Mairesse, J., & Peters, B. (2006). Innovation and productivity across four European countries. *Oxford Review of Economic Policy, 22*(4), 483–498.

Hall, B. H. (2011). Innovation and productivity. *Nordic Economic Policy Review, 2*, 167–208.

Legros, D., & Galia, F. (2012). Are innovation and R&D the only sources of firms' knowledge that increase productivity? An empirical investigation of French manufacturing firms. *Journal of Productivity Analysis, 38*(2), 167–181.

Lööf, H., & Heshmati, A. (2006). On the relationship between innovation and performance: A sensitivity analysis. *Economics of Innovation and New Technology, 15*(4/5), 317–344.

Mairesse, J., & Mohnen, P. (2010). Using innovation survey for econometric analysis. In B. H. Hall & N. Rosenberg (Eds.), *Handbook of economics and innovation* (pp. 1130–1155). Amsterdam: Elsevier.

Mairesse, J., Mairesse, J., & Robin, S. (2009). Innovation and productivity: A firm-level analysis for French manufacturing and services using CIS3 and CIS4 data (1998–2000 and 2002–2004). Working paper.

Marques, C. S., Gerry, C., Covelo, S., Braga, A., & Braga, V. (2011). Innovation and the performance of Portuguese business: A 'SURE' approach. *International Journal of Management and Enterprise Development, 10*(2/3), 114–128. Elsevier.

MINECOFIN (2013). *Economic development and poverty reduction strategy II: 2013–2018*. Kigali.

Mohnen, P., & Hall, B. H. (2013). Innovation and productivity: An update. *Eurasian Business Review, 3*(1), 47–65.

Morrar, R. (2014). Innovation in French services compared to manufacturing: An empirical analysis based on CIS4. *Journal of Innovation Economics & Management, 1*(13), 175–203.

OECD, E. (2005). Oslo manual: Guidelines for collecting and interpreting innovation data. In *Paris 2005, Sp, 46*. D. B. Audretsch, & M. Keilbach (Eds.) (2006), *Entrepreneurship, growth and restructuring* (No. 1306). Papers on Entrepreneurship, Growth and Public Policy.

Schumpeter, J. (1940). *Capitalism, socialism and democracy*. New York: Harper & Row.

Tuan, N., Nhan, N., Giang, P., & Ngoc, N. (2016). The effects of innovation on firm performance of supporting industries in Hanoi. *Vietnam. Journal of Industrial Engineering and Management, 9*(2), 413–431.

Van Stel, A. (2006). *Empirical analysis of entrepreneurship and economic growth* (Vol. 13). Springer Science & Business Media.

Waheed, A. (2011). Innovation and firm-level productivity: Econometric evidence from Bangladesh and Pakistan. Working paper series no. 2011-061, UNU-MERIT.

Zemplinerova, A., & Hromadkova, F. (2012). Determinants of firm's innovation. *Prague Economic Papers, 4,* 487–503.

Chapter 7
Business Networks and Small and Medium Enterprise Growth in Rwanda

Olivier Mugwaneza and Olof Brunninge

Abstract Networking has been found to be an important source of SME's growth and development, both in developed and developing countries. This study discusses the importance of networking in the context of Rwanda's SMEs. Literature on firm growth and business networks discusses networks that the SMEs are involved in, and how these networks help them grow. This study which is set in the context of a developing country follows a *case study approach* in studying SMEs. Using a cross-case analysis, its findings show that networks remain important and contribute toward the growth of SMEs because they help them address most of their identified growth challenges. However, networks can address some but not all growth challenges and they can address these challenges differently for different SMEs. One case in this study brought together players that would not have been able to meet without the networks. Hence, the study suggests that complementary solutions need to be found for addressing all growth challenges faced by SMEs holistically.

Keywords Networks · Growth · Small and medium enterprises (SMEs)

JEL Classification Codes M12 · M31 · M37

1 Introduction

The creation of business networks is a topic of growing interest in light of economic convergence and enterprise development across the world. In developed economies, networks form a vital basis for facilitating SMEs' development (Senik et al. 2011). Some SMEs even build their growth strategies on developing networks (Achtenhagen

O. Mugwaneza (✉)
School of Business, University of Rwanda, Kigali, Rwanda
e-mail: mugwaolivier@yahoo.fr

O. Brunninge
Jönköping International Business School, Jönköping, Sweden
e-mail: olof.brunninge@ju.se

© Springer Nature Singapore Pte Ltd. 2020
G. G. Das and R. B. Johnson (eds.), *Rwandan Economy at the Crossroads of Development*, Frontiers in African Business Research,
https://doi.org/10.1007/978-981-15-5046-1_7

et al. 2017). Like for many other sub-fields of management research, scholarly investigations of SMEs' growth and business networks have mostly been carried out in the North American/European context. However, we cannot take for granted that these research results are transferrable to a developing economy or a specific country without any problems. Welter (2011) emphasizes that a contextualized perspective critically contributes to an understanding of entrepreneurship. Hence, she calls for discussing the diversity of contexts of entrepreneurship, as rules of the game change depending on time, place, culture, and other factors. Researchers of business networks point out that the way businesses interact in networks is determined by their circumstances and context (Håkansson and Ford 2002). Changes cannot be made in some of the citations for consistency.

Hence, exploring the role of business networks in SMEs growth in the Rwandan context can make a two-fold contribution. Firstly, it can highlight how the specific features of the Rwandan context impact how entrepreneurial ventures develop and leverage their business growth. Secondly, by pointing out the similarities and differences with extant research conducted in the context of industrialized countries, it can highlight the diversity of entrepreneurship and thus enrich literature on business networks and firm growth.

In Rwanda, approximately 98% of all firms are SMEs including formal and informal businesses, providing more than 41% employment to Rwandans (MINICOM 2010). Despite their importance, SMEs in Rwanda face several constraints including those in technical and management skills, limited business development services, high costs of doing business, inability to access finance, challenges in getting access to market information, inadequate entrepreneurial skills, and lack of appropriate technologies (Donatus 2011; MINICOM 2010). This study qualitatively investigates the role of networking in SMEs' growth. Clearly, contextual differences go beyond a mere dichotomy of developing and developed economies. Even within these general contexts, countries and regions are characterized by their unique contextual characteristics, involving combinations of, for example, space, traditions, religion, and history (see Welter 2011, p. 166). This means that Rwanda as a country has its own context and situation and how the networks can be managed by SMEs' owners to reap benefits from them, and growth in Rwanda might be different from other contexts. The aim of this study is exploring different forms of business networks that SMEs in Rwanda are involved in, and analyzing how those networks help SMEs to grow/develop. The study did semi-structured interviews with the owners of two selected SMEs.

The rest of the chapter is organized as follows. The next section gives a literature review which is followed by a description of the research method in Sect. 3. The next section presents the findings from the two Rwandan SMEs selected as cases. In Sect. 5, these cases are then discussed with respect to extant literature on business networks and SMEs' growth; this serves as the basis for suggesting topics for future research. Section 6 concludes.

2 Literature Review

2.1 What Is a Network?

The concept of a network is not new, and it is extensively discussed in the literature. A network can be defined differently depending on the perspective used. For example, (Axelsson and Easton 1992, p. xiv) define a network as "a model or a metaphor which describes a number, usually a large number, of entities, which are connected." Håkansson and Ford (2002, p. 133) describe a network as a make-up where companies or other business entities are nodes and the relations between them are the threads that link them.

Other authors define networks as "a set of interdependent actors, activities and resources" (Groen 2005; Håkansson 1989). This definition is in line with a network model known as the "A-R-A Framework" (Axelsson and Easton 1992) which follows the idea that actors/entities control different resources. As resources are distributed heterogeneously, actors need to cooperate in networks to perform their activities.

In this study, the actors are SMEs and the entities that they network with. The simplest relationship that the actors have is a dyad where only two actors perform activities together. However, the idea of a network makes it possible to extend the network's exchange from its format of having two actors (Emerson 1976). This means that there is no upper limit to the number of actors in a network and the roles that they assume in their cooperation.

Networks are also referred to as "connections and interactions between individuals, groups and organizations" (Širec and Bradač 2009, p. 60). This definition brings out the role of individuals/owners in networks. The next section discusses how individual/personal networks play an important role in building organizational network for SMEs. The form a network takes depends on the aims of the actors in the network. Literature shows that networks are efforts to access information, assistance, and direction on developmental issues (Chell and Baines 2000; Covin and Slevin 1991). Depending on the aims of the actors, networks have different ways of manifesting themselves. They appear in different forms. Networks may take the form of licensing or sub-contracting agreements, joint research and development activities, strategic alliances, or shared marketing endeavors (Groen 2005). Networks can also be channels through which materials, goods, and information circulate, they can be part of the processes, and they can also be platforms for power or influence (Havnes and Senneseth 2001). This means that networks can include relations with customers, suppliers, owners, partners, government institutions, and even competitors. One aspect that is common in these explanations is that networks help actors/entities that are involved in them to get access to resources and perform activities that would not be possible outside a network.

2.2 Business Networks in SMEs

Literature on SMEs' network shows that personal relations play an important role in building the networks. According to Biggiero (2001) there is an overlap between entrepreneurs' personal networks and those of the SMEs that they are involved in. The argument of the entrepreneurship theory is that an entrepreneur uses his personal networks while building his venture (Johannisson et al. 1994). It is also argued that a SME's growth depends on how much the owner is determined, how ambitious he is, what he aspires to achieve, and his determination to make it work, and so growth is not a result of chance (Širec and Bradač 2009). This also shows that for a SME, networking and growth are more likely to be attributed to the efforts of the owner. The way a firm grows is closely linked to its owner's goals (Davidsson 1989). Since SMEs mostly rely on personal information, it is difficult for them to link with big institutions and have access to market information. For SMEs in sub-Saharan Africa, approaching formal market supporting institutions like insurance companies, courts, or lending institutions is expensive. Instead, SMEs use their own networks(Barr 1999). Besides personal relations which play an important role, SME networks may also originate from other sources. Senik et al. (2011) found three main sources of networking for SMEs: (a) institutions—supporting government agencies, ministries, SME supporting agencies; (b) personal relations—relations with other entrepreneurs, friends, colleagues, and relatives; and (c) business associations—links with large foreign and local companies.

Another aspect discussed in the literature is that SMEs in networks behave differently from large entities. Unlike large entities, networks help improve performance and SMEs also build networks to reduce uncertainties (Barr 1999). Larger firms are perceived to possess advantages that determine their behavior in networks compared to small firms (Wincent 2005). It is also argued that SMEs working in traditional sectors network to "reduce information asymmetries, improve contract discipline and support informal credit and risk sharing arrangement" (Barr 1999, p. 123). The next section discusses some works that illustrate the linkages between SMEs' networks and their growth.

2.3 Business Networks and SME Growth

This study puts particular emphasis on how networking contributes to SMEs' growth. Business networks are considered as one of the best ways for SMEs to improve their level of competition and acquire the most important assets that they usually lack such as management skills, technical know-how, technologies, and finance (UNCTAD 2010). Networks are mostly favorable to micro, small, and medium enterprises since they help such enterprises overcome the challenges that they face due to their size (Schulenburg 2006). According to Havnes and Senneseth (2001) there is an assumption in research on SMEs that networks are particularly good for them.

Networks provide entrepreneurs with information about the markets and technologies, thus affecting their performance (Barr 1999). Achtenhagen et al. (2017) found that network-based growth was a *resource-saving* alternative to organic or acquired growth for SMEs. While such firms often lack the financial means to grow organically or to buy other companies, their network partners may allow them to expand their businesses even to foreign markets.

The growth that results from being a part of networks for an SME largely depends on how much investment the SME or any other entity in the network has made. Håkansson and Ford (2002, p. 135) argue that the "opportunities and limitations for a company are related both to the resources invested in the relationships and to the companies' internal capabilities." This means that the extent to which a SME has invested in a network determines how much it will reap from the network. The features of the relationships in a network shape what happens in the business (Håkansson and Ford 2002). If relationships are strong then the entities can also grow as a result.

SMEs' networks and growth are linked. Literature shows that networks affect SMEs' growth; however, these results are not conclusive. Premaratine (2001) found that those SMEs in Sri Lanka which were involved in networks were likely to get access to more resources, and were most likely to run growth-oriented firms with a probability of 0.98. The study called for more comparative studies in less-developed countries. Širec and Bradač (2009) looked at how networking affected SMEs' growth and explored the extent to which networking affected past growth and future aspirations. Their findings showed that past growth and future growth aspirations were seen in companies (SMEs) that were part of networks (frequent cooperation) with educational institutions, research institutions, support institutions, final users of their products, suppliers, and agents. They recognized that SME growth is a complex phenomenon that might go beyond the effects of these networks leaving a huge scope for further research on the effects of networks on SMEs' growth.

Havnes and Senneseth (2001) also investigated the assumption that networking enhanced small firms' performance and therefore their growth. Their argument is that if networks bring specific benefits to small firms, these should be perceived and/or manifested through (a) increase in market share (b) and/or increase in sales (c) and/or increase in the number of employees (Mazzarol 1998). Havnes and Senneseth's (2001) study shows that networks only helped SMEs in achieving long-term growth objectives of extending their markets, that is, increasing their market share but did not help SMEs in achieving short-term objectives of increasing sales and the number of employees. The study recommended that policymakers should focus on long-term objectives if they want to help SMEs grow through networks given that there is no evidence that networking activities can help SMEs achieve short-term objectives like increasing sales and the number of employees.

As this literature review shows, there is some evidence that SMEs' networks contribute to their growth. However, as indicated earlier the results of previous studies are not conclusive on this point. This study responds to requests by scholars that case studies should be considered in a developing country like Rwanda to understand SMEs' networks and their effects on growth at the firm level.

2.4 The Context of Developing Economies in General and of Rwanda in Particular

SMEs in developing countries face similar problems/challenges. The most commonly discussed of these include lack of capital/finance, low technological capabilities, lack of access to market/business information, high costs of doing business, and lack of management skills (Ghauri et al. 2003; MINICOM 2010; Tambunan 2008). In a study in 119 developing countries, lack of access to finance was found to be the biggest challenge along with others like taxes, competition, political factors, and access to electricity (Wang 2016). These constituted growth challenges in developing countries. Several solutions have been put in place in developing countries to address these challenges to allow SMEs to grow. However, some of these have proven to be unsuccessful, for example, protection of SMEs has seen some of the SMEs becoming inefficient, and stringent regulations have benefited strong multinationals that can comply with such regulations and helped those large enterprises to bring monopolies in developing countries. In other cases, the suggested solutions have led to dominance of state-owned enterprises and some SMEs with good connections have grown at the expense of most of the other SMEs (Tambunan 2008). Network is an alternative solution that might work differently in developing countries and specifically in Rwanda.

Rwanda is a developing country in East Africa which is a landlocked and not endowed with many natural resources. Lack of connection to water and to main ports means that Rwandan firms, whether small or large, need networks with other players to access resources and markets. Hence, after the 1994 genocide against the Tutsi that led to massive destruction and left the country with extreme poverty encouraged the government to promote the private sector. The Rwandan government put in place Vision 2020 that required private-sector-led economic development. The Rwandan private sector is dominated by SMEs which form approximately 98% of the businesses, including formal and informal businesses providing more than 41% employment to Rwandans (MINICOM 2010). These SMEs face the challenges identified in developing countries and others that are more specific to Rwanda given her history and context. In a search for solutions to these challenges the Government of Rwanda put in place the SME development policy. The policy has five objectives: promoting an entrepreneurial culture among Rwandans; facilitating SMEs' access to development services; putting in place mechanisms that help SMEs to get appropriate finance; simplifying SMEs' fiscal and regulatory framework to ease their development; and developing an appropriate institutional framework for their development (MINICOM 2010). These objectives require strategic approaches. Business networks are one of the best strategies to help SMEs increase their level of competition(UNCTAD 2010). This study investigates two cases to see how networks have worked in ensuring SMEs' growth in the Rwandan context.

3 Research Methodology

This study follows an exploratory approach as it investigates the forms of business networks that SMEs in Rwanda are involved in and the extent to which these networks have helped the SMEs to grow. To achieve this objective, the study adopted a case study approach. "Case studies are preferred when 'how' or 'why' questions are being posed" (Yin 1994, p. 1). Case studies can also be used for describing a situation. We chose a case study approach to describe the types of networks that SMEs in Rwanda are involved in and also to answer the question of how these networks helped these two SMEs to grow. The case study approach is in line with suggestions made by Havnes and Senneseth (2001), who say that more case study research should be conducted to investigate the mechanisms of networks at the firm level and the motives behind working with networks.

The cases selected for this study were chosen based on information that was available to the researchers that these were SMEs which were actively building networks and thus they could inform research on how business networks help SMEs grow. Of the two SMEs studied, one is in the transport industry supplying speed governors and other technologies to transport companies while the other is in coffee making industry. The two cases were chosen because multiple cases are helpful in studying a phenomenon and analyzing it across cases to understand similarities and differences (Yin 1994). However, multiple cases can also be complex and time-consuming (Gustafsson 2017), which is also the reason why only two cases were studied. We plan to add additional cases to our study and also collect additional data on the cases already included.

Semi-structured interviews with owners/entrepreneurs of the two SMEs were conducted to collect data. We also conducted interviews with the operations manager of RTC, an important partner in a network of the second case to understand how the network is structured. The main questions related to are: "What forms of networks do you get involved with?" and "How do they help your company to grow?" (The interview schedule is given in Appendix.) The study also used information from media reports and the websites of the two cases.

We chose Rwanda for this study as its focus is on Rwanda's environment and context as a developing country and since less work has been done on networks and SMEs' growth in this country. Hence, this study can be a steppingstone to finding out more about the role of networks in this context. The choice of context was also informed by previous research which suggested that the way businesses interact in networks is determined by their circumstances and context (Håkansson and Ford 2002).

We used a cross-case synthesis to analyze the data. A cross-case synthesis as an analytical technique allows for an analysis of multiple cases (Yin 1994). A word table was used for synthesizing the findings of both the cases and for drawing conclusions on how networks helped these cases to overcome growth challenges. Word tables provide a possibility of analyzing data in a certain framework (Yin 1994). The framework used looks at the types of networks that exist in the two cases, how they help them in overcoming growth challenges, and how similar these findings are for both the cases.

4 Findings

This section presents the findings of the interviews done for the two cases. These findings are structured as: (a) a brief background of the company, (b) types and sources of networks, and (c) networks and their role in the growth of the company.

4.1 Company A

4.1.1 Background

Company A operates in transport technology. It specializes in automotive solutions. It was established in 2015 for making speed governors and fleet tracking solutions in Rwanda. The use of speed governors in Rwandan public transport since then has made tremendous contributions to reducing road accidents. The company trades in two main products: speed governors and global positioning systems (GPS). A speed governor is a micro-controller-based electronic unit which continuously monitors the speed of a vehicle and maintains it within the preset limit. In Rwanda, the preset limit for vehicles used in public transport and transport of goods is 60 km/h. GPS is an electronic device which is normally carried by a moving vehicle or person. It uses the global positioning system to establish and track its exact location, and thus that of its carrier, at intervals.

Data recorded by the GPS can be stored within the tracking unit/device, or it may be transmitted to a central location database, or to an internet-connected computer using cellular means (GPRS or SMS), radio, or a satellite modem embedded in the unit/device. Company A shares the data it collects with the National Police and the Rwanda Utilities Regulating Authority (RURA) for real-time control and road security purposes. The National Police and RURA are the main users of the information recorded using the GPS. In addition, the company also shares its information with its customers especially car owners who need to follow their cars used in public transport without following them physically. The company is still growing and is introducing new products and services; currently it is working in partnership with the Rwanda Management Institute and wants to start a professional driving training.

When Company A started it brought a new technology to Rwanda to overcome the problems of road accidents that were mainly caused by speeding. The introduction of speed governors was made possible in partnership with National Police and RURA. Both the institutions helped put in place legal instruments that determine the legal and regulatory framework under which public transport operates. The company has grown and the number of its employees as well as the customers has increased.

The owner says *".... When we started, we only had 3 employees including myself, but now the company has 27 employees. We started with zero vehicles but now we have 2,500 vehicles with speed governors.... I want to see my company growing to the Africa level, it is my dream and I believe we will reach there."*

4.1.2 Sources and Types of Networks

There are several sources and types of networks—individual/personal networks, networks with businesses on the supply and market sides, networks with government institutions, and networks with international organizations.

Company A has personal networks that are basically made by the owner of the company. These personal networks existed before the company started and became strong and helpful after it introduced the new technology. As the founder of the company states, he did not have to rely much on personal networks to start his business *"At the start, I did not have strong personal contacts, but as I brought new technology that was important at the national level, I built several strong personal contacts which are now of much help in creating other business networks."*

Company A is also involved in networks with other businesses. It has got into business relationships with businesses across the country who work as agents and distributors of its products. *"We have representatives in the South (Butare, Gitarama), North (Musanze), and West (Cyangugu) of the country,"* the managing director says *"These agents have served as distributors of speed governors and GPS across the country and they have also helped during sensitization programs through road shows that were organized to make the products known."*

In addition to the agents, the company has also been involved in business relationships with two international companies Tramigo, a Finnish multinational company known as the world's best-selling fleet tracking solutions provider which helped Company A get access to fleet tracking systems. Company A has also entered into and is still in partnership with Bump Recorder, a Japanese company with its headquarters in Tokyo which specializes in road-level measurement technology. Besides, the company also has ongoing business relations with its customers and suppliers.

Company A also uses its networks with government institutions. The main government institutions that Company A currently works with include National Police, RURA, ICT Chamber, and Rwanda Management Institute (RMI). As the founder explains, the connections with all these institutions were made possible by the new technology that the company brought to Rwanda. *"When we brought the idea, the first beneficiary was National Police because of the effect of the technology in reducing road accidents, and then later RURA had to join as a regulating authority. The introduction of the speed governor technology could not be possible without the involvement of these two institutions. Concerning the ICT Chamber, that is where we belong, all our products are based on information technology and thus we have to work closely with the responsible chamber in the Private Sector Federation (PSF)."*

Further, Company A has just entered into a partnership with RMI. RMI provides professional training mainly to civil servants and it has also started working with civil society organizations as well as the private sector. Company A has embarked on a partnership with RMI to serve as RMI's consultant providing professional driving training. *"We want to work with RMI to upgrade the knowledge and attitude of drivers to the level of professional drivers through defensive driving and maintaining their vehicles properly."*

Lastly, Company A also has relationships with international organizations. Currently, it has a contract with the World Bank. The founder explains, *"We have a project where we currently supply it with data on a monthly basis and we want to see how we can operate together more."*

All these networks have helped Company A in its growth agenda.

4.1.3 Networks and Their Roles in the Growth of the Company

Personal networks primarily help Company A access right information and right people which are important for any business.

"Currently personal contacts help me to get an audience with decision makers in different institutions. With the technology that I have brought I have built trust and so far, the people I have met, for example, in the police, RURA or elsewhere give it a priority when they see my call because they think I can contribute in their daily activities and responsibilities. So personal contacts make it easy to introduce my new products to relevant stakeholders, especially those I am working with now." Hence, personal networks help the company access both information and people. They also help Company A to know about the current developments, challenges, and desires of the clients for their products. *"For example, our company started with speed governors but the police and RURA brought in the idea of GPS and later customers also raised a need to know whether their vehicles were offline or online, and the provision of this information is billed. All this information on current trends and current needs can only be accessed and used if your personal networks work properly otherwise the business can even be taken to other companies,"* says the managing director.

Networking with businesses has also helped Company A mainly to get access to technology. Tramigo helped it get access to GPS (a fleet tracking technology that it did not have) and to distribute it on behalf of Tramigo, not only in Rwanda but also in other African French-speaking countries opening a room for growth for Company A beyond Rwandan boundaries. Bump Recorder will help it gather data that can be useful and which will be supplied to governments and other partners in roads construction maintenance *"… we plan to assist in efficiently diagnosing the state of the roads, as well as improving safety conditions and smoothing travel for all those using roads in Rwanda. Bump Recorder will provide us with the software that helps measure the quality standards of constructed roads and tell us when a road needs repair."*

Networks with government institutions too have helped Company A in several ways. Normally, these networks help companies get access to local markets, they also connect companies to the international arena, provide access to information, and provide companies access to technology either directly or indirectly. Relations with government institutions helped Company A secure access to the local market. When the company introduced the speed governor technology, there was market resistance. *"Given that it was a new technology it was not easy to make the beneficiaries including both passengers and transport companies understand what it was. Transport companies saw it as a threat to their businesses saying speed governors will damage their vehicles and reduce their revenues due to reduced speed, and passengers saw that their travel time will increase and affect their daily programs. So through law making and sensitization, government institutions, especially the police and RURA played an important role,"* said the MD of Company A. Secondly, contact with government institutions helped take the company to an international level as affirmed by its founder and owner, *"For example, our connections with the ICT Chamber provide us with an opportunity to go with His excellency the President of the Republic and meet other partners from other countries and learn as we looked at possibilities of expansion, this is a golden business opportunity for us."* Thirdly, relations with government institutions provide access to information—these networks help the company get new ideas from the new information that is available. *"For example, through the existing networks I have been able to get information that Rwanda needs to find a solution for reducing transport-based pollution and I am trying to respond to this problem,"* says the owner of Company A.

Networks with international organizations are new to Company A and thus we could not find the contributions made by this network. The discussion so far shows that Company A has got several networks and each of them has contributed to the growth of the company. However, the extent to which each has contributed is not clear even though one can see that all of them are important.

4.2 Company B

4.2.1 Background

Company B is a coffee washing firm. It started as a farming business where the owner cultivated and harvested coffee cherries that were taken to the market for the production stage. As the volume of harvested cherries grew, the owner started a washing station in 2005. At the same time, he also started collecting cherries from several other farmers and washing them to supply them as fully washed coffee beans. Since then, Company B has been supplying full washed coffee berries. Some of the coffee is produced by the owner of the washing station. In addition, he also collects cherries from other small farmers who do not possess washing stations. At the beginning, the washing station could collect coffee cherries from a 5 km radius, but the space has now reduced due to the entry of new washing stations which has led to an almost 50% reduction in the production of the station. In 2009, an international company called the Rwanda Trading Company (RTC) started operating in Rwanda. RTC works directly with over 50 independent wet mills throughout the country to help improve production and quality and also helps market their coffee around the globe. Among those working stations is Company B. RTC is the most important network partner that Company B has.

4.2.2 Sources and Types of Networks

Like Company A, for Company B too there are individual/personal networks, networks with businesses on the supply and market sides, and networks with government institutions but we could not see any networks with international organizations.

The company's owner has personal networks that he uses in his business. He considers personal networks to be the ones driving his business since the beginning, *"Since the beginning I have relied on my personal networks, I always worked as an individual and my networks in business have always been personal and were this way even before we registered the company."*

As the farming business grew, Company B started working in partnership with the Rwanda Trading Company. This has been its main network and the most important partner on the market side. On the supply side, Company B works with small farmers who supply it with coffee cherries. These are important players in the network because both Company B and RTC depend on their production. Lastly, the company has relations with government institutions. It mainly interacts with the National Agricultural Export Development Board (NAEB). NAEB serves several purposes in line with agriculture export products' development, and coffee is one of the main export products.

4.2.3 Networks and Their Role in the Growth of Company B

Different networks play different roles for Company B. Personal networks have more of a role in connecting the company to people and also providing access to other resources. *"Because I started as an individual farmer, I owe all my contacts to the connections I had as a person and not as a company. These connections have helped me get to others and to know where to direct my coffee business,"* says the owner.

Business networks helped Company B get access to finance management oversight and securing a market for its washed coffee as well as access to raw material (coffee cherries). The owner of Company B attests that the relationship with RTC has helped it in several ways, *"RTC provides us with finance to buy coffee cherries from small farmers and we pay a lower interest rate which is around 12 percent and it is comparatively lower because banks could ask for an interest rate of around 19 percent, so this has helped us a lot in our operations."* RTC confirmed this as, *"Our suppliers receive financing, we want to give them working capital and we also provide them with management oversight – we monitor how they collect coffee, how they process it and follow them up to the time they deliver it to ensure quality."* RTC normally signs an agreement with washing stations like Company B which provides a guarantee that the washing stations will sell all the coffee that they process to RTC unless their processed coffee goes beyond the limit fixed in terms of tons that should be supplied to RTC. This has reduced unpredictability for both Company B and RTC. As the owner of Company B says, the network with RTC has ensured sustainability of the business since it is assured of a market for its products. In addition, the partnership with RTC also helps Company B train the farmers it works with. We were informed that RTC provides training to farmers from time to time since it has expertise in the field; this improves the quality of coffee and benefits all the stakeholders in the network.

Business connections with farmers have helped Company B to reduce unpredictability about the quantity of coffee cherries it gets. The owner says, "*I build good connections with my farmers to ensure they supply to me. I give them cows that help them get manure. I am sure that we will get the needed quantities to deliver to RTC.*"

For Company B, networking with government institutions mainly works for regulating the sector, like setting prices for coffee. However, there are other roles that NAEB plays, like establishing relations and cooperation with regional and international organizations with the aim of improving operations and collaborating with regard to exports of agricultural and livestock products including coffee. Further, the government also helps in providing fertilizers, facilitating workshops with farmers, and promoting their coffee at the international level. We were also informed that in case of an excess harvest, NAEB helps keep the coffee in its premises and continues to advise on its sale in international markets.

5 Discussion

This study found several patterns of networks and their relation to SMEs' growth. This section first discusses the findings from a general perspective and then discusses the findings using a word table to synthesize cross-case findings on how networks address growth challenges that SMEs in Rwanda face.

When it comes to building networks, the study found that despite the fact that both Company A and B had networks from which they benefitted, we observed that it was easier for Company A to create networks as compared to Company B. This was mainly because Company A was bringing a non-traditional, innovative technology to the country which was addressing a national issue. So, it was easy for Company A to enter into relationships. This is in agreement with Barr (1999) who found that it was easy for SMEs that are involved in new as opposed to traditional technologies to make networks.

Based on our findings, we agree with Barr (1999) that some SMEs build networks to reduce uncertainty. We found that when Company B established relations with RTC, it was mainly to avoid unpredictability and ensure sustainability of its sales. However, SMEs also build networks for growth purposes and as Achtenhagen et al. (2017) found, network partners can help SMEs to expand to foreign markets. This was the case for Company A that worked with Tramigo to distribute GPS among African

French-speaking countries. On the importance of personal networks for SMEs that has been emphasized in the literatures (Barr 1999; Biggiero 2001; Johannisson et al. 1994; Širec and Bradač 2009), this study too found that there was an overlap between the owner's personal networks and company networks. For example, the owner of Company B confirmed that all networks he was a part of were driven by his personal networks. What is interesting is that not personal networks had to come first and drive other networks but personal networks could also be made after business networks had been established. We found that in Company A, the owner did not have strong personal networks but because of the new technology that he brought to the country he was able to build strong personal networks that currently help him in his business. This explains the overlap between personal networks and other networks and also explains that there is interdependence among the networks (Senik et al. 2011).

On growth in general, as Premaratine (2001) concluded, SMEs in networks are likely to get access to more resources and run growth-driven firms with very high probability of success of registering growth. The views of the owners interviewed in this study argued that networking had been critical to their firms' growth. As self-reported estimates, both the companies' owners were certain that networks had contributed more than 60% to their growth. This means that at least in these two cases, networking was critical for the firms' growth strategies. Achtenhagen et al. (2017) found network-based growth where firms' growth and the size of their businesses grew through a network of partners, as they lacked the resources to grow organically. In our two cases, rather than substituting organic growth, networking served as a catalyst for organic growth by increasing the firms' customer base and by channeling resources to them.

Looking at the sources of the networks that contributed to growth, the cases under study showed that their growth could primarily be a result of business networks and partly because of networks with the government. This is in line with what Širec and Bradač (2009) found that growth aspirations were observed in companies that networked with educational institutions, support institutions, end users of their products, and agents. There were no networks with educational institutions in the two cases that we studied. Our findings on whether the networks helped SMEs only in achieving their long-term growth objectives of expanding markets and not-short term growth objectives, like increasing sales, are different from literature, especially for Company B because this company entered into a network with RTC mainly to increase its sales and not necessarily to expand.

To focus more on the Rwandan perspective and looking at the growth challenges that SMEs in Rwanda face, we now discuss how the networks helped SMEs in Rwanda. As Senik et al. (2011) found, networks play a vital role in facilitating SMEs' development. Networks also help address the challenges that SMEs face (Schulenburg 2006; UNCTAD 2010). We found that for both Company A and Company B the networks helped address their existing growth challenges (Table 1).

As can be seen in Table 1, there were three main types of networks that the SMEs were involved in personal networks, business networks, and networks with government institutions. Company A started networking with the World Bank, but this network was new and had not yet produced growth benefits for the company.

Table 1 Networks and addressing the existing growth challenges

Source/type of networks	Existing growth challenges for SMEs in Rwanda to be addressed by the type of network	Findings on how the source of network addresses the challenge		Conclusion whether the network addresses the existing challenge	
		Findings for company A	Findings for company B	Company A	Company B
Personal networks					
	Lack of technical and managerial skills	☐	☐	☐	☐
	Lack of access to market information	The owner gets a lot of market-related information from personal contacts. For example, customer feedback and government's priorities and needs	The owner relies on personal networks from time to time, and any new relevant information is most likely to come from personal contacts than from any other source	☐	☐
	Inadequate entrepreneurial skills	☐	☐	☐	☐
	Inability to access finance	Personal networks help access finance through facilitation and easing procedures when such contacts are part of financial institutions but cannot help for more substantial issues, like securing a loan, providing interest free loans, and others	☐	☐	☐
	Lack of appropriate technology	☐	☐	☐	☐
Business networks					
	Lack of technical and managerial skills	☐	The network with RTC gives the company access to training and management oversight which helps it improve both technical and managerial skills	☐	☐

(continued)

Table 1 (continued)

Source/type of networks	Existing growth challenges for SMEs in Rwanda to be addressed by the type of network	Findings on how the source of network addresses the challenge		Conclusion whether the network addresses the existing challenge	
		Findings for company A	Findings for company B	Company A	Company B
	Lack of access to market information	Business networks provide market information, especially networks with customers and suppliers	The company can access market information without going through business networks but there is some information that it gets through business networks, like current developments in international prices of coffee	☐	☐
	Inadequate entrepreneurial skills	☐	☐	☐	☐
	Inability to access finance	☐	The partnership with RTC has been a main source of finance since it no longer uses its own money or banks' money to buy coffee cherries. The finance comes from RTC. The company found it difficult to deal with banks at the small firm level and RTC made it possible to get finance without going through banks' procedures that were complex and costly	☐	☐

(continued)

Table 1 (continued)

Source/type of networks	Existing growth challenges for SMEs in Rwanda to be addressed by the type of network	Findings on how the source of network addresses the challenge		Conclusion whether the network addresses the existing challenge	
		Findings for company A	Findings for company B	Company A	Company B
	Lack of appropriate technology	To a large extent the company is dependent on business networks for accessing the technology it uses – first with Tramigo to access GPS and now with Bump Recorder to access road standards measurement software that it is yet to start using	☐	☐	☐
Networks with government institutions					
	Lack of technical and managerial skills	☐	Government institutions that work with the company organize workshop to increase technical and managerial skills of the stakeholders	☐	☐
	Lack of access to market information	Working with government institutions helps get market information whether local or international	Government institutions help get market information at the international level because coffee is an international commodity	☐	☐
	Inadequate entrepreneurial skills	☐		☐	☐
	Inability to access finance	☐	☐	☐	☐

(continued)

Table 1 (continued)

Source/type of networks	Existing growth challenges for SMEs in Rwanda to be addressed by the type of network	Findings on how the source of network addresses the challenge		Conclusion whether the network addresses the existing challenge	
		Findings for company A	Findings for company B	Company A	Company B
	Lack of appropriate technology	Working with the ICT chamber has helped the company to travel around the globe and learn about new technologies as it signs agreements with foreign companies, for example, Bump Recorder on how the technology can be imported	☐	☐	☐
Networks with International organizations	Lack of technical and managerial skills	☐	N/A	☐	N/A
	Lack of access to market information	☐	N/A	☐	N/A
	Inadequate entrepreneurial skills	☐	N/A	☐	N/A
	Inability to access finance	☐	N/A	☐	N/A
	Lack of appropriate technology	☐	N/A	☐	N/A

Keys
X: The network exists but is not currently solving this growth challenge for the company
☐: The network exists and is currently solving this growth challenge for the company
N/A: The network does not exist currently for the company

In addition, a Finnish company was an important network partner for Company A that had been able to establish a link between the foreign firm and African customers including government institutions. Company A in particular shows how an owner's personal networks became a resource that he could use to better serve his other network partners. A Finnish firm could hardly establish contacts with African government institutions on its own, while at the same time it would be challenging for African governments and institutions to establish their own networks with foreign suppliers of new technologies. In Company A the relationships between both the market and supply sides helped the company perform an intermediary function for its growth.

Table 1 looks at the similarities and differences in how the sources addressed the growth challenges that SMEs in Rwanda face. These challenges were identified by MINICOM's 2010 SMEs policy. The challenges include lack of technical and managerial skills, lack of access to market information, inadequate entrepreneurial skills, inability to access finance, and lack of appropriate technologies. Looking at how different types of networks addressed these challenges, we found more differences than similarities across cases. There were only two similarities between the two cases studied. Firstly, all the three types of networks helped the studied SMEs get access to market information, like changes in customer needs, prices, and others. Secondly, none of the networks addressed the challenge of lack of entrepreneurial skills. Other types of networks addressed the challenges differently for the two cases and there were challenges that were not completely addressed for each case apart from the common one of lack of entrepreneurial skills which was not addressed for both. For Company A, as Table 1 shows, none of the networks could address the challenge of technical and managerial skills, while for Company B, none of the networks could address the challenge of accessing appropriate technologies.

The differences in the networks can be looked at by comparing the two cases for each type of network. The study found that personal networks helped Company A access finance but this was not the case for Company B. Business networks could provide access to technology to Company A but it could provide access to technical and managerial skills and access to finance to Company B. Networks with government institutions could provide access to technology for Company A and could provide access to technical and managerial skills to Company B. It can thus be seen that depending on the type of network and the nature of the entity, different networks contributed differently to the growth of SMEs in Rwanda.

6 Conclusion and Recommendations

Networks remain important for SMEs' growth. This study showed that networks contributed to SMEs' growth by providing them access to finance, technology, technical and managerial know-how, and access to market information. This study also found that personal networks remained important SME networks but were different in how they were built by the two SMEs. The study also found that networks contributed toward both short-term and long-term growth objectives of the two SMEs.

Though networks remained important and contributed to the growth of SMEs, they could address only some growth challenges, and further, they addressed those challenges differently for different SMEs as seen from the cases. Hence, the study shows that networks are one way of helping SMEs to grow, and thus complementary solutions need to be considered if growth has to be achieved.

While this study emphasized on the implications of networks in the Rwandan context, there is potential for further research on Rwandan business networks to get insights that are valuable in developed economies as well. For instance, the cases studied highlighted the interplay of different SME growth modes that Achtenhagen et al. (2017) identified, but which were not fully analyzed in their study. Hence, practices developed by Rwandan entrepreneurs could help us to better understand how growth modes such as organic growth and network-based growth are combined and simultaneously exploited.

This study is the beginning of exploring the dynamics of Rwandan SMEs' networks. Future research should continue conducting in-depth case studies that show the contextual influence of networking. In addition, quantitative studies could make an important contribution to our knowledge by estimating the percentage that networks contribute to the growth of SMEs and thus find out other variables that can contribute to SMEs' growth in Rwanda as well as in other developing countries (Table 2).

Table 2 List of abbreviations

Abbreviations	Full text
GPS	Global Positioning System
ICT	Information and Communication Technology
MD	Managing Director
MINICOM	Ministry of Trade and Industry
NAEB	National Agricultural Export Development Board
PSF	Private Sector Federation
RMI	Rwanda Management Institute
RTC	Rwanda Trading Company
RURA	Rwanda Utilities Regulating Authority
SME	Small and Medium Enterprise
UNCTAD	United Nations Conference on Trade and Development

Appendix

Interview Guide

Title: Business Networks and SMEs' Growth in Rwanda

Part 1: Researchers' Introduction

Dear Respondent,

I am Olivier MUGWANEZA, a researcher as well as an Academic Staff at the University of Rwanda College of Business and Economics (UR-CBE) and Associate Professor Olof BRUNNINGE is a researcher as well as an Academic Staff in the Jonkoping International Business School (JIBS)/Sweden.

In collaboration with the University of Rwanda and the Jonkoping International Business School (JIBS), we are conducting a research that explores the role of business networks for SMEs' growth in Rwanda. "Business networks" can be relevant in facilitating SMEs' growth. Hence, the main purpose of this study is understanding how business networks have helped SMEs to grow. Your firm has been chosen as one of our cases for study and we want to interview you to get detailed information. The interview will last one hour at the most.

After the interview, I will leave my contact details in case you need to know more about this research.

Part 2: General Information

1. *Could you please introduce yourself?*
2. *What is your position in the company?*
3. *How long have you been working in this company?*

Part 3: Background of the Company

4. *When did the company start to operate? Please tell us a bit about how it has developed since then.*
5. *What activities/businesses does the company carry out?*
6. *Who are your main suppliers?*
7. *Who are you main customers?*
8. *Do you have other stakeholders that are important to your company?*
9. *What do you think are your strengths as a company? And what are your weaknesses?*

Part 4: Business Networks

10. *Is your company involved in any kind of relationship with other companies or institutions? Please tell us about these relationships, with whom you have them, what they are about and for how long they have been going on.*

11. *Could you please describe for us the type of relationship you have with these companies? (Customer or supplier relationship? Ownership network? Partnership? ....)*
12. *Do you have personal contacts or relationships that are important for your business? IF yes, can you please describe those relationships to us and how important they are for your company?*

Part 5: Business Networks and SMEs Growth

13. *Is it important for you that your business grows? IF so, why is this important? Do relationships with other organizations help you growing?*

    Do they bring new business to you? How?
    Do they help you to get access to finance? How?
    Do they help you to get access to new technology? How?
    Do they help you acquire management skills? How?

14. *How much value addition in your company can be attributed to engaging in business networks? Or to what extent do you think you have grown after entering into networks?*
15. *What do you think networks should be helping you but is not happening now?*
16. *How do you think networks can be structured to be more beneficial to your company?*
17. *How do you compare your company with an SME in Rwanda that does not have networks?*
18. *Is there anything else that you think can be helpful in our research as far as networks are concerned?*

Thank you very much for your time!

References

Achtenhagen, L., Brunninge, O., & Melin, L. (2017). Patterns of dynamic growth in medium-sized companies: Beyond the dichotomy of organic versus acquired growth. *Long Range Planning, 50*, 457–471.

Axelsson, B., & Easton, G. (1992). *Industrial networks—A new view of reality*. London and New York: Routledge.

Barr, A. (1999). Do SMEs network for growth? In K. King, & S. A. McGrath (Eds.), *Enterprise in Africa: Between poverty and growth* (Vol. 121, No. 131, pp. 121–131). London: Intermediate Technology Development Group Publishing.

Biggiero, L. (2001). Self-organization process in building entrepreneurial process; A theoretical and emprical investigation. *Human Systems Management, 20*(3), 209–222.

Chell, E., & Baines, S. (2000). Networking, entrepreneurship and microbusiness behaviour. *Entrepreneurship and Regional Development, 12*(3), 195–206.

Covin, J. G., & Slevin, D. P. (1991). A conceptual model of entrepreneurship as firm behavior. *Entrepreneurship Theory and Practice, 16*(1), 7–26.

Davidsson, P. (1989). *Continued enterpreneurship and small firm growth*. Stockholm: Ekonomiska Forskningsinstitutet.
Donatus, M. (2011). *Challenges and barriers facing entrepreneurship development through public investment: A case of millenium development villages project Mayange*. Rwanda: Mastricht School of Management (MSM-Rwanda Campus).
Emerson, R. M. (1976). Social exchange theory. *Annual Review of Sociology, 2*(1), 335–336.
Ghauri, P., Lutz, C., & Tesfom, G. (2003). Using networks to solve export-marketing problems of small-and medium-sized firms from developing countries. *European Journal of Marketing, 37*(5/6), 728–752.
Groen, A. (2005). Knowledge intensive entrepreneurship in networks, towards a multi-level/multi dimensional approach. *Journal of Enterprising Culture, 13*(01), 69–88.
Gustafsson, J. (2017). Single case studies vs. multiple case studies: A comparative study.
Håkansson, H. (1989). *Corporate technological behavior; Co-operation and networks*. London: Routledge.
Håkansson, H., & Ford, D. (2002). How can companies interact in business networks? *Journal of Business Research, 55*(2), 133–139.
Havnes, P.-E., & Senneseth, K. (2001). A panel study of firm growth among SMEs in networks. *Small Business Economics, 16*(4), 293–302.
Johannisson, B., Alexanderson, O., Nowicki, K., & Senneseth, K. (1994). Beyond anarchy and organization-entrepreneurs in contextual network. *Entrepreneurship and Regional Development, 6*(4), 329–356.
Mazzarol, T. (1998). Partnerships—A key growth in small businesses. In *43rd ICSB Conference*. Singapore.
MINICOM. (2010). *Small and medium entrprises (SMEs) development policy*. https://www.minicom.gov.rw/fileadmin/minicom_publications/policies/SME_Devt_policy_V180610.pdf.
Premaratine, S. (2001). Networks, resources and small businesses growth. *Journal of Small Business Management, 39*(4), 363–371.
Schulenburg, D. (2006). *Promoting business linkages—Overview and tool*. Deutsche Gesellschaft für.
Senik, C., Brenda, S. L., Entrekin, L., & Adham, K. A. (2011). Networking and internationalization of SMEs in emerging economies. *Journal of International Entrepreneurship, 9*(4), 259–281.
Širec, K., & Bradač, B. (2009). How does networking impact SMEs growth. *Organizacija, 42*(2), 59–66.
Tambunan, T. (2008). SME development, economic growth, and government intervention in a developing country: The indonesian story. *Journal of International Entrepreneurship, 6*(4), 147–167.
UNCTAD. (2010). *Creating business linkages—A policy perspective*. Geneva: United Nations.
Wang, Y. (2016). What are the biggest obstacles to growth of SMEs in developing countries?—An empirical evidence from an enterprise survey. *Borsa Istanbul Review, 16*(3), 167–176.
Welter, F. (2011). Contextualizing entrepreneurship—Conceptual challenges and ways forward. *Entrepreneurship Theory and Practice, 35*(1), 165–184.
Wincent, J. (2005). Does size matter? A study of firm behavior and outcomes in strategic SME networks. *Journal of Small Business and Enterprise Development, 12*(3), 437–453.
Yin, R. K. (1994). *Case study research design and methods* (3rd ed.). London: Sage.

Chapter 8
Cost-effectiveness of Optimizing a Network of Drone-Aided Healthcare Services in Rural Rwanda

Chinasa I. Ikelu and Eugene C. Ezin

Abstract Maternal mortality is one of the leading causes of death among childbearing women in Africa. One of the major challenges facing women in rural areas in Africa is delivering their babies safely, thereby curtailing excessive bleeding during birth. This paper focuses on optimizing costs related to delivery of blood using drone technology by determining how much blood is shipped from the distribution center to each destination center to help minimize total shipping costs. We envisage that drone-aided healthcare services can reduce the shipping costs associated with transporting blood from the point of origin to the centers. This paper also examines a classical optimization problem referred to as the transportation model in which the supply depends on the demand in the various facilities in rural Rwanda. Our study focuses from the start of drone operations in Rwanda in 2018. Using this model, we observe that data is critical for the success of any facility location analysis. Our preliminary results show that the associated travel from the second distribution point of origin to all destination centers (except the third destination) is optimal since the quantity of blood transported from the same point of origin to the same centers is zero. The results of the integer linear programming show optimality. Drone-aided networks using a mathematical optimization model and a simulation analysis help in understanding transportation costs associated with transporting blood in Rwanda so as to reduce maternal mortality.

Keywords Healthcare services · Operations research · Simulation · Drones · Mathematical modeling · Africa

JEL Classification Nodes I11 · C44 · C53 · N7 · C63 · O55

C. I. Ikelu (✉)
Institut de Mathematiques et de Sciences Physiques (IMSP), Porto Novo, Republic of Benin
e-mail: ignatius.chinasa@imsp-uac.org

E. C. Ezin
Institut de Formation et de Recherche en Informatique (IFRI), Universite de Abomey Calavi, Cotonou, Republic of Benin
e-mail: eugene.ezin@uac.bj

1 Introduction

Despite several challenges encountered in expanding telehealth and distance care in most countries in sub-Saharan Africa (SSA), the benefits of these approaches are undeniable and could contribute to the strengthening and better functioning of most health systems in these countries. This will be an asset in achieving the goals of universal health coverage (UHC) and sustainable development to which all these countries have agreed and subscribed. The opportunities for presenting evidence-based results, especially from rural areas, remain wide open for researchers to explore and study. Some of the difficulties faced by homecare services in rural areas are because of an environment that is different from the one in urban areas, including lower population and lack of transportation, medical facilities and pharmacies, as well as long distances between patients and medical facilities in the rural areas (Arcury et al. 2005; Goins et al. 2005). Recently, a new research topic has emerged on the numerical application of patients' dependence on drones for healthcare services. A current improvement in such studies looks at testing solution approaches for improving the models' computational performance by performing a numerical experiment to show its applicability (Kim et al. 2017) and eventual reliability.

Since our research interests are most grounded in operations research applied to healthcare, this study looks at how the problem of transportation in rural areas can be addressed and solved with the use of innovative technologies like drones. Hence, this study examines why transportation of healthcare services is significant, what do we know about the reasons for this, what theories can help one understand the issue, where can better solutions be found, what methods have been used to investigate this issue, and how is it being currently addressed.

Our research is based on some key variables for which we did a simulated analysis which involved using digital and interactive models to replicate an existing or proposed healthcare service or system. Hospitals and healthcare systems are complex with a huge range of variables that impact performance and patient care. Managing variability, understanding its impact on departments and organizations, and implementing existing process improvements are difficult without the right tools. That is why healthcare organizations rely on simulations to better understand how processes and systems work and how these will behave when changes occur. Simulations have the ability to test 'what-if'[1] experiments and safely assess the impact of changes across a unit, hospital, or the entire health system without any risk to the patients or staff. Simulations incorporate real-life variations that the healthcare systems experience every day. By taking account of these variabilities, simulations reflect the reality and behave the same way in real life.

---

[1] Agent-based models support a 'what-if' analysis which allows the impact of unexpected perturbations to be studied (Iturriza et al. 2018).

2 Literature Review

Each year, postpartum hemorrhaging (PPH) causes millions of preventable deaths across both the developed and developing worlds. Throughout both the developed and developing worlds, access to life-saving and critical health products is hampered by what is known as the last-mile problem or the inability to deliver needed medicines from the city to rural or remote locations due to lack of adequate transportation, communication, or supply chain infrastructure. The result is that all too often someone in need of life saving care does not receive the medicines needed in time.

The use of drones to facilitate blood for transfusion has the potential to lower the maternal mortality rate even further. The report also stated that blood delivery by drones was just the beginning as this innovative technology can be used for delivering vaccines and treatment for HIV/AIDS, malaria, tuberculosis, rabies, and other life-threatening illnesses not only in Rwanda but also in the neighboring countries that aim to use this technology as a supply chain mechanism for transporting products. Some questions that arise here include: Can drone technology increase the availability of automated external defibrillators (AEDs) and reduce the delivery time, thereby improving out-of-hospital cardiac arrests (OHCAs)?[2] Boutilier et al. (2017) discovered that an optimized drone network designed with the aid of a novel mathematical model can substantially reduce the AED delivery time for an OHCA event.

Although ReVelle and Hogan (1989) note that the location set covering problem and maximal covering should be used with caution in congested systems, this study implements a variety of model corrections to address this congestion effect[3] proposed by Daskin and Stern (1981) after checking if they are a set covering problem or not.[4] In solving the problem of where to locate emergency service stations and the problem of vehicles to have in each station, the integer programming optimization model proposed by Ball and Lin (1993) which uses the Branch and Bound procedure was effective. The Branch and Bound algorithm intelligently searches for a feasible region for an integer solution by implicitly enumerating most such solutions and enumerating a few of them explicitly.

Moving away from these studies since they all study reliability in varying forms but not in the form of an innovative technology, our paper studies reliability[5] in the form of drone technology that saves the lives of mothers and infants in rural

---

[2] Church and ReVelle's proposed method for answering this question is using a binary optimization model known as the Maximal Covering Location Model for identifying locations for public access defibrillators.

[3] Other correction measures for the congestion effect were proposed by Hogan and ReVelle (1986) and Daskin et al. (1988).

[4] The importance of doing so has been described by Jacobsen (1990) who points out that formulating a problem incorrectly (e.g., failing to account for important problem factors) is likely to be far more important than whether or not you obtain an optimal or sub-optimal solution to a particular problem's formulation (Daskin 2013).

[5] This study follows Snyder and Daskin (2004) who formulated reliability models based on both the P-median problem (PMP) and the uncapacitated fixed-charge location problem (UFLP) and presented an optimal Lagrangian relaxation algorithm to solve them.

areas. It does an in-depth analysis by visiting all centers where drone technology is distributing health-related products so as to understand how this innovative way of transporting medical products affects the lives of patients who need them and of health practitioners in general. The study investigates this nouvelle phenomenon in rural Rwanda and makes some recommendations for its scaling-up to other areas in the region and in Africa in general since maternal mortality and cardiac arrests are common in developing countries.

3 Modeling the Drone-Aided Healthcare System

The transportation problem is important in location modeling for satisfying all the demand and supply and also for keeping the total costs as low as possible. The transportation problem is: given a set of suppliers I, each with supply S_i, a set of demand points J, each with demand D_j, and the unit cost c_{ij} of shipping from supply point $i \in I$ to demand point $j \in J$. Suppose we are asked to locate facilities with known capacities C_i, if a facility is located at candidate site $i \in I$, to serve demand sites with known demands D_j, to minimize the combined facility location and transport costs, the transportation problem of such a scenario can be formulated mathematically using the notations in Daskin (2013).

3.1 Model Notations

The following symbols are used for defining the transportation problem identified in this study.

Inputs:

n: set of distribution plants
m: set of destination centers
I: supply capacity for node $i\,(\forall i = 1, \ldots, n)$
J: demand capacity for node $j\,(\forall j = 1, \ldots m)$
f_{ij}: unit cost of shipping blood from supply node $i \in I$ to demand node $j \in J$

Outputs:

X_{ij}^*: optimal solution

$$X_{ij} = \begin{cases} 1, & \text{if plant } i \text{ is allocated to unit } j \\ 0, & \text{otherwise} \end{cases}$$

ϑ: value of the objective function

Decision Variables:

X_{ij}: number of units of blood shipped from plant i to centers j (integer variable)

3.2 Model Formulation

The transportation problem may be formulated mathematically as:

$$\text{Maximize} \sum_{i \in I} f_{ij} \sum_{j \in J} X_{ij} \tag{1}$$

subject to:

$$\sum_{j=1}^{m} X_{ij} \leq S_i \quad \forall i = 1, \ldots, n \tag{2}$$

$$\sum_{i=1}^{n} X_{ij} \geq D_j \quad \forall j = 1, \ldots, m \tag{3}$$

$$X_{ij} \geq 0 \ \forall i = 1, \ldots, n \ \text{ and } \ \forall j = 1, \ldots, m \tag{4}$$

$$X_{ij} - C_i * t_r \leq 0 \ \forall i = 1, \ldots, n \ \text{ and } \ \forall j = 1, \ldots, m \tag{5}$$

$$C_i * (t_r - 1) \leq X_{ij} \ \forall i = 1, \ldots, n \ \text{ and } \ \forall j = 1, \ldots, m \tag{6}$$

$$t_r \leq X_{ij} \ \forall i = 1, \ldots, n \ \text{ and } \ \forall j = 1, \ldots, m \tag{7}$$

This function is an integer linear problem. The objective function (1) minimizes the total cost. Constraint (2) states that the total amount of blood shipped from each distribution plant $i \in I$ must be less than or equal to the supply of distribution plant $i \in I$. Further, Constraint (3) stipulates that the total amount of blood shipped from each distribution plant $i \in I$ must be greater than or equal to the demand capacity of the facility centers. Constraint (4) is the non-negative integers. Constraint (5) states that the total amount of blood shipped from each distribution plant $i \in I$ minus the capacity of the drone multiplied by the number of travel trips is less than or equal to zero (0). Constraint (6) ensures that the left tail of the allocations are met, that is, the capacity of the drone multiplied by the number of travel trips minus 1 is less than or equal to the total amount of blood shipped from each distribution plant $i \in I$. Constraint (7) states that the number of travel trips is less than or equal to the total amount of blood shipped from each distribution plant $i \in I$.

We make a general assumption that the total supply equals the total demand, that is:

$$\sum_{i \in I} S_i = \sum_{j \in J} D_j$$

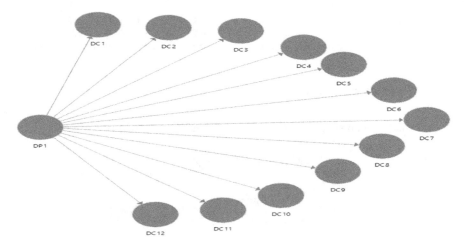

Fig. 1 An architectural structure of a distribution plant and several destination centers. *Source* Author's representation using SmartPLSSmartPLS

4 Simulated Analysis

Many optimization problems are too large to solve either effectively or efficiently in Excel (Daskin 2013). Hence, we used the optimization modeling language in carrying out the analysis along with the Python language for generating data for the simulation. The architectural design was produced using SmartPLS (Fig. 1).

For planners and decision makers to communicate and take decisions about the drone system, we identified an optimal solution by including discussions on the mathematical models in clear non-technical terms; identifying the limitations of the modeling process; identifying the non-modeled impacts; presenting predicted solutions in both objective space[6] and solution space[7]; and recommending the scaling, financing, and implementation of the predicted solutions.

4.1 Interpretation of the Results

Table 1 gives the quantity of blood that will move from the distribution plants to the destination centers. In column one, row one represented by X_{11}, the quantity supplied to the destination center is 54; in the last column represented by X_{112}, the quantity supplied to the destination center is 12.

---

[6]Objective space is the space spanned by the objective function values corresponding to each point in the solution space.

[7]Solution space is a set of all feasible solutions to a problem.

Table 1 Units of blood shipped

$N=2$	$M=12$ (value for x)											
	1	2	3	4	5	6	7	8	9	10	11	12
1	54	30	13	41	97	11	62	59	35	42	19	12
2	0	0	30	0	0	0	0	0	0	0	0	0

Source Authors' calculations

Table 2 Distance covered

$N=2$	$M=12$ (value for travel)											
	1	2	3	4	5	6	7	8	9	10	11	12
1	4	2	1	3	7	1	5	4	3	3	2	1
2	0	0	2	0	0	0	0	0	0	0	0	0

Source Authors' calculations

Table 3 Blood supply value

Value for supply	
N (size 2)	Value
1	475
2	30

Source Authors' calculations

Table 2 gives the number of travel trips that the drone will make from the point of origin to the destination. For example, the number of travel trips from origin one to destination one is four, while the number of travel trips from origin one to destination 12 is one.

Following that the quantity transported from the second origin to all the destinations—except the third destination—is zero, the associated number of travel trips from these origins to the destinations is also zero. This is also clear from the value of cost obtained; to minimize the cost of transporting blood from origin to destination, the cost-effective optimal point is the value with the minimum 22—found in row two, column three (Tables 3, 4, and 5).

Table 4 Cost of the blood

$N=2$	$M=12$ (value for cost)											
	1	2	3	4	5	6	7	8	9	10	11	12
1	49	94	90	24	6	63	17	65	72	40	67	99
2	97	53	22	47	60	36	54	67	46	55	42	70

Source Authors' calculations

Table 5 Demand for blood

Value for demand	
M (size 12)	Value
1	54
2	30
3	43
4	41
5	97
6	11
7	62
8	59
9	35
10	42
11	19
12	12

Source Authors' calculations

5 Summary and Conclusion

This research investigated blood transportation through an innovative technology called drones in rural Rwanda. The purpose of the study was ascertaining if drone-aided healthcare services can reduce the shipping costs associated with transporting blood from the point of origin to the various centers. The study showed that an optimal solution is possible when examining the likely link between health and technology. Using agent-based and input–output models, we presented and studied the modeling and simulations of the transportation problem for the drone-aided healthcare system in rural Rwanda. We solved the integer linear programming and showed how a simulated analysis can be applied to real data for taking practical decisions on optimal costs for the drone system.

In general, therefore, our results show that the associated travel trips from the second distribution point of origin to all destination centers (except the third destination) is optimal since the quantity of blood transported from the same point of origin to the same centers is zero. However, these findings are subject to some limitations, the most significant of which is data. Since data[8] is critical for the success of any facility location analysis, we conclude that the planning process[9] used in the simulation exercise will enable us to make good predictions about what we might see when real data

---

[8]Good data on customer demand, distances, costs, and other relevant inputs are essential for developing credible solutions and recommendations.

[9]The planning process includes identifying the problem; analysis; communication and decisions; and implementation (Daskin 2013). The process of identifying goals, actors, objectives, constraints, and options is of considerable value in and of itself, even if no model is solved.

is used for the exercise.[10] Hence, a direction for further research[11] is calibrating this exercise as part of the validation process taking into account network-based models (proposed in Ouyang 2014) that are built on the mathematical network theory.

References

Arcury, T. A., Preisser, J. S., Gesler, W. M., & Powers, J. M. (2005). Access to transportation and health care utilization in a rural region. *Journal of Rural Health, 21*(1), 31–38.

Ball, M. O., & Lin, F. L. (1993). A reliability model applied to emergency service vehicle location. *Operations Research, 41*(1), 18–36.

Boutilier, J. J., Brooks, S. C., Janmohamed, A., Byers, A., Buick, J. E., Zhan, C., et al. (2017). Optimizing a drone network to deliver automated external defibrillators. *Circulation, 135,* 2454–2465.

Daskin, M. S., & Stern, E. (1981). A hierarchical objective set covering model for EMS vehicle.

Daskin, M. S., Hogan, K., ReVelle, C. (1988). Integration of multiple, excess, backup, and expected covering models. *Environment and Planning B: Planning and Design, 15*(1), 15–35.

Daskin, M. S. (2013). *Network and discrete location: Models, algorithms, and applications*. New Jersey: Wiley.

Goins, R. T., Williams, K. A., Carter, M. W., Spencer, S. M., & Solovieva, T. (2005). Perceived barriers to health care access among rural adults: A qualitative study. *Journal of Rural Health, 21*(3), 206–213.

Hogan, K., ReVelle, C. (1986). Concepts and applications of backup coverage. *Management Science, 32*(11), 1434–1444.

Iturriza, M., Labaka, L., Sarriegi, J. M., & Hernantes, J. (2018). Modelling methodologies for analysing critical infrastructures. *Journal of Simulation, 12*(2), 128–143.

Jacobsen, S. K. (1990). Multiperiod capacitated location models. In P. B. Mirchandani & R. L. Francis (Eds.), *Discrete location theory* (pp. 173–208). New York: Wiley.

Kim, S. J., Lim, G. J., Cho, J., & Côté, M. J. (2017). Drone-aided healthcare services for patients with chronic diseases in rural areas. *Journal of Intelligent and Robotic Systems, 88*(1), 163–180.

Ouyang, M. (2014). Review on modeling and simulation of interdependent critical infrastructure systems. *Reliability Engineering and System Safety, 121,* 43–60.

ReVelle, C., & Hogan, K. (1989). The maximum availability location problem. *Transportation Science, 23*(3), 192–200.

Snyder, L. V., & Daskin, M. S. (2004). *Reliability models for facility location: The expected failure cost case*. Technical Report #04T-016. Lehigh University, Department of Industrial and Systems Engineering.

---

[10] Models and data should be tested by using them to represent existing conditions. This process is known as calibration and it enables us to compare the model's predictions with measured and actual performance. For example, we can compare the predicted or modeled average response time for a drone system with the actual average response time. If the two numbers are close enough, we may be willing to accept both the validity of the model and the data (Daskin 2013). This then leads to actionable recommendations for policy and program design based on a simulated study and its findings.

[11] With the recent launch of a similar technological advancement in Ghana, it will be good to understand how these technological systems work following the introduction of more products like vaccines. More research is needed in this regard to further understand what impact the addition of more products like vaccines for treating ailments can have on patients' well-being.

Chapter 9
Effect of Transfer Pricing on Profit Shifting by Multinational Companies in Developing Countries: A Case of Rwanda

Daniel Twesige, Faustin Gasheja, Jonas Barayendema, and Alexis Uwamahoro

Abstract Transfer pricing is the price between two related parties. Multinational companies have a tendency to shift their profits from the country where they operate to their home countries. The objective of this study is to examine the effects of transfer pricing on profit shifting by multinational enterprises in Rwanda. The study tests transfer pricing's factors such as finance costs, intra-group transactions/services costs, and royalty expenses on profit shifting by multinational companies in Rwanda. The study is guided by the theory of optimal transfer prices, agency theory, and accounting theory. The study adopts a quantitative research design with a target population of 72 Multinational Enterprises registered in the large taxpayer's offices. It collected data from financial statements and uses inferential statistics to ascertain the effects of transfer pricing on profit shifting. The study finds that multinational companies shift profits through royalties, finance costs, and intra-group services. The study concludes that a unit change in the independent variables influences total costs as well as taxable incomes. The study recommends that the Rwanda Revenue Authority (RRA) should come up with a clear law or legislation on transfer pricing.

Keywords Profit shifting · Transfer pricing · Multinational companies · Intra-group transactions · Rwanda

JEL Classification codes M11 · M13 · M16 · M38

1 Introduction

Thanks to globalization, there is no country, industry, or nation, which has not been touched by its positive or negative externalities (Pryma 2017). Multinational corporations are key players in the changing economic environment due to their ambiguous

D. Twesige (✉) · F. Gasheja · J. Barayendema · A. Uwamahoro
School of Business, College of Business, University of Rwanda, Kigali, Rwanda
e-mail: twesiged@yahoo.com

© Springer Nature Singapore Pte Ltd. 2020
G. G. Das and R. B. Johnson (eds.), *Rwandan Economy at the Crossroads of Development*, Frontiers in African Business Research,
https://doi.org/10.1007/978-981-15-5046-1_9

role in the globalization process (Pryma 2017). The relationships between multinationals and states are becoming more complex. One of the aspects of current interest refers to taxation of international corporations, in particular income tax.

Several studies have identified the creative use of transfer prices to shift profits from higher tax locations to more desirable locations. The Chinese government's official website states that tax evasion through transfer pricing accounts for 60% of total tax evasions by multinational companies. Richardson and Taylor (2015) studied income shifting where they took a sample of 286 multinationals. Their study showed that multinational companies shifted profits through thin capitalization and intangible assets.

Cristea and Nguyen (2016) used a firm-level panel dataset covering the entire Danish exports sector between 1999 and 2006. Their results provided evidence of profit shifting by multinational corporations (MNCs) through transfer pricing. They observed that once they own an affiliate in a country with a corporate tax rate lower than in the home country, Danish multinationals reduced the unit value of their exports there between 5.7 and 9.1%, on average. This reduction corresponded to $141 million in under-reported export revenues in 2006, which translated into a loss in tax income of 3.24% in Danish MNEs' tax returns.

A survey carried out by Clausing (2015) on US multinationals on the effect of profit shifting on corporate tax base in the United States showed a high sensitivity of foreign incomes to the tax burden on major foreign direct investments. The study used data from the Bureau of Economic Analysis survey on US multinational corporations in the period 1983–2012. It used estimates of tax sensitivity together with data on reported foreign incomes to calculate how much 'extra' income was booked in low-tax countries due to profit shifting. Clausing (2015) also estimated what the tax base would be in the United States without profit shifting. He found that profit shifting likely cost the US government between $77 and $111 billion in corporate tax revenue by 2012, and these revenue losses increased substantially in recent years. These findings are consistent with stylized facts about large quantities of income booked in tax havens.

A 2018 study by Blouin et al. (2018) on "Conflicting Transfer Pricing Incentives and the Role of Coordination" showed that the presence of a coordinated income tax and customs enforcement regime or coordination between income tax and customs functions altered transfer prices for firms. Their analysis had implications for both firms and taxing authorities. Specifically, their findings suggested that MNCs might decrease their aggregate tax burdens by increasing coordination within the firm, or that governments might increase their aggregate revenues by improving coordinating enforcement across taxing authorities.

Richardson et al. (2013) showed that tax havens may impose none, or only nominal amounts of corporate tax and have laws or administrative practices which prevent the effective exchange of information. Tax havens also promote tax avoidance via transfer pricing by permitting the reallocation of taxable incomes to low-tax jurisdictions and by reducing the amount of domestic taxes paid on foreign incomes (PwC 2011). Specifically, tax avoidance can be achieved by manipulating transfer pricing by transferring goods to countries with low income tax rates (for example, tax havens) at the lowest possible transfer price and by transferring goods out of these countries at the highest possible transfer price. Tax havens may thus facilitate aggressiveness in transfer pricing by acting as a conduit for the flow of goods and services between countries with established operations and parent firms domiciled in higher taxed countries (OECD 2014). It is possible that utilization of tax havens may act as a substitute for transfer pricing's aggressiveness in terms of achieving reduced group tax liabilities.

KPMG (2014) identified adoption of profit shifting strategies by MNEs as one of the main causes of base erosion. Transfer pricing forms a significant portion of tax planning strategies. According to OECD's (2010) report, abusive tax avoidance by MNEs raises serious issues of fairness and compliance. Transfer prices serve to determine the income of both parties involved in cross-border transactions. Transfer prices, therefore, tend to shape the tax bases of the countries involved in cross-border transactions.

Flows of goods and services among related entities of an MNE across different tax jurisdictions are referred to as intra-firm trade and the prices at which these goods and services are transferred at are called transfer prices (OECD 2010). Multinationals operate in different tax jurisdictions and as such their commercial transactions should be subject to different market forces which influence the nature of the relationships among them. To enhance compliance and fair distribution of the tax base among the related entities in a multinational, it is imperative that the transactions among the related entities are carried out at an arm's length (OECD 2014). Failure to comply with this principle may lead to double taxation where tax authorities from both sides insist on taxing the profits generated to get their share. To avoid this, multinationals come up with various means of reducing their tax liabilities through manipulation of transfer prices (Azémar and Corcos 2009).

In Rwanda, most multinational enterprises make losses and their income tax payable on a self-assessment basis is very low. In addition, controlled transactions that they enter into with their affiliates abroad have always gone untested to confirm whether they respect the arm's length principle. It is also a big challenge for the Rwandan tax administration to obtain pertinent information located outside Rwanda in situations of risks assessment, audits, or investigations regarding controlled cross-border transactions.

Figure 1 shows how multinational enterprises in different sectors make losses or very low profits due to untested high expenses incurred even after the expected breakeven period. The information used is sourced from filed income tax returns for the period 2010–17.

As can be seen in Fig. 1 the telecommunication sector contributed almost no income tax to the tax administration during 2010–17. It can also be noted that in some instances the expenses exceeded sales whereas losses were persistent. These are all multinational enterprises whose costs and operating expenses originate in their ultimate parents. This may be due to huge investments but transfer prices also need to be tested.

Figure 2 shows how the mining sector in Rwanda is less productive in terms of contributions to income tax. Most of the time sales equal the expenses incurred.

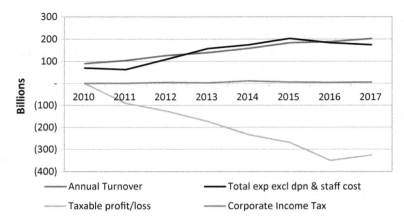

Fig. 1 Income tax contributions by the telecommunication sector. *Source* RRA systems, income tax returns for the period 2010–17

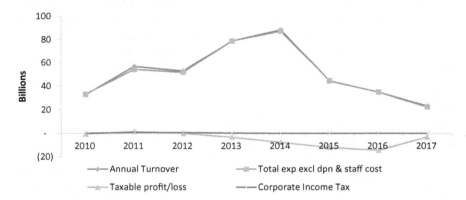

Fig. 2 Income tax contributions by the mining sector. *Source* RRA systems, income tax returns for the period 2010–17

This situation is sometimes normal due to high exploration and analysis expenses. However, companies which were established some before 2010, should be breaking even and making profits or else, they should sell abroad. Most of the transactions taking place in this sector need to be tested to confirm whether they respect the arm's length principle.

The construction sector in Rwanda is booming but it is shocking how less profitable it is even though most of the companies' contracts with the government. In this sector, expenses grow as the turnover grows over the years. However, profits are very low and hence their income tax contributions are insignificant (Fig. 3). Most of the services and materials are imported from related parties whose prices can easily be manipulated. Construction sites in Rwanda mostly last for more than six months but the tax administration has never endeavored to determine the existence of PEs

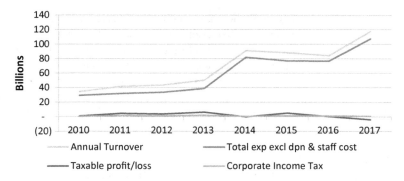

Fig. 3 Income tax contributions by the construction sector. *Source* RRA systems, income tax returns for the period 2010–17

so that profits attributable to such PEs can be taxed in Rwanda. Therefore, all these transactions need to be tested.

The banking sector shows a growth trend in turnover/sales in the study period but its profitability seems to be very low and hence the income tax payable is very small (Fig. 4). This is due to the continuous growth of expenses. Banks, however, do not undertake huge investments other than in software which is mainly purchased by the parent company and the cost is shared by all the group companies. The cost-sharing mechanism may be not at arm's length in this sector.

From Figs. 1, 2, 3, and 4 which give details of some sectors' contributions to income tax per year in Rwanda, one thing in common that most of them incur losses for a long period perhaps because of huge investments but the reasons may also be profit shifting through service fees, business restructuring, transfer pricing, and duplication of some expenses.

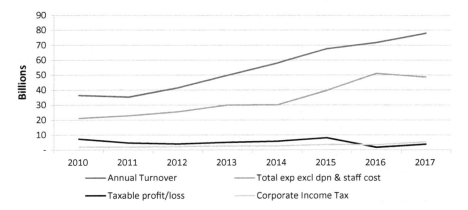

Fig. 4 Income tax contributions by the banking sector. *Source* RRA systems, income tax returns for the period 2010–17

Readhead's (2016) study of public finance policies in developing nations showed that although MNCs contributed to government revenue in the form of taxes, they generally tended to pay much less than what they ought to pay due to long tax concession periods, transfer pricing practices, huge investment allowances, disguised public subsidies, and tariff protection from the government. These companies lobbied using their economic powers for policies that were unfavorable for development and they could avoid local taxation and shift profits to their affiliates in low-tax jurisdictions. This led to a negative effect on the revenues collected by the governments from taxation and therefore developing countries were unable to effectively fund their development goals.

According to Niyibizi (2017), the value of transactions between associated enterprises was, on average, 82.3% in relation to total expenses in 2015 whereas in 2013, the value was 63.3% This confirms that MNEs operating in Rwanda have business relationships with their affiliates and the issue is knowing if their transactions are carried following the arm's length principle. Transacting with related parties is not illegal, but the tax administration has to ensure that these transactions are at arm's length. This study examines the effects of transfer pricing practices on profit shifting by multinational companies in Rwanda. The study was guided by the following research questions:

i. What are the effects of transfer pricing practices on profit shifting by multinational companies in Rwanda?
ii. What are the determinants of multinational companies' total costs in Rwanda?

2 Theoretical and Conceptual Framework

Profit shifting can be in the form of tax evasion or tax avoidance. These two practices are used for reducing or avoiding tax obligations. Tax evasion refers to failure to pay taxes which are legally due and therefore is a criminal offence; this involves practices like deliberate non-payment of taxes due, declaring lesser incomes, profits or gains in the returns, and overstating deductions in the financial returns produced for tax purposes for achieving non-compliance (Uwimbabazi 2017).

Transfer pricing has been under scrutiny at any given point in time and in any society, regardless of the degree of democracy that the country has. However, without taxes, modern societies cannot survive. Several transfer pricing theories have been elaborated on to find out their determinants. Theoretical approaches followed in transfer pricing are commonly divided into three main approaches: the economic deterrence approach, accounting approach, and the agency relationship approach.

Economic approach
Literature on economic theory is based on the Hirshleifer's 1965 model which uses the manufacturing division and the distribution division. This model was used for developing the theory that uses buying and selling divisions as profit centers. According to

Schjelderup and Sorgard (1997), under a competitive market structure, the strategy to be employed is transferring the resources at market prices while for intra-company transfers the prices are placed along the marginal cost curve.

The basic concept for determining the transfer price is the marginal cost which is an economic aspect. A company is supposed to manage its scarce resources effectively and produce the right amounts that maximize its profits. Members of a firm are questioned about their best inputs for achieving an output that achieves these returns. In this theory, prices are used as a measure for distributing scarce resources. This theory is criticized because of its focus on short-term profit maximization and not on the long-term effects that it has. Therefore, the model is only effective in simple case situations (Hirshleifer et al. 2006).

Accounting approach

Pricing is made up of cost-plus margins. Further, transfer pricing requires constant control over the activities involved. Expectations of tax rules are a crucial factor in multinationals' transfer prices. Transfer prices in accounting theory have two main functions which are profit allocations and maximization. Profit allocation is meant to follow the decisions taken by the management while profit maximization in relation to taxation systems transfers the returns between individuals so as to reduce the tax base in line with the multinational level to reorganize the returns in a lesser tax rate economical setting (Veres 2011).

According to Milner and Tingley (2011) MNEs in Africa have the liberty to change transfer prices in their favor. In this case, transfer pricing becomes a major loss of returns in many African nations. However, with the aim of protecting profits and encouraging growth, African nations are taking measures used in the rest of the world related to transfer pricing (Veres 2011). The target of the accounting theory is the impact of transfer prices on economic decisions that are used for determining how much a company can produce. Further, it is also used for determining the type of market price that should be used by a firm.

Agency theory

The agency theory emanates from corporate governance principles. According to this theory, there is always a conflict of interest between different participating subjects and stakeholders. Richardson et al. (2015) applied the theory of the firm concept based on conflict of interest among different participating subjects. These subjects were specified as stockholders, managers, and creditors. Based on the agency theory, the principal and agents were individual utility maximizers. Therefore, they will always follow their self-interests which may not be identical. Richardson et al. (2015) assert that the existence of agency costs is based on an incompatibility between agents and principals' individual interests. The transfer pricing policy will never be effective if it is set by the parent company (Clausing 2015). In a situation where transfer prices differ from market ones, this leads to a deformation of supply and demand. When the motivation of subsidiary firms' management is based on the profits of the subsidiary firms, a conflict of interest arises.

This study applied the agency theory to assess the motivating factors that the parent company can use to motivate subsidiary companies so that they can act in the same interests. It can be stated that there must exist an optimal transfer pricing so that the profit of the concern is maximal. The principals motivate agents to act in their best interests. Agents create systems which convince the principal that they are acting in their best interests.

Determinants of profit shifting by multinational companies
In a global economy where MNEs play a prominent role, governments need to ensure that MNEs' taxable profits are not artificially shifted out of their jurisdiction and that the tax base reported by MNEs in their country reflects the economic activity undertaken therein (OECD 2010).

The Rwanda tax law has adopted the arm's length principle in Article 8 to ensure that transfer prices between related companies are established on a market value basis. In this context, the principle means that prices should be the same as they would have been had the parties to the transaction not been related to each other. This is often seen as being aimed at preventing profits from being systematically deviated to lowest tax countries.

The arm's length principle is instrumental in determining how much of the profits should be attributed to one entity and, consequently the extent of a country's tax claims on such an entity. OECD (2010) developed thorough guidelines on how the arm's length principle should be applied in this context. Under this approach, price is considered appropriate if it is within a range of prices that would be charged by independent parties dealing at an arm's length. This is generally defined as a price that an independent buyer would pay an independent seller for an identical item under identical terms and conditions, where neither is under any compulsion to act.

Intra-group transactions
According to OECD (2010), companies are required to conduct their related party transactions at an arm's length. This means that the conditions made or imposed between two or more CTPs in their commercial or financial relations should be similar to those which would exist between independent enterprises. Broadly, related party transactions may be grouped into four categories: (i) tangible goods: these relate to transactions involving purchase/sale of finished goods, raw materials, fixed assets, and spare parts; (ii) intangible properties: involves know-how (professional and technical support), trademark, and trade name; and (iii) financing arrangement: includes transactions such as loans, guarantees, and cash pooling arrangements.

Existing corporate tax systems permit deduction of interest payments from the tax base, whereas equity returns to investors are not tax-deductible (Mintz 2004). This asymmetric treatment of alternative means of financing investments offers firms a fundamental incentive to increase their reliance on debt finance (Mintz 2004). For multinational companies, this incentive is further strengthened by the opportunity to use internal debt as a means of shifting profits from high-tax to low-tax countries. Most of the time, debts are in foreign currency and from there foreign currency risk is obvious. By foreign currency risk, we mean the risk that an investment's value may change due to changes in the value of two different currencies (Engel 2015). Losses because of fluctuations in foreign exchange on outstanding foreign currency loans are allowed as business expenditure in accordance with Chapter 2, Section 3(23) of Rwanda's income tax law No. 016/2018 of 13 April 2018.

Recent empirical research provides conclusive evidence that international tax differentials affect multinationals' financial structures in a way that is consistent with overall tax minimization (Desai et al. 2004; Egger et al. 2010; Huizinga et al. 2008). Moreover, while profit shifting within multinationals can occur through a variety of channels, there are clear empirical indications that the use of financial policies plays an important role in this process (Grubert 2003; Mintz 2004; Mintz and Smart 2004). For this reason, international debt is a core factor in empirical findings that multinational firms seem to pay substantially lower taxes as a share of pre-tax profits as compared to nationally operating firms (Egger et al. 2007).

Intangible assets
An increasing number of MNEs' tax planning strategies involve the relocation of intangible properties to low-tax affiliates (Dischinger 2008). Others have found trademark holding companies in tax havens that own and administer the group's brands and licenses. Several studies explain how MNEs shift intangibles related profits from high-tax to low-tax countries. Fuest et al. (2013), discuss prominent models for IP-based profit shifting. In a nutshell, the parent transfers the right to use its intellectual property to a subsidiary located in a low-tax country at a reasonable price and a 'reasonable tax payment' because determining the arm's length price for partially developed intangibles is quite difficult.

The other companies in the group will then pay high tax-deductible royalties for the use of the IP held by the IP holding company. The IP holding company will pay little or no tax because it is located in a tax haven. For jurisdictions where the operating companies are located there will be little or no corporation tax paid as well. According to Fuest et al. (2013), multinational corporations set up branches and subsidiaries in Africa that make a lot of profits, which are 'shifted' along such avenues.

2.1 Determinants of Profit Shifting

The model proposed in this study (see Fig. 5) is made up of variables from models tested in earlier studies. The independent variables used in the study are factors of transfer pricing while the dependent variable is profit shifting by MNEs which was measured on the basis of total costs and taxable profits/losses. Independent variables are factors of transfer pricing which contain elements like intra-group transactions/services, finance costs, and royalty expenses.

According to OECD (2010), intra-group transactions are financial or commercial transactions which involve two companies of the same group simultaneously. The most common example is the issuing of a sales invoice for the supply of goods and

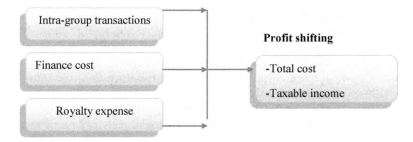

Fig. 5 Conceptual framework. *Source* Author's framework

services (OECD 2010). The company issuing the invoice will recognize a receivable in its balance sheet and revenue from the sale in its income statement whereas the purchasing company will have a payable on its balance sheet and an expense on its income statement.

Financing cost (FC), also known as the cost of finances (COF), is the cost, interest, and other charges involved in the borrowing of money to build or purchase assets (Mintz 2004). In this study, finance costs include interests, foreign exchange losses accruing from debt finance, and other financing fees involved in the borrowing of money.

Royalty fee can be defined as periodic charges that the owner of a franchised business needs to pay to remain part of the franchise system that provides branding, advertising, and administrative support (OECD 2010).

3 Methodology

This section gives the methods and techniques used in the data collection.

3.1 Research Design

This study adopted a descriptive/diagnostic research design. According to Hajase and Hajase (2003), a descriptive study describes the existing conditions and attitudes through observations and interpretation techniques. Therefore, a descriptive/diagnostic design was adopted in this study to describe the characteristics of intra-group transactions, finance costs, and royalty expenses as well as for finding out their possible associations.

3.2 Study Population and Sampling

The population was 72 multinational companies registered on the basis of their corporate income tax reported by the large taxpayer offices of the Rwanda Revenue Authority under the Domestic Taxes Department. This population only consisted of MNEs registered as large taxpayers. Due to the small population, all companies were considered as the sample. Simple random sampling was used for selecting the respondents.

3.3 Data Sources and Research Instruments

Data was gathered from audited financial statements including income statements, balance sheets, statements of cash flows, and statements of changes in equity. Quantitative data on intra-group services/transactions, foreign exchange risks, and royalty expenses were collected from secondary sources (audited financial statements) to measure their effect on profit shifting by MNEs in Rwanda. Data was also derived from statistical abstracts (NISR) as well as from the Rwanda Revenue Authority's systems.

3.4 Data Analysis

The study used inferential statistics using IBM's Statistical Product and Service Solutions (SPSS) software (Hejase and Hejase 2013). Data was analyzed by a multiple regression analysis. A multiple regression analysis was used for investigating the extent to which independent variables were associated with the dependent variables (Hejase and Hejase 2013: 433). The findings were presented using tables and graphs. The following ordinary least squares (OLS) regression model was used in analyzing the relationship between the dependent and independent variables:

$$\text{TC} = \beta_o + \beta_1(\text{Royl}) + \beta_2(\text{Finc}) + \beta_3(\text{Intrgrptrans}) + \varepsilon \qquad (1)$$

$$\text{TI} = \beta_o + \beta_1(\text{Royl}) + \beta_2(\text{Finc}) + \beta_3(I\text{ntrgrptrans}) + \varepsilon \qquad (2)$$

where

TC	Total costs
TI	Taxable income
Royl	Royalty payment
Finc	Financial costs
Intrgrptrans	Intra-group transactions/services

ε	Error term
β_0	Intercept (value of *TC* or *TI* when independent variables $= 0$)
β_1, β_2 and β_3	Are the regression coefficients included in *TC* or *TI* by each independent variable.

4 Results and Discussion

4.1 Multicollinearity Test

The variance inflation factor (VIF) was analyzed to test for the existence of multicollinearity. Multicollinearity occurs when "two or more independent variables (or combination of independent variables) in a multiple linear regression are highly correlated with each other" (Hejase and Hejase 2013: 482), that is, one can be linearly predicted from the others with a substantial degree of accuracy. This leads to problems of understanding which independent variable contributes to the variance explained in the dependent variable, as well as technical issues in calculating a multiple regression model. VIF for each predictor is quite low compared to the maximum acceptable value of 5, hence there is the absence of co-linearity among them (Table 1).

Testing violation of the normality assumption of the error term in the model
We now examine the assumption of the error terms in the model. These are assumed to be normally distributed with constant variance. Figure 6, shows that these are close to being normally distributed. In fact, the right-hand side graph reveals that the standard deviation of the residual is small, since its density tends to concentrate around the center or the mean.

Hence, we conclude that there has not been any violation of the normality assumption of the error terms in the model. This validation of the model confirms that all predictors used have no linear relationship among them, that is, they are not collinear with respect to one another. Moreover, the normality assumption of the error terms in the model is checked and the findings show that this is close to normal distribution. Hence, the model is valid, and its results can be trusted.

Table 1 Variance inflation factor values for each predictor coefficients

Model		Collinearity statistics	
		Tolerance	VIF
1	Royalties	0.953	1.049
	Finance cost	0.950	1.053
	Intra-group transactions	0.908	1.101

Source Survey data (2019)

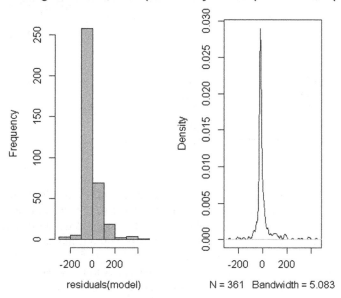

Fig. 6 Histogram and density display of the residuals generated by the model. *Source* Authors' output

4.2 Determinants of Profit Shifting and Total Costs

The purpose of this study was to examine the determinants of profit shifting in multinational companies in Rwanda.

Table 2 shows the correlation coefficient and the coefficient of determination. As can be seen in the table the correlation coefficient is very high (0.889). This means that transfer pricing factors and total costs are highly positively correlated. The coefficient of determination is 0.790 which implies that 79% of the variations in total costs are determined by variations in intra-group transactions, finance charges, and royalties.

We conduct the ANOVA test to assess whether the data was consistent with the model's assumptions or not. This was done on the basis of the null hypothesis which stated that "there is no difference between the model without independent

Table 2 Model summary on the determinants of profit shifting

Model	R	R square	Adjusted R square	Std. error of the estimate
1	0.889[a]	0.790	0.788	7859283909.46074

[a] are the predicators of the model which are intratransactions, finance cost, and royalties
Source Survey data (2019)

Table 3 Significance of the model for determining profit shifting (ANOVA[a] Table)

Model		Sum of squares	df	Mean square	F	Sig.
1	Regression	$5779728517865679 \times 10^7$	3	$1926576172621893 \times 10^7$	311.903	0.000[b]
	Residual	$15318549205238122 \times 10^6$	248	$6176834356950856 \times 10^4$		
	Total	$7311583438389491 \times 10^7$	251			

[a] is the dependent variables which is total cost
[b] are the predicators intratransactions, finance cost, and royalties
Source Survey data (2019)

variables and the model with independent variables." As can be seen in Table 3, the *P*-value (0.000) is less than the significance level (0.05), thus there is enough evidence for rejecting the null hypothesis. We therefore conclude that there is a significant statistical difference between the model without independent variables and a model with independent variables. Hence, the model fits the data.

Table 4 shows the significance of the independent variables. This was done on the basis of the null hypothesis that "the independent variable has no effect on total costs." The table shows that the *P*-values for intra-group transactions/services and finance costs are (0.000) which are smaller than the significance level (0.05), thus there is enough evidence to reject the null hypothesis for these independent variables. We therefore conclude that intra-group transactions/services and finance costs have significant effects on total costs. The coefficients of these variables are positive meaning that their increase leads to an increase in total costs. The *P*-value for royalties (0.221) is greater than the significance level (0.05) so we conclude that royalties had no significant effect on total costs and therefore may be removed from the equation. This study's findings are similar to Bennett's (2015) study which concluded that aggressive intra-group pricing especially for debt and intangibles played a major role in corporate tax avoidance and it was one of the issues identified when the OECD released its BEPS's action plan in 2013. Niyibizi's (2017) research findings too

Table 4 Determinants of profit shifting

Model		Unstandardized coefficients		Standardized coefficients	t	Sig.
		B	Std. error	Beta		
1	(Constant)	2004136077.975	643387036.508		3.115	0.002
	Intrgrtrans	0.995	0.037	0.818	26.834	0.000
	Finance cost	1.271	0.200	0.190	6.373	0.000
	Royalties	0.567	0.462	0.036	1.226	0.221

Source Survey data (2019)

confirmed that in 2013 the value of the transactions between associated enterprises was, on average, 82.3% in relation to total expenses whereas in 2013, the value was 63.3%. This study confirms that MNEs operating in Rwanda have business relationships with their affiliates and the question is how to know if their transactions are carried following the arm's length principle.

$$TC = 2004136077 + 1.271(\text{Financecost}) + 0.995(\text{Intrgrtrans}) \quad (3)$$

From the regression Eq. (3), we can say that: a unit change in finance costs increases TC by 1.271 units and vice versa keeping all other variables constant. A unit change in intra-group transactions/services increases TC by 0.995 units and vice versa keeping all other variables constant.

4.3 Determinants of Profit Shifting and MNEs' Taxable Incomes in Rwanda

Table 5 shows the correlation coefficient and the coefficient of determination. The correlation coefficient is −0.574 which means that transfer pricing factors and taxable income are negatively correlated. The coefficient of determination is 0.329 which implies that 32.9% of the variations in taxable income is determined by variations in transfer pricing factors. This means that variations in intra-group transactions, finance costs, and royalty costs only explain 32.9% of the variations in taxable income.

ANOVA was conducted to assess whether the data was consistent with the model's assumptions or not. This was done on the basis of the null hypothesis that "there is no difference between the model without independent variables and the model with independent variables." Table 6 shows that the P-value (0.000) is less than the significance level (0.05), thus there is enough evidence for rejecting the null hypothesis. We therefore conclude that there is a significant statistical difference between the model without independent variables and a model with independent variables hence the model fits the data.

Table 7 shows the significance of the independent variables. This was done on the basis of the null hypothesis that "the independent variables have no effect on taxable incomes". The table shows that the P-values for intra-group transactions/services and finance costs are (0.000) which are less than the significance level (0.05), thus

Table 5 Transfer pricing factors and taxable income

Model	R	R square	Adjusted R square	Std. error of the estimate
1	−0.574[a]	0.329	0.321	6773219025.88304

[a] are the the predicators which are intratransactions, finance cost, and royalties
Source Survey data (2019)

Table 6 Anova test results

Model		Sum of squares	df	Mean square	F	Sig.
1	Regression	$55843227551001 \times 10^8$	3	$18614409183667 \times 10^8$	40.575	0.000^b
	Residual	$113773710012008 \times 10^8$	248	458764959726×10^8		
	Total	$169616937563009 \times 10^8$	251			

[a] is the dependent variables which is Taxable income
[b] are the predicators intratransactions, finance cost, and royalties
Source Survey data (2019)

Table 7 Determinants of profit shifting

Model		Unstandardized coefficients		Standardized coefficients	T	Sig.
		B	Std. error	Beta		
1	(Constant)	−998294219.941	554478164.536		−1.800	0.073
	Intrgrtrans	−136	0.032	−233	−4.269	0.000
	Finance cost	−1.866	0.172	−0.579	−10.856	0.000
	Royalties	−0.054	0.398	−0.007	−0.135	0.893

Source Survey data (2019)

there is enough evidence to reject the null hypothesis for these independent variables. We therefore conclude that intra-group transactions/services and finance costs have significant effects on taxable incomes. The coefficients for intra-group transactions/services and finance costs are negative meaning than an increase in these variables leads to a decrease in taxable income and vice versa. The P-value for royalties (0.893) is greater than the significance level (0.05), so we conclude that royalties had no significant effect on taxable incomes and therefore may be removed from the equation.

This study's findings are similar to Bennett's (2015) study which concluded that aggressive intra-group pricing especially for debt and intangibles played a major role in corporate tax avoidance Clausing (2015) study confirmed that one of the tools used by MNEs is issuing big loans to subsidiaries resulting in thin capitalization which leads to tax avoidance. A survey by Richardson and Taylor (2015) showed the association between a series of income shifting incentives including multinationality, aggressiveness in transfer pricing, thin capitalization, intangible assets, and use of tax havens.

$$TI = -998294219 - 1.866(\text{Financecost}) - 136(\text{Intrgrtrans}) \quad (4)$$

From the regression Eq. (4), we can say that: a unit change in finance costs leads to a decrease in TI by 1.866 units and vice versa keeping all other variables constant. A unit change in intra-group transactions/services leads to a decrease in TI by 136 units and vice versa keeping all other variables constant.

5 Conclusion and Policy Recommendations

This section presents a summary of the study and makes policy recommendations based on its findings.

5.1 Conclusion

This study investigated the effects of transfer pricing factors on profit shifting by MNEs in Rwanda. It was conducted on taxpayers registered with the Large Taxpayer Department. They were all registered in the corporate income tax operational office. A survey was done using 72 multinational companies (registered on the basis of their corporate income taxes reported with the Large Taxpayer Office under the Domestic Tax Department of Rwanda Revenue Authority. This population only consisted of MNEs registered as large taxpayers. The study used secondary data with the objective of assessing the effects of intra-group transactions to determine the effects of finance costs for examining the effects of royalty charges and predicting profit shifting in Rwanda. Five quantitative models were tested, and the descriptive statistics of the data were given. The research findings suggest that profit shifting is highly affected by finance costs and intra-group transactions/services are the leading determining factor of such activity.

5.2 Policy Implications and Recommendations

Based on the study's findings we put forward some recommendations to check profit shifting as the tax administration strives to increase MNEs' tax compliance levels especially in corporate income tax so that the government can raise the required tax revenue to finance its national expenditure. The recommendations of this study include but are not limited to the following:

(i) RRA should look at the loopholes in the current ITA, especially in the thin capitalization rule which sets a limit on the interest deductible on loans from related parties that is currently set at 4:1 the amount of equity. This should be the same for foreign exchange losses accruing from interest-bearing loans as

well as free interest loans. This will limit the finance costs normally claimed by MNEs.
(ii) RRA should closely follow up on Rwanda's treaties with regard to selecting who to conclude a treaty with, when to conclude it, what to forego, what to achieve from the concluded treaty, and when to terminate a treaty. There is also a need to closely monitor the country's treaty network for RRA to better understand how the tax base is being narrowed and/or expanded.
(iii) The tax administration has to have in place a clear mechanism for accessing current information regarding international taxation where most multinationals post information regarding their businesses including databases. Information exchange tools and procedures are an important aspect to be considered at an earlier stage since information needed during the audit process cannot be available only within the country (Rwanda).
(iv) There should be a focus on the use of intangible properties by Rwandan subsidiaries of foreign MNEs to ensure that no royalties are paid above what would be paid under the arm's length principle.
(v) RRA should put in place transfer pricing guidelines that will guide MNEs on how to prepare and keep contemporaneous transfer pricing documentation. Preparing and maintaining transfer pricing documentation will show that related party transactions are conducted at an arm's length and will facilitate reviews by tax authorities and help resolve any transfer pricing issues that may arise.

References

Azémar, C., & Corcos, G. (2009). Multinational firms' heterogeneity in tax responsiveness: The role of transfer pricing. *World Economy, 32*(9), 1291–1318.

Bennett, M. (2015). The OECD's BEPS final report. *Tax executive, 67*(6), 22.

Blouin, J. L., Robinson, L. A., & Seidman, J. K. (2018). Conflicting transfer pricing incentives and the role of coordination. *Contemporary Accounting Research, 35*(1), 87–116.

Clausing, K. A. (2015). The effect of profit shifting on the corporate tax base in the United States and beyond. *SSRN*.

Cristea, A. D., & Nguyen, D. X. (2016). Transfer pricing by multinational firms: New evidence from foreign firm ownerships. *American Economic Journal: Economic Policy, 8*(3), 170–202.

Desai, M., Foley, F., & Hines, J. (2004). A multinational perspective on capital structure choice and internal capital markets. *Journal of Finance, 59*, 2451–2487.

Dischinger, M. (2008). *Corporate taxes and the location of intangible assets within multinational firms*. Munich: University of Munich.

Egger, P., Eggert, W., Keuschnigg, C., & Winner, H. (2010). Corporate taxation, debt financing and foreign-plant ownership. *European Economic Review, 54*(1), 96–107.

Egger, P., Eggert, W., & Winner, H. (2007). *Saving taxes through foreign plant ownership* (CESifo Working Paper No. 1887). Munich.

Engel, C. (2015). Exchange rates and interest parity. *Handbook of International Economics, 4*, 453–522.

Fuest, C., Spengel, C., Finke, K., Heckemeyer, J., & Nusser, H. (2013). Profit shifting and'aggressive'tax planning by multinational firms: Issues and options for reform. *ZEW-Centre for European Economic Research Discussion Paper* (13-078).
Grubert, H. (2003). Intangible income, intercompany transactions, income shifting, and the choice of location. *National Tax Journal, 56,* 221–242.
Hejase, A., & Hejase, H. (2013). *Research methods: A practical approach for business students* (2nd ed.). Philadelphia: Masadir Inc.
Hirshleifer, D., Subrahmanyam, A., & Titman, S. (2006). Feedback and the success of irrational investors. *Journal of Financial Economics, 81*(2), 311–338.
Huizinga, H., Laeven, L., & Nicodµeme, G. (2008). Capital structure and international debt shifting. *Journal of Financial Economics, 88,* 80–118.
KPMG International (2014). Planning for the recovery: Examining transfer pricing in the current environment and beyond.
Milner, H. V., & Tingley, D. H. (2011). Who supports global economic engagement? The sources of preferences in American foreign economic policy. *International Organization, 65*(1), 37–68.
Mintz, J. (2004). Conduit entities: Implications of indirect tax efficient financing structures for real investment. *International Tax and Public Finance, 11,* 419–434
Mintz, J., & Smart, M. (2004). Income shifting, investment, and tax competition: theory and evidence from provincial taxation in Canada. *Journal of Public Economics, 88,* 1149–1168.
Niyibizi, O. (2017). *La problématique des prix de transfert dans le contrôle des sociétés multinationales au Rwanda: dispositifs et méthodologies de contrôle* (unpublished Master's dissertation). Universite Alioune Diop De Bambey, Cameroun.
OECD. (2010), *Transfer Pricing Guidelines for Multinational Enterprises and Tax Administration.* Paris: OECD Publishing.
PwC. (2011).Transfer pricing and developing countries-final report. Europeaid-Implementing the Tax and Development policy agenda (pp. 1–119).
Pryma, K. (2017). *Transfer pricing and its effect on financial reporting and taxation* (unpublished diploma thesis). Mendel University, Brno.
Readhead, A. (2016). *Preventing tax base erosion in Africa: A regional study of transfer pricing challenges in the mining sector.*
Richardson, G., Lanis, R., & Taylor, G. (2015). Financial distress, outside directors and corporate tax aggressiveness spanning the global financial crisis: An empirical analysis. *Journal of Banking & Finance, 52,* 112–129.
Richardson, G., & Taylor, G. (2015). Income shifting incentives and tax haven utilization: Evidence from multinational U.S. Firms. *International Journal of Accounting, 50*(4), 458–485.
Richardson, G., Taylor, G., & Lanis, R. (2013). Determinants of transfer pricing aggressiveness: Empirical evidence from Australian firms. *Journal of Contemporary Accounting and Economics, 9*(2), 136–150.
Schjelderup, G., & Sorgard, L. (1997). Transfer pricing as a strategic device for decentralized multinationals. *International Tax and Public Finance, 4*(3), 277–290.
Uwimbabazi, H. (2017). *The determinants of tax compliance on corporate income tax in Rwanda* (unpublished master's dissertation). INES Ruhengeri, Musanze.
Veres, T. (2011). Accounting aspects of pricing and transfer pricing. Annals of the University of Petrosani. *Economics, 11*(2), 289–296.

Part III
Entrepreneurship and Business Performance: Strategies and Polices

Chapter 10
Determinants of Entrepreneurship Sustainability Among Family Businesses in Rwanda: Case of Small and Medium Family Businesses in Kigali

Alexis Uwamahoro and Daniel Twesige

Abstract Most of the businesses in Rwanda are family owned and managed. These businesses fall in the category of Small and Medium-sized Enterprises (SMEs). They face a lot of challenges including in their initiation, management, and lifespan, leading to most of them collapsing leaving many people jobless. Given that this study is an exploratory research, it uses a combination approach composed of positivism. The study's sample is 49,000 SMEs registered on the Rwanda Revenue Authority (RRA) portal in Nyarugenge district. However, the study targets the managers/owners of these businesses. It uses simple random sampling to select the respondents. It did the Chi-square test to test for the determinants of entrepreneurship sustainability among family businesses. The results show a significant association between training and mentorship in entrepreneurs involving family members in the management, good family relationships, financial discipline, education levels, innovations, and business sustainability. The results also show that there is no significant relationship between financial resources and a business' sustainability and that although the educational levels are significant for a business' sustainability, these do not contribute much to its sustainability. The key factors that determine a business' sustainability are innovations, involvement of family members in the management, training and mentorship of entrepreneurs, good family relationships, and financial discipline.

Keywords Family business · Family entrepreneurship · Entrepreneurship sustainability · Sustainability · And SMEs

JEL Classification M10 · M13 · M19 · L2

A. Uwamahoro (✉) · D. Twesige
School of Business, College of Business, University of Rwanda, Kigali, Rwanda
e-mail: uwamahoro231@yahoo.fr

D. Twesige
e-mail: twesiged@yahoo.com

© Springer Nature Singapore Pte Ltd. 2020
G. G. Das and R. B. Johnson (eds.), *Rwandan Economy at the Crossroads of Development*, Frontiers in African Business Research,
https://doi.org/10.1007/978-981-15-5046-1_10

1 Introduction

Family businesses are a part of entrepreneurship development and an important aspect of economic development and economic transformation offering jobs and creating wealth for families and other people working in the family businesses (Aronoff et al. 2003). Family-owned businesses are those in which two or more family members have control over the financial resources (Fuller 2011).

Family businesses are an important part of the world's economy and the backbone of the economic systems in most countries. In fact, they make up more than 60% of all companies in Europe and the Americas, and they account for about 50% of their employment, encompassing a vast range of firms of different sizes and in different sectors. For instance, the engine of Germany's economy, the largely family-owned Mittelstand businesses, are the envy of Europe because of their reliability, excellence, and ability to penetrate emerging markets.

In emerging markets, local family businesses are thriving as the entrepreneurs' hand on fast-growing companies to their ambitious and well-educated offspring (Arifin et al. 2013). In an ideal situation, family-owned businesses aim to "grow leaders" within their organizations, and the objective is to ensure that there is continuity of the leadership in the future so that their turnover rates are reduced (Miller and Rollnick 2003).

Small and Medium-sized Enterprises (SMEs) and micro enterprises in the Organization for Economic Cooperation and Development (OECD) countries account for over 95% of all firms, 60–70% of the employment, 55% of the GDP, and create the maximum number of new jobs, showing the impact that SMEs have on employment. In contrast, currently over 80% of Rwandans are engaged in agricultural production. The SME sector, including formal and informal businesses, comprises 98% of the businesses in Rwanda and 41% of all private-sector employment though the formalized sector has a lot of growth potential with only 300,000 currently employed in this sector. Most micro and small enterprises employ up to four people, showing that growth in the sector will create significant private sector non-agricultural employment opportunities (MINICOM 2010).

Family businesses face a major threat which emanates from the succession of the management. Studies show that only 30% of the family businesses survive till the second generation, only 12% of the family businesses make it to the third generation, and only 3% survive to the fourth generation and beyond. Inadequate planning and a failure to create management succession plans are the main factors that affect the continuity of family businesses. Family businesses can avoid such a destruction of valuable assets if their founders develop plans for the management's succession long before retirement (Fuller 2011).

Entrepreneurship sustainability is defined as a process of business creation that meets current needs without compromising the next generation's abilities to meet their own needs (O'Neill et al. 2009); the World Commission on Environment and Development 1987). In literature, entrepreneurship sustainability is also defined as a concept that links sustainability development to entrepreneurship (Majid et al. 2012).

Crals and Vereeck (2005) define sustainable entrepreneurship from the perspective of sustainable development which is mainly concerned with the triple bottom line meaning people, planet, and profits. The first P (People) is linked to an enterprise's behavior in social and ethical dimensions; how the organization treats its employees and promotes social cohesion; and the protection of human rights and gender relationships. The second P (Planet) is concerned with the disposition of the organization toward the environment, while the last P (Profits) relates to what the organization gets as financial returns and the allocation and distribution of returns to relevant stakeholders. while Madjid and Koe (2012) define entrepreneurship sustainability in the context of preserving those domains in an equal manner through continuous commitment of entrepreneurs who are innovative enough to make changes in their enterprises, processes, and products for sustainability.

A 2008 Private Sector Federation (PSF) study estimated that there were over 72,000 SMEs operating in Rwanda, while only 25,000 of them were formally registered. The study also found that most of the small enterprises in Rwanda started off as micro businesses and grew into small businesses or they were formed to supplement the incomes of middle to upper income households. Rwandan small and micro businesses comprise 97.8% of the private sector and account for 36% of the private sector employment. They often lack proper accounting and financial systems. In contrast, Rwandan medium-sized enterprises are well-established businesses that are individually or jointly owned. They have set administrative processes, qualified personnel, and trained staff, employ between 50 and 100 people, and account for 0.22% of the businesses in Rwanda contributing 5% to the total private sector employment. Combining these categories shows that SMEs comprise approximately 98% of the total businesses in Rwanda and account for 41% of all private-sector employment (MINICOM 2010). A study by NISR (2017) indicated that more than 95% of the business enterprises in Rwanda were family businesses. The private sector was the biggest employer in Rwanda, and more than 90% were family-owned establishments. The informal sector in Rwanda constituted 90.8% of the total establishments. This implies that the informal sector was one of the leading sectors that contributed to the country's (GDP). This means that family businesses in Rwanda contribute much to its growth. Therefore, family businesses and entrepreneurship sustainability are seen as the engines of employment, helping in alleviating poverty and improving equalities (Ayyagari et al. 2011).

Family-owned and managed businesses in Rwanda face the same issues that plague such businesses around the world given that they face a considerable number of challenges ranging from their initiation to management and consequently their lifespan. This situation has been observed in many family businesses in Rwanda. Given the importance of this sector and its contribution to Rwanda's economy, the worry is that most of the family businesses in Rwanda close down when their initiators die, leaving many people unemployed. This inevitably has a negative impact on the country's economic development.

Despite the importance of sustainability and continuity of family businesses, studies which focus on family businesses' sustainability in developing countries particularly in Rwanda are scarce. Section 2 offers review of literature. Methodology is spelt out in Sect. 3. Section 4 discusses results while the concluding section offers summary and policy insights.

2 Literature Review

Most of the businesses in Rwanda are family owned and managed. These family businesses fall in the SME and micro enterprises categories which account for over 95% of all firms in the country (MINICOM 2010). The management of family businesses poses a serious problem as an individual may have multiple roles and responsibilities (MINICOM 2010). These multiple roles are usually associated with different incentives, which increase the challenges that family businesses face as opposed to their non-family counterparts (Acs et al. 2008). Most founders of family businesses want their companies to stay within their families, but in some cases maintaining family control is not practical. Sometimes no one in the next generation has an interest in managing the company or he/she does not have the required skills and experience to manage the business. Under these circumstances family-owned businesses have to look outside their families for leadership if they have to survive (Fuller 2011).

This situation looks different from the perspective of an owner who does not work in the business and relies on dividends as a main source of income. Such an owner is interested in receiving higher and more frequent dividends. Matters usually get more complex as a family business grows and its owners hold different roles with different incentives (Gersick and Feliu 2014). Managers in a family business also have different motivations depending on their roles in the business. A common issue in this area is the unequal treatment of family and non-family managers. In many family businesses, part or all of the senior management positions are strictly reserved for family members (Anderson and Reeb 2004). This can negatively impact non-family managers' motivations and performance who know that no matter how hard they work they will never be part of the senior management of the company. As a result, many family businesses find it very hard to attract and retain talented non-family managers.

Setting up clear and fair employment policies (for both family and non-family employees) will make it easier for family businesses to keep their very best employees motivated and interested in the growth of the company. Such policies will also align employees' incentives to their performance regardless of whether they are part of the family or not.

When it comes to board membership, most family businesses reserve this right for members of the family and in a few cases for some well trusted non-family managers. This practice is generally used as a way of keeping family control over the direction that a business takes. Most decisions are usually taken by family-member directors. When it comes to dividend distribution, family directors who are also managers in the business naturally encourage reinvesting profits in the company so as to increase its growth potential. On the contrary, family directors who do not work in the business would rather take a decision of distributing the profits as dividends to family shareholders. These contradicting views can lead to major conflicts in the board and negatively impact its way of functioning (Sharma 2004).

Failure in succession represents a serious problem not only for the family enterprises, but also for the health of the economy. Owner-managers are often not aware of the problems of securing the continuity of their enterprises. Because they are busy with daily operational problems, they often cannot or do not want to start preparing for changes in the ownership and management of their enterprises early enough. They are often not aware of the crucial importance of solving succession issues on time. Although many problems are linked to family business' succession, according to Duh et al. (2010), this should not necessarily be seen as a negative event in the lifecycle of a family business as no evidence has been found that a family firm's profitability is affected by succession. The succession is more a process than an event of transferring ownership and management control to the successor; planning for succession reduces the tensions and stress created by negative events/conflicts of a changing guard (Fuller 2011).

In family-owned businesses, parent–child succession in management and leadership entails ensuring a continuous diachronic process of socialization to ensure that the family's successors are gradually prepared for leadership continuity in key positions, retaining and developing intellectual and knowledge capital for the future, and encouraging individual advancement (Onuoha and Segun-Martins 2013). This preparation covers many years and several successive positions, from non- or informal involvement to a successor's functional roles to early and mature succession when a successor actually takes over the leadership position and is relatively autonomous in that role. Handler (1994) discusses the need for a mutual role adjustment between predecessor/transferor and the successor. She developed a model according to which the transferor evolves from the role of a monarch to a delegator to an advisor; the successors in turn evolves from a helper to a manager to a leader.

The transfer of ownership (that is, succession in ownership) can take place within the family, through management buyouts (like a sale to non-family management/employees), and a sale to outside persons or existing companies, including takeovers and mergers (Duh 2012). Hence, succession in the management within the family is only one of the options. However, ownership in family businesses has a special meaning because it involves a strong "personal" factor. When an enterprise is transferred within the family, the financial capital is transferred with "social and cultural capital" that usually results in an enhanced personal commitment to the enterprise as well as to the community. Family owners do not think that they possess just capital. They are aware that ownership encompasses persons, products, and responsibilities. Ownership of a family business is a property built and developed by the family over several generations (Pounder 2015).

Although succession within the family is only one of the many possibilities, most of the family enterprises' leaders have been found to be desirous of retaining family control past their tenures (Bjuggren and Sund 2001). According to Gersick et al. (1997) nepotism is one of the reasons why succession takes place within the family. Next to this purely nepotistic explanation, Bjuggren and Sund (2002) show that a family member as a successor is preferable when so-called idiosyncratic knowledge is considered highly relevant for the successful functioning of an enterprise. Referring to the experts' opinions, Duh (2012), argues that the necessary preparation period for succession may take from 5 to 10 years and if the preparation and planning also include the qualifications of a potential successor then it can take even longer.

Many studies show that successions are not planned in time (Bjuggren and Sund 2001; Sharma et al. 2003) and first-generation family enterprises do less succession planning than the second and third-generation family enterprises (Sonfield and Lussier 2004). The first type of problems in succession are psychological and emotional ones. Many owner-managers, who have created and built their businesses over a number of years, are very reluctant to let go and prepare for transferring their businesses. The transfer of know-how and skills takes place very late, if at all. There are many invisible, "soft", or emotional problems that play a major role in succession, especially where family enterprises are concerned (Dyck and Zingales (2003), owner-managers being too busy running and controlling the enterprise; owner-managers' fears of losing a central role in the family; owner-managers' different excuses which are more or less connected to feelings of rivalry and jealousy toward potential successors; and owner-managers' very often associating retirement with their mortality.

The second type of problems relate to the complexity of the succession process and to the fact that the owner-managers have no (or just limited) experience or knowledge of handling such a situation and scarce external support for facilitating the succession process. The owner-manager very often does not know who to contact for help or where to find information (Dyer 2006; Malinen 2004). The third type of problems stem from national legislations, in particular company law, taxation, and administrative formalities. Examples of problems of this kind include high inheritance and gift taxes and problems preventing a change in the legal form of a business when preparations are being made for succession (Bjuggren and Sund 2001). The fourth set of problems is based on the understanding that entrepreneurship consists of many complex activities in which involve a lot of tacit knowledge that cannot be easily transferred from one generation to the next. There are many deeply ingrained routines and experiential knowledge that make a company successful and can be acquired only by learning by doing in which younger family members work together with elders adopting their experiential knowledge and skills. Family culture is an important constituent of tacit knowledge (Duh 2012).

According to Wanjohi (2018), succession planning in essence is the art of grooming tomorrow's leaders today and should be a part of every company's strategic plans for sustaining family businesses. Planning for the future is a key activity for any successful family business/organization that wants to maintain a stable and effective workforce. Succession planning is a part of the strategic process of preparing for a company's future.

Kirsipuu (2012) argues that family businesses can be sustainable when members are prepared for a generational change. It has been found that the main challenge in succession is addressing the changes in generation related problems. Family enterprises are characterized primarily by their small size; they usually employ up to 10 people, but there are also exceptions. One of the most positive qualities of family enterprises is their short decision-making chains. A specific feature of family enterprises is that the business and personal activities are intertwined, for example, use of time, common living space, and operating and production facilities. In addition to entrepreneurship, family members are connected by friendship and family relations and marriages, and the owner of a family is often the manager of the family enterprise. The latter determine the business' objectives based on his/her personal ambitions and prefers keeping the business small to maintain control over what he/she owns. Thus, a family business is rendered sustainable by the division of roles between family members, in particular appreciating the role of the women as housewives (Rautamäki 2007); women take care of cozy homes and at the same time make a major contribution to the development of family businesses. However, inter-generational problems prevent family enterprises from being sustainable (Kirsipuu 2012).

The sustainability of a family enterprise can be seen only when family entrepreneurs are aware of the factors that ensure sustainability as well as those that restrain sustainable development, recognizing the role of women in the family, involvement of children in the business, and the problem of succession. In his research on transfer of management in family enterprises, Hautala (2006) found that family enterprises can be sustainable only when ownership, management, and knowledge are turned over to the descendants, meaning children. Problems arise when the transfer is made to non-family members; Hautala also found that sustainability can be ensured only when mentors are included in the transfer process. The investigation based on consolidation of wage labor and family interests, a woman's role in the family, integration of children in the family business' activities, and succession problems show that succession planning is important for ensuring the success of a generational transition. Family business' continuity, strategic planning and corporate governance, leadership, and family values help in family enterprises' sustainability (Rautamäki 2007).

Researchers like Kakkonen (2006) argue that family businesses are more sustainable when all family members work for a common objective. Their research concluded that if children want to continue what their parents started, then parents have to pass on knowledge and skills to them. When children do not wish to participate in a family business, the issue of continuing the business, whom to leave the business to, and whom to appoint the manager come up on the agenda sooner or later. The issue whether to close the business or bring a person from outside the family may lead to conflicts and prevent a family business from being sustainable (Niemela 2004). In this context, sustainability covers preserving domains[1] in an equal manner through continuous commitment of the entrepreneurs who are innovative in making changes in their enterprises, processes, or products for sustainability. A relationship has been found between entrepreneurship, economic performance, and sustainability in terms of growth, an enterprise's survival, innovations, employment creation, technological changes, productivity increases in assets, and exports (Baran and Velickaite 2008).

---

[1] Refer to strategic planning and corporate governance, leadership, economic performance, inter-generational knowledge transfers for continuity, succession planning, and family values.

According to Sonfield and Lussier (2004) a surprisingly small number of family-owned businesses survive a transition to the second generation. There are two common reasons why families cannot retain their businesses. The first is that there is no qualified successor. However, even if a business is not passed down to the next generation, ensuring that the family take steps to ensure that the value of the business survives is just as important and is another form of succession planning. The second major reason for unsuccessful business transitions is more unfortunate. In many cases, family businesses fail or are sold off because of lack of planning.

Though most families are careful in safeguarding their personal assets, for example, insuring their homes, many businesspeople do not plan ahead to safeguard the value of their businesses. Determining whether succession to a family member is a viable alternative seems an obvious first step but doing so is not always straightforward. Many business owners do not carefully consider all the issues when deciding whether succession to a family member is a viable alternative (Gilding 2005). Business owners often have plans in their own minds. Alternatively, some children may be overlooked as successors because their views and general outlook on business issues differ greatly from that of the founder (due to human nature, families often relate better to people who share the same style and values) (Bocatto et al. 2010).

A specific feature of SMEs is that business and personal activities are intertwined, for example, use of time, a common living space, and operating and production facilities. In addition to entrepreneurship, family members are connected by friendship, family relations, and marriages (Kaseorg and Raudsaar 2008). The owner of a family enterprise is often the manager of the family enterprise (Gersick et al. 1997) and his/her personal ambitions determine the enterprise's business objectives (Chrisman et al. 2003) and he/she prefers keeping the enterprise small to maintain control over what he/she owns (Kaseorg and Raudsaar 2009).

According to Koe et al. (2015), the determinants of entrepreneurship are that attitudinal factors and perceptual factors are important in influencing a person's level of propensity for entrepreneurship sustainability. This is without prejudicing the other dimensions of sustainable entrepreneurship such as employees, suppliers, and clients (direct stakeholders), and larger society. Entrepreneurship sustainability in family businesses has a significant positive relationship between motivating factors, personality characteristics, management skills, level of education, and entrepreneurial sustainability and success as indicated by Dionco-Adetayo (2004).

In the context of access to finance, Dalberg (2011) explains that SMEs' inability to access formal banks is because of debt financing barriers; high risk profiling of the SMEs market; challenges in satisfying the requirements for a collateral; banks' preference for earning higher returns on traditional activities; high administrative costs of lending to SMEs; banks' inability to provide long-term capital due to significant short-term liabilities in their deposit mix; lack of adequate skills; and lack of? regulatory support for lending to SMEs. According to Sunday (2011), SMEs' survival is predicated on appropriate standard credit policies; effective management of the working capital (which goes a long way in guaranteeing continuity, growth, and solvency); and articulated financial reports and control systems. In the Rwandan context, SMEs lack access to financial services.

Financial institutions perceive SMEs as high risk and are therefore inflexible in terms of collateral and repayment terms. This is compounded by the fact that most small borrowers in Rwanda lack experience and an understanding of financial institutions and do not have the necessary technical skills to make successful loan applications because of lack of technical and business skills. SMEs themselves identify a variety of skill gaps in areas including ICT, technical and industrial knowledge, finance, accounting, and management. Many SMEs have rudimentary production facilities, low-quality products, and underutilization of appropriate technologies. There are also limited innovations and competitiveness in the SMEs sector because of lack of technical and managerial skills (MINICOM 2010).

In the context of a family's involvement and relationships in mentorship on entrepreneurship sustainability, Kirsipuu and Silberg (2013) show that family businesses become sustainable through a division of roles between family members, especially appreciating the role of the woman as a housewife and because she takes care of a comfortable home, at the same time contributing to the development of a family business. Entrepreneurship sustainability in family enterprises is attributed to a woman's role in the family, involvement of the children in the business, and the problem of succession. According to Haggard and Turban (2012), mentoring is most often defined as a professional relationship in which an experienced person (the mentor) assists another (the mentored or mentee) in developing specific skills and knowledge that will enhance the less-experienced person's professional and personal growth.

According to Emeraton (2008) the main aim of mentoring is developing requisite entrepreneurial skills, attitudes, competencies, and disposition that compel an individual to be a driving force in managing a business. Schaltegger and Wagner (2011) explain entrepreneurship sustainability in the framework of innovation through the application of the entrepreneurial approach toward meeting societal goals and toward changing market contexts, and technology. Capabilities in these are particularly important in making innovations in the management, processes, and procedures, all of which can lead to economic success and a sustainable business. If the children want to continue the businesses that their parents started, the parents pass on knowledge and skills to them. Research shows that when children do not wish to participate in family businesses, the issue of whether to close the business or bring a person from outside the family may lead to conflicts and prevent a family business from being sustainable (Littunen 2001).

According to Majid and Koe (2012), sustainability covers preserving domains in an equal manner through the continuous commitment of entrepreneurs who are innovative in making changes in their enterprises, processes, and products for sustainability please rephrase sentence for more clarity.

Sonfield and Lussier (2004), show that a surprisingly small number of family-owned businesses survive a transition to the second generation. There are two main reasons why families cannot sustain their businesses. The first is that there is no qualified successor. However, even if the business cannot be passed down to the next generation, making sure the family take steps to ensure that its value survives is just as important and is another form of succession planning. The second major reason for unsuccessful business transitions is more unfortunate. In many cases, family businesses fail or are sold off because of lack of planning. Though most families are careful in safeguarding their personal assets, for example, insuring their homes, many businesspeople do not plan ahead to safeguard the value of their businesses. Determining whether succession to a family member is a viable alternative seems an obvious first step but doing so is not always straightforward. Many business owners do not carefully consider all the issues when deciding whether succession to a family member is a viable alternative Gilding (2005). Developing a succession plan and preparing a successor requires a wide variety of skills, some of which the business founder will not have.

Family businesses focus on long-term sustainability rather than the realization of short-term profits. Experts on family businesses are of the opinion that the main characteristics of family businesses which differentiate them from non-family businesses are that they are run and managed without the intention of selling them. This attitude toward the longevity of a firm (in terms of decades and generations instead of years and a focus on the professional lifetime of an entrepreneur in non-family businesses) influences everything related to the business activity (that is, not only the core production/service delivery processes but also the treatment of employees, other stakeholders, and the local community). According to Mosbah et al. (2017) most of the family entrepreneurs see themselves as momentary caretakers of the company who have the responsibility of maintaining and further developing the enterprise for the following generation while non-family business managers often focus on the sustainability of the business during their own professional lifetime and opt for selling the company if this turns out to be a good bargain.

3 Methodology

This section gives the methods used in collecting the data. It also presents the research design, the sample and its design, data collection methods, and data analysis. This study uses a combination approach composed of positivism and a phenomenology approach. According to Saunders and Vincent (1999) a positivism approach is good when the emphasis of the study is on explaining some theories. On the other hand, the phenomenology approach is good when the study involves explaining why something is happening rather than describing what is happening. Because this study involves both developing and explaining theories, a combination approach is preferred. The study's design is based on a multi-method strategy which uses both qualitative and quantitative research designs. It uses a case study and a survey approach. This helps in triangulating the different strategies. According to Bryman and Bell (2003), a multi-method approach uses more than one research strategy and data source in a study of a social phenomenon. A multi-method approach can be followed within a single research strategy by using multiple sources of data or across research strategies (Bryman and Bell 2003; Carter and Marlow 2006). A combination of qualitative and quantitative design strategies is recommended and used in situations where one approach is insufficient in finding out all that is required to be known about a phenomenon (Bryman et al. 1996).

The data used in this study is from a survey of family-owned and family-managed businesses, the 49,000 SMEs registered with the Rwanda Revenue Authority (RRA) portal in Nyarugenge district. The study targeted the managers/owners of these businesses. In selecting the sample an optimum sample size was considered. According to Kothari (2000) an optimum sample is one which fulfills the requirements of efficiency, representativeness, reliability, and flexibility. The sample size was decided using Solvin and Yamen's $S = N/[1 + N(e)^2]$, where S is the sample size, N is the total population, and e is the sampling error. A simple random sampling was used to select the respondents:

$$S = 49000/\left[1 + 49000(0.05)^2\right] = 397$$

To address the objectives of the study, primary data was collected using one set of questionnaires, which were administered to the managers of family businesses. This study used both structured and unstructured self-administered questionnaires. These two types of questionnaires were used because of the advantages that they have over other instruments (Kasomo 2006; Kothari 2000; Mugenda 2008; Saunders and Vincent 1999). The last approach that was used in the data collection was documentation or desk research. This data may be used as raw data if there has been some—if any processing or compiled data—collection or summaries of data that have been received.

The survey data that was generated from the questionnaires was analyzed using both exploratory and confirmatory statistical techniques. After receiving the completed questionnaires from the field, a data entry capture template was designed in the Statistical Package for Social Scientists (SPSS) which was used for data entry. After data entry and cleaning up, an inferential statistical data analysis was done using a Chi-square test.

4 Results and Discussion

4.1 Training and Mentorship in Entrepreneurship and a Business' Sustainability

The results of the survey using the Chi-square test showed that there was a significant effect of training and mentoring entrepreneurs and business sustainability as indicated by the *P*-values of 0.000. The symmetric measure through Phi showed that there was a strong relationship between training and mentorship and business sustainability. The Phi value indicates that training and mentoring entrepreneurs contributed 68% to the sustainability of the business (Table 1). .

Table 1 Effects of training and mentoring entrepreneurs on a business' sustainability all tables need to be mentioned in text

Chi-square tests			
	Value	df	Asymp. Sig. (2-sided)
Pearson Chi-square	55.541[a]	12	0.000
Likelihood ratio	55.639	12	0.000
Linear-by-linear association	0.567	1	0.451
N of valid cases	397		
Symmetric measures			
		Value	Approx. Sig.
Nominal by Nominal	Phi	0.680	0.000
	Cramer's V	0.393	0.000
N of valid cases	397		

[a]Ten cells (50%) have the expected count less than 5. The minimum expected count is 0.88
Source Survey data (2019)

4.2 *Involving Family Members in the Management of the Business and the Sustainability of the Business*

The results of the survey showed that there was an association between involvement of family members in business management and business sustainability as indicated by the *P*-value of 0.000. The results further show that the involvement of family members in the management of the business contributed to the business' sustainability as indicated by the Phi value of 78.3%. This means that there was a strong relationship between involvement of family members in business management and business sustainability (Table 2)..

4.3 *Good Family Relationships and a Business' Sustainability*

Family relationships is another important factor for a business' sustainability. There is no empirical evidence in literature based on an analysis of this relationship. The results in Table 3 tested whether good family relations had a significant relationship with the sustainability of the business. The results of the Chi-square test show a *P*-value of 0.000. This shows that there was a significant relationship between family relationships and a business' sustainability. Good family relationship enhanced a business' sustainability and poor family relationships had a negative effect on its sustainability. A symmetric measure for the strength of the relationship showed that good family relationships contributed 63.5% to the business' sustainability.

Table 2 Association between family involvement and sustainability

Chi-square tests

	Value	df	Asymp. Sig. (2-sided)
Pearson Chi-square	73.506[a]	12	0.000
Likelihood ratio	76.854	12	0.000
Linear-by-linear association	8.726	1	0.003
N of valid cases	397		

Symmetric measures

		Value	Approx. Sig.
Nominal by nominal	Phi	0.783	0.000
	Cramer's V	0.452	0.000
N of valid cases		397	

[a]Seven cells (15%) have the expected count less than 5. The minimum expected count is 5.75
Source Survey data (2019)

Table 3 Relationship between good family relationships and sustainability

Chi-square tests

	Value	df	Asymp. Sig. (2-sided)
Pearson Chi-square	48.370[a]	12	0.000
Likelihood ratio	58.471	12	0.000
Linear-by-linear association	6.754	1	0.009
N of valid cases	397		

Symmetric measures

		Value	Approx. Sig.
Nominal by Nominal	Phi	0.635	0.000
	Cramer's V	0.367	0.000
N of valid cases		397	

[a]Eight cells (10%) have the expected count less than 5. The minimum expected count is 0.70
Source Survey data (2019)

4.4 Financial Resources and a Business' Sustainability

The results in Table 4 are of the tests done to find out the strength of the association between financial resources and business sustainability. The results show that

Table 4 Relationship between financial resources and a business' sustainability

Chi-square tests

	Value	df	Asymp. Sig. (2-sided)
Pearson Chi-square	4.558[a]	3	0.207
Likelihood ratio	4.697	3	0.195
Linear-by-linear association	0.883	1	0.347
N of valid cases	397		

Symmetric measures

		Value	Approx. Sig.
Nominal by nominal	Phi	0.195	0.207
	Cramer's V	0.195	0.207
N of valid cases		397	

[a]Zero cells (0.0%) have the expected count less than 5. The minimum expected count is 8.40
Source Survey data (2019)

there was no significant relationship between financial resources and a business' sustainability. This is indicated by *P*-values of 0.207 which are greater than 0.05. The results further show that there was a weak relationship between financial resources and business sustainability as only 19.5% of the variations in a business' sustainability were because of financial resources as measured by the Phi value. The results also show that although financial resources are important in running a business, they do not define its sustainability. This means that the sustainability of a business does not depend on how much one has invested in the business, but on how the money invested has been used.

4.5 *Financial Discipline and a Business' Sustainability*

Two critical issues in the theory of finance need to be clearly distinguished—raising the funds needed to do business and using the raised funds in a business. As shown in Table 5, the issue is not how many funds you have raised to do the business but how these funds have been used. Use of funds in a business requires respect and discipline more especially in small businesses where it is hard to separate the owner from the business. Financial discipline is all about the respect that entrepreneurs have for money. The Chi-square test shows that there was a significant relationship between financial discipline and business sustainability as indicated by the *P*-value of 0.001 which is less than 0.05. A symmetric measure of the strength of the relationship using

Table 5 Financial discipline and a business' sustainability

Chi-square tests

	Value	df	Asymp. Sig. (2-sided)
Pearson Chi-square	34.696[a]	12	0.001
Likelihood ratio	38.350	12	0.000
Linear-by-linear association	0.057	1	0.812
N of valid cases	397		

Symmetric measures

		Value	Approx. Sig.
Nominal by Nominal	Phi	0.538	0.001
	Cramer's V	0.310	0.001
N of valid cases		397	

[a]Twelve cells (10%) have the expected count less than 5. The minimum expected count is 4.18
Source Survey data (2019)

the Phi value shows that financial discipline contributed 53.8% to a business' sustainability. These results also show that entrepreneurs who have financial discipline can sustain their businesses as compared to those with no financial discipline.

4.6 Education Levels and a Business' Sustainability

There has been a lot of debate among academicians on whether the level of education affects a business' sustainability. The Chi-square test in Table 6 shows that there is a significant association between the level of education and a business's sustainability as shown by the *P*-value of 0.007 which is less than 0.05. A test of the strength of the relationship using the Phi value shows that the level of education did not contribute much to a business' sustainability by 43.5%. This means that although there is a significant relationship between the level of education and a business' sustainability, being successful in achieving a business' sustainability does not depend on the level of education as indicated by lower symmetric measures value of 0.435.

4.7 Innovations and a Business' Sustainability

The results in Table 7 are of the test of association and strength between innovations and business sustainability. The Chi-square test shows that there was a significant relationship between innovations and business sustainability as indicated by the *P*-value of 0.005 which is less than 0.05. The results further show that there was a

Table 6 Relationship between education level and a business' sustainability

Chi-square tests

	Value	df	Asymp. Sig. (2-sided)
Pearson Chi-square	22.751[a]	9	0.007
Likelihood ratio	29.742	9	0.000
Linear-by-linear association	0.865	1	0.352
N of valid cases	397		

Symmetric measures

		Value	Approx. Sig.
Nominal by Nominal	Phi	0.435	0.007
	Cramer's V	0.251	0.007
N of valid cases		397	

[a]Six cells (17.5%) have the expected count less than 5. The minimum expected count is 5.28
Source Survey data (2019)

Table 7 Relationship between innovations and a business' sustainability

Chi-square tests

	Value	df	Asymp. Sig. (2-sided)
Pearson Chi-square	18.777[a]	6	0.005
Likelihood ratio	24.060	6	0.001
Linear-by-linear association	12.269	1	0.000
N of valid cases	397		

Symmetric measures

		Value	Approx. Sig.
Nominal by Nominal	Phi	0.896	0.005
	Cramer's V	0.680	0.005
N of valid cases		397	

[a]One cell (8.3%) has the expected count less than 5. The minimum expected count is 4.38
Source Survey data (2019)

strong relationship between innovations and business sustainability as indicated by the Phi value of 89.6%. This means that for an entrepreneur to remain in business for a long time, he must be innovative since innovations contribute a lot to a business' sustainability.

5 Conclusion and Policy Recommendations

5.1 Conclusion

The results of this study show a significant association between training and mentorship in entrepreneurship, involving family members in the management, good family relationships, financial discipline, education levels, innovations, and business sustainability. The results also show that there was no significant relationship between financial resources and a business' sustainability and although the level of education was significant in a business' sustainability, it did not contribute much to its sustainability. This means that even if an entrepreneur is not educated but pays attention to the significant factors mentioned earlier, he/she can still succeed in the business. The key factors that determine a business' sustainability are innovations, involvement of family members in the management, inter-generational skill or knowledge transfer via mentorship in succession good family relationships, and financial discipline.

5.2 Policy Recommendations

i. Entrepreneurs should be financially literate so that they are equipped with skills in financial discipline.
ii. Most African businesses die with their owners. Involvement of family members in the management and having good family relationships can be key to the continuity of a business after the death of its founder.

References

Acs, Z. J., Desai, S., & Hessels, J. (2008). Entrepreneurship, economic development and institutions. *Small Business Economics, 31*(3), 219–234.
Anderson, R. C., & Reeb, D. M. (2004). Board composition: Balancing family influence in S&P 500 firms. *Administrative Science Quarterly, 49*(2), 209–237.
Arifin, J., Yazid, A. S., & Sulong, Z. (2013). A conceptual model of literature review for family Takaful (Islamic Life Insurance) demand in Malaysia. *International Business Research, 6*(3), 210.
Aronoff, C. E., McClure, S. L., & Ward, J. L. (2003). *Family business succession: The final test of greatness* (No. 1). Family Enterprise Publisher.
Ayyagari, M., Demirguc-Kunt, A., & Maksimovic, V. (2011). *Small versus young firms across the world: Contribution to employment, job creation, and growth*. Washington, DC: The World Bank.
Baran, D., & Velickaite, R. (2008, May). Building the theoretical framework of entrepreneurship. In *The 5th International Scientific Conference/Business and Management, Faculty of Business Management*. Lithuania: Vilnius Gediminas Technical University.
Bjuggren, P. O., & Sund, L. G. (2001). Strategic decision making in intergenerational successions of small-and medium-size family-owned businesses. *Family Business Review, 14*(1), 11–23.

Bjuggren, P. O., & Sund, L. G. (2002). A transition cost rationale for transition of the firm within the family. *Small Business Economics, 19*(2), 123–133.

Bocatto, E., Gispert, C., & Rialp, J. (2010). Family-owned business succession: the influence of pre-performance in the nomination of family and nonfamily members: Evidence from Spanish firms. *Journal of Small Business Management, 48*(4), 497–523.

Bryman, A., & Bell, E. (2003). Breaking down the quantitative/qualitative divide. *Business Research Methods, 2*(1), 465–478.

Bryman, A., Stephens, M., & Campo, C. (1996). The importance of context: Qualitative research and the study of leadership. *The Leadership Quarterly, 7*(3), 353–370.

Carter, S., & Marlow, S. (2006). Female entrepreneurship: Theoretical perspectives and empirical evidence. In *Female Entrepreneurship* (pp. 27–52).

Crals, E., & Vereeck, L. (2005). Taxes, tradable rights and transaction costs. *European Journal of Law and Economics, 20*(2), 199–223.

Dalberg, H. (2011). Report on support to SMEs in developing countries through financial intermediaries. *SME Briefing Paper, EIB Draft version (Geneva: European Investment Bank), 35*, 392–416.

Dionco-Adetayo, E. A. (2004). *Determinants of small firms' entrepreneurial success in a developing economy*. Ile-Ife: Obafemi Awolowo University.

Duh, M. (2012). Family businesses: The extensiveness of succession problems and possible solutions. *Entrepreneurship-gender, geographies and social context, 210*–234.

Duh, M., Belak, J., & Milfelner, B. (2010). Core values, culture and ethical climate as constitutional elements of ethical behaviour: Exploring differences between family and non-family enterprises. *Journal of Business Ethics, 97*(3), 473–489.

Dyck, A., & Zingales, L. (2003). The bubble and the media. *Corporate governance and capital flows in a global economy*, 83–104.

Dyer, W. G. Jr. (2006). Examining 'Family Effect' on firm performance. *Family Business Review, 19*(4), 253–273.

Emeraton, U. G. (2008). Re-thinking higher education management for poverty reduction among the youth in Africa. In *The 3rd Regional Conference of Higher Education for Youth Empowerment, Opportunities, Capabilities and Second Chance. Organized by Higher Education Research and Policy Network (NERPNET) at IITA* (pp. 18–21). Ibadan, and Oyo State.

Fuller, T., Warren, L., & Norman, S. J. (2011). Creative methodologies for understanding a creative industry. *Entrepreneurship and the creative economy: Process, policy and practice*, 79–96.

Gersick, K. E., & Feliu, N. (2014). Governing the family enterprise: Practices, performance, and research. *The SAGE handbook of family business*, 196–225.

Gersick, K. E., Davis, J. A., McCollom, H. M., & Lansberg, I. (1997). *Generation to generation: Life cycles of the family business*. Boston: Harvard Business School Press.

Gilding, M. (2005). Families and fortunes: Accumulation, management succession and inheritance in wealthy families. *Journal of Sociology, 41*(1), 29–45.

Haggard, D. L., & Turban, D. B. (2012). The mentoring relationship as a context for psychological contract development. *Journal of Applied Social Psychology, 42*(8), 1904–1931.

Handler, W. C. (1994). Succession in family business: A review of the research. *Family business review, 7*(2), 133–157.

Hautala, T. M. (2006). The relationship between personality and transformational leadership. *The Journal of Management Development, 25*(8), 777–794.

Institute of Statistics for Rwanda (2017) Enterprise survey, annual report

Kakkonen, M. L. (2006). *Intuition and entrepreneurs: A phenomenological study of managerial intuition of Finnish family entrepreneurs* (No. 49). University of Jyväskylä.

Kaseorg, M., & Raudsaar, M. (2008). Family firm as social entrepreneur in post-communist transition society: The case from Estonia. In *European Summer University (ESU) conference in Entrepreneurship* (Vol. 21, No. 26.08, p. 2008).

Kaseorg, M., & Raudsaar, M. (2009). Entrepreneurial skills education process and support in pilot project of entrepreneurship home for young people. *ICERI2009*, 16–18.

Kasomo, D. (2006). *Research methods in humanities and education.* Egerton: Egerton University.

Kirsipuu, M. (2012). Sustainability of rural family enterprises. *Discussions on Estonian Economic Policy: Theory and Practice of Economic Policy, 20*(1).

Kirsipuu, M., & Silberg, U. (2013). Women in family enterprises in Estonia. *Estonian Discussions on Economic Policy, 21*(2).

Koe, W. L., Omar, R., & Sa'ari, J. R. (2015). Factors influencing propensity to sustainable entrepreneurship of SMEs in Malaysia. *Procedia-Social and Behavioral Sciences, 172,* 570–577.

Kothari, S. P. (2000). The role of financial reporting in reducing financial risks in the market. In *Conference Series-Federal Reserve Bank of Boston* (Vol. 44, pp. 89–102). Federal Reserve Bank of Boston; 1998.

Littunen, H. (2001). *The birth and success of new firms in a changing environment* (No. 8). University of Jyväskylä.

Majid, I. A., & Koe, W. L. (2012). Sustainable entrepreneurship (SE): A revised model based on triple bottom line (TBL). *International Journal of Academic Research in Business and Social Sciences, 2*(6), 293.

Majid, I. A., Kamaludin, M. H., Saad, M. S. M., & Aziz, N. A. (2012). Sustainability-driven Entrepreneurship: The mediating effect of opportunity based management structure on the relationship between entrepreneurial orientation and environmental sustainability management of SMES: A conceptual framework. *European Journal of Business and Management, 4*(13), 148–155.

Malinen, P. (2004). Problems in transfer of business experienced by Finnish entrepreneurs. *Journal of Small Business and Enterprise Development, 11*(1), 130–139.

Miller, W., & Rollnick, S. (2003). Motivational interviewing: Preparing people for change. *The Journal for Healthcare Quality (JHQ), 25*(3), 46.

MINICOM. (2010). *Small and medium enterprises (SMEs) development policy.* Rwanda: Kihgali.

Mosbah, A., Serief, S. R., & Wahab, K. A. (2017). Performance of family business in Malaysia. *International Journal of Social Sciences Perspectives, 1*(1), 20–26.

Mugenda, A. G. (2008). *Social science research: Theory and principles.* Nairobi: Kijabe printers.National.

Niemelä, T. (2004). Interfirm cooperation capability in the context of networking family firms: The role of power. *Family Business Review, 17*(4), 319–330.

Onuoha, U. C., & Segun-Martins, I. O. (2013). Predicting job satisfaction of married female employees: The role of age and emotional intelligence. *Gender and Behaviour, 11*(2), 5745–5751.

O'Neill Jr., P. G. D., Hershauer, J. C., & Golden, J. S. (2009). The Cultural Context of Sustainability Entrepreneurship. *Greener Management International* (55).

Pounder, P. (2015). Family business insights: An overview of the literature. *Journal of Family Business Management, 5*(1), 116–127.

Private sector Federation. (2008). Annual business report.

Rautamäki, H. (2007). Psykologinen omistajuus ja työnilo perheyrittäjyydessä. *Jyväskylän yliopisto. Yrittäjyyden tutkimus XXIII taloustutkijoiden kesäseminaarissa, 160,* 37–47.

Routledge.Chrisman, J. J., Chua, J. H., & Steier, L. P. (2003). An introduction to theories of family business. *Journal of Business Venturing, 4*(18), 441–448.

Saunders, B. R., & Vincent, B. (1999). Microgel particles as model colloids: theory, properties and applications. *Advances in Colloid and Interface Science, 80*(1), 1–25 (Says et al. in text).

Schaltegger, S., & Wagner, M. (2011). Sustainable entrepreneurship and sustainability innovation: Categories and interactions. *Business Strategy and the Environment, 20*(4), 222–237.

Sharma, P. (2004). An overview of the field of family business studies: Current status and directions for the future. *Family business review, 17*(1), 1–36.

Sharma, P., Chrisman, J. J., & Chua, J. H. (2003). Predictors of satisfaction with the succession process in family firms. *Journal of Business Venturing, 18*(5), 667–687.

Sonfield, M. C., & Lussier, R. N. (2004). First-, second-, and third-generation family firms: A comparison. *Family Business Review, 17*(3), 189–201.

Sunday, K. J. (2011). Effective working capital management in small and medium scale enterprises (SMEs). *International Journal of Business and management, 6*(9), 271.

Wanjohi, M. (2018). The role of succession planning in family enterprises performance: A case study of Bidco oil refineries limited Kenya. Nairobi-Kenya.

World Commission on Environment and Development. (1987). *Our common future the Brundland report*. Oxford, UK: Oxford University Press.

Chapter 11
Assessing the Role of Positioning Strategy on Market Performance of Soft Drink Manufacturing Enterprises (SDMES) in Rwanda

Nimusima Pereez, Karuhanga Nathan, Mukarutesi Dative, Gasana Charles, Kampire Charity, and Turyamushanga Labson

Abstract This study empirically answers two questions: Does a positioning strategy influence market performance? Do a firm's resources have a directional influence on positioning its strategy-performance relationship? It uses a sample of 149 marketing/sales and corporate staff members of two soft drink manufacturing enterprises in Rwanda—Urwibutso Enterprises Ltd. and Inyange Industries Ltd. It uses a structured questionnaire to collect primary data from the two enterprises and uses multiple and simple regression models to estimate the nature of the relationship between the dependent and independent variables. It uses market share, sales, and profitability as comprehensive measures for market performance, and applies Aaker and Shansby's model 1982 as a measure for the positioning strategy. The results confirm that a firm's assets and capabilities have a strong and significant association with its positioning decisions and targets. The results also show that managers can use resources and capabilities to strengthen an enterprise's positioning strategy decision-making function. Further, the study observes that 57.5% of the variations in performance in these enterprises are largely explained by product quality, price, and cultural symbols. If an enterprise emphasizes a limited number of positioning dimensions, its performance results in terms of market share, sales, and profitability are better.

Keywords Rwanda · Positioning strategy · Market performance · Soft drinks · Manufacturing

JEL Classification Code D13 · D63 · H53 · I131 · I138 · J13

N. Pereez (✉) · K. Nathan · M. Dative · G. Charles · K. Charity
University of Rwanda, College of Business and Economics, Butare, Rwanda
e-mail: pereeznimusima@gmail.com

T. Labson
Department of Business Studies, Faculty of Arts and Social Sciences, Kabale University, Kabale, Uganda

1 Introduction

Conceptually, companies exist through, with, and by the product sales that they make. But sales figures or numbers realized are a function of many marketing factors including positioning. Though sales performance per se as a construct falls outside this study's scope, variations in contextual sales trends on the one hand, and adopting exit strategies by some soft drink manufacturing enterprises (SDMEs) in Rwanda on the other, form the foundation of this study. For example, Bralirwa, a long-standing hard and soft drink manufacturing enterprise exhibited variations in its sales performance over years with a 0.6% decline in sales in 2013; a 1.4% decrease in total sales volume in 2016; and a 12.4% reduction in total sales volume in 2017 (Bralirwa Annual Reports 2013, 2016, 2017). On the other hand, some products have not lived to see their first anniversary in Rwanda like Marakujya Passion Juice launched in 2010 and Ingenzi Pineapple Juice launched in 2016. They closed their doors and exited the market a few months after launching their products in the local market. Amazi ya Huye, also a highly recognized and visible brand with high demand in 2002 through 2010, is almost a fading name.

As researchers, we are preoccupied with the *whys* of such a mix of the market phenomena and the choice of a study's subject, and how it is constructed hinges on this reality. Admittedly, the current performance of manufacturing enterprises in Rwanda like in the other countries in the region manifests some critical challenges including low production capacity due to inadequate financial resources, unreliable supplies, lack of market information, and high transport costs (Sophia 2013). Considering the entrepreneurial significance of these manufacturing enterprises for the economy in general as they represent 69% of all formal business establishments in the industry sector in Rwanda, contributing 6% to the national GDP (NISR 2018),[1] and providing 14.3% of the formal private sector employment (IBES 2014), trying to understand the theoretical and empirical strategies that they can employ to improve their performance is a worthy subject of study.

Reasons for enterprises' market performance remain unclear in the existing literature. The resource-based theory (RBT) confirms that a firm's resources and capabilities determine its competitive advantage and firms that enjoy superior capabilities relative to their competitors have a significant advantage over them. This theory advocates using a company's internal resources, competencies, and capabilities as essential determinants for formulating strategies. This line of thinking argues that differences in a firm's performance can be traced back to heterogeneous assets and capabilities owned by the company. It assumes that each firm has unique resources and capabilities (Wernerfelt 1984) and its growth is subject to the efficient use of resources and deployment of its capabilities. However, according to Porter (1991), resources are not valuable in and of themselves but because they allow firms to perform activities that create advantages in particular markets; even the competitive value of resources can be enhanced or eliminated by changes in technology, competitors' behavior, or buyers' needs which the theory overlooks. The theory does

---

[1] National Institute of Statistics of Rwanda, Gross Domestic Product—2017.

not specify which type of resources and capabilities lead a firm to attaining market success. While researchers are engraved into these resource-based theory issues, they strongly believe that resources have the ability to create market power for an organization which is an inside-out perspective that Grant (1991) emphasizes. Grant (1991) explains that incumbent firms' possession of specific resources helps build entry barriers based on scale economics, patents, advantages of experience, and brand reputation. He also asserts that even other structural sources of market power, that is, financial and other resources are based on a firm's resources. Birger (1984) uses the words *"resource position barrier"* to explain the same phenomena to indicate a potential for high returns, since one competitor will have an advantage like entry barriers in the traditional market context. He, however, maintains that a firm's ability to exploit this resource position barrier is what is most important, that is, its ability to create a situation where its own resource position directly or indirectly makes it more difficult for others to catch up. While resource-based and market-based theories tend to be contradictory in some respects (the former emphasizing the need to base strategy on external market considerations and the latter on internal organizational resources and capabilities), Hooley et al. (1998) maintain that positioning decisions seek to find a match between market requirements and a company's abilities in seeking a competitive position for the company. They emphasize that *positioning strategies* need not choose between these two approaches and maintain that by placing same value on market demand and capability profiles when selecting the markets to enter and implementing positioning strategies, firms can enduringly match their offerings and their markets.

On the basis of these arguments this study poses the question: Do a firm's resources have a directional influence on the relationship between positioning strategy-performance? Positioning scholars have tried to link a firm's long-term success with its positioning strategy. Brooksbank (1994) specifically emphasizes that market tastes and preferences must tally with a firm's offerings. Fisher (1991) and Hooley et al. (1998) report a strong relationship between positioning strategy and a firm's performance, while Hooley et al. (2001a) and Blankson and Crawford (2012) associate a firm's chosen positioning strategy with the creation of a competitive advantage. These scholars observe and argue that there has been a change in marketing world over. They observe that as features of market offerings become less distinctive, intangible factors gain importance, that is, managing one's reputation and manipulating consumer perceptions and the positioning of the firm and what it offers in the marketplace become important. Additionally, in markets where rivalries intensify day-in-day-out and more pronounced competition and buyers have a greater choice, a product must occupy an explicit, distinct, and proper place in the minds of potential and existing consumers relative to other rival products in the market to be successful. Ries and Trout (2001) argue that in an *"over-communicated society"* in which the volume of commercial messages far exceeds an individual's mental processing capacity, marketers must focus on how to get into the minds of the consumers. Doing so requires taking challenging decisions about how a brand might stand out among its competitors, and how it might be perceived as superior in a consumer choice dimension. Positioning then becomes a tool for achieving these results. A product will not only be purchased but can also warrant a larger margin through increased added value. Hence, this study seeks to answer the question: *Does a firm's positioning strategy influence its market performance?*

There are differing views on the application of the positioning concept: product positioning seems to dominate in business marketing (specific product positioning) literature with little emphasis on company positioning, yet there is a general belief that the positioning concept is equally relevant for companies and their activities (Hayes et al. 1996). It is believed that the operationalization of positioning deals with modifying tangible characteristics and intangible perceptions of a market offering in relation to the competition. For Solomon (2007) all the marketing activities which potentially change or improve perceptions about a brand form the positioning of a brand. While pioneers of the positioning concept (Ries and Trout 1981) maintain that positioning is a mere communication issue that involves manipulating consumer perceptions about a certain good or service (that is, focusing on consumer attitudes and preferences) for some other scholars, positioning relates to all marketing activities that potentially create or change associations in a consumer's mind (Solomon et al. 2006). They refer to positioning as an activity that takes place in consumers' mindsets. Contenders of this view see positioning as a *consumer concept* rather than a management concept. A similar view is shared by Day (1981) who argues that product positioning refers to the customer's perception of the place that a product or brand occupies in a given market.

Understanding whether and how positioning strategies affect enterprises' market performance is an important research subject which has unceasingly prompted many empirical studies. For example, Blankson and Crawford (2012) did an exploratory qualitative case-based study in which they examined the effects of positioning strategies on service retail firms' performance in Dallas–Fort Worth Metroplex, one of the fastest-growing metropolitan areas in the US, where they found that "branding", "service", "value for money" and, to a lesser extent, "reliability" and "attractiveness" as positioning strategies had a significant and positive impact on desired profit levels, returns on investments (ROI), market shares, and consumer perceptions; although emphasis placed on each strategy varied from firm to firm. Their study shows that pursuing multiple positioning strategies related to multiple performance indicators presupposing that pursuing more strategies was better in terms of yielding performance outcomes than the other way around.

In a cross-sectional survey of 500 CEOs of supplier companies operating at all levels of the UK timber trade, Kalafatis et al. (2000) show that the domineering and most differentiating strategies related to hard-choice criteria, for example, product performance and pricing, and/or relationship building factors, for example, easy to do business with and personal contacts in terms of specific positioning strategies. Though they focused on the positioning of suppliers rather than of products in their study, they showed the dynamic nature of a positioning strategy, since no strategy was found to be dominant among the nine companies sampled: they found that easy to do business with was associated with three companies while personal contacts, product performance, pricing, and a range of offerings were associated with two companies. Their results led them to conclude that strategic market considerations (for example, product performance) rather than image building factors (for example, attractiveness) helped determine perceived positioning strategies. They also remind us that positioning is a matter of corporate strategy and not sales tactics; it is a crucial *strategic choice* that is not simply a question of marketing communication but encompasses the entire behavior of a firm. Earlier Bennion and Redmond (1994) and Bingham et al. (1995) unveiled similar positioning dimensions (price and product quality) in their positioning conceptualizations.

In a study conducted with 1,000 executives and owner-managers of service industries in the United States, Blankson and Crawford (2012) found that positioning strategies (that is, top of the range, service, value for money, reliability, and the brand name) significantly and positively influenced a firm's performance in terms of sales, profits, ROI, market share, company image, and consumer perceptions. Their study confirmed that there was a positive relationship between a company's performance and the positioning activities that it adopted. Some, if not, all of these positioning alternatives/types reviewed in literature represent *abstract attributes* (often seen as a bundle of concrete attributes) which form part of a consumer's purchase evaluation criteria and are frequently comparable across product categories. They are *not tangible* (performance, quality, style, sporty, fast acceleration) and instead they depend on core product features. Sacco (1986) advises that companies should not put their strategic focus on a number of claims when positioning a brand because using too many dimensions may lead to disbelief (Kotler 2003), confusion (Ghose 1994), or lowered memory (Meyers-Levy and Tybout 1989), often described as the enemies of positioning (Evans et al. 1996) because consumers do not have a clear picture of the brand in their minds. According to Trout and Rivkin (1996) the human brain only has a limited capacity to remember multiple brand associations. This discussion shows that positioning has no rule, save for every business playing its games, and resisting temptations to be all things to all people (Czepiel 1992). Empirical literature provides evidence of the claim that consumers perceive *brands* that are positioned on attributes as superior. This means that in these specific dimensions, they perform better relative to a multiple positioning option, even when the dimension is exactly the same for both the options (Chernev 2007).

The demanding conditions in which firms operate have been challenging and how organizations are responding to the changing environment in terms of their strategic positioning is a critical directional question of their success or failure. Hamel and Prahalad (1990) argue that the *functional and key role* of strategic positioning is identifying an organization's place in its operating environment which essentially depends on its mission and distinctive/core competencies. It has often been pointed out that positioning is a significant driver of a firm's performance and some scholars argue that positioning activities that are needs-based and resource-based guarantee long term financial and competitive rewards (Porter 1996). Brooksbank (1994) and Porter (1996) provide evidence of a close association between a company's performance in terms of profitability and its well-articulated positioning strategy activities. Cravens (1998), perceived positioning as a means of selecting an appropriate marketing strategy geared by the zeal to strengthen the organization's position in competitive markets. Other scholars like Brown and Sims (1976) link performance with positioning as its processes lead to competitor analysis and identifying customer needs which have market share and sales implications. Hofer and Schendel (1978) found a relationship between positioning strategy and competitive advantage. The same view is shared by Hooley et al. (1998) who argue that a positioning strategy is one of the sources of a competitive advantage over rivals in commercial organizations.

While in reality there are a never-ending number of ways in which firms might position themselves in their markets, Hooley et al. (1998) highlight six *differentiation-based positioning strategies*: price, quality, service, grade, tailored offerings, differentiated benefits, and innovations. These positioning alternatives/options seemingly tend to fall on the side of the claim of viewing positioning as part of setting sales objectives, demand forecasting, and response modeling and or, as part of the general claim that positioning is affected predominantly through the activities of the sales force (Dovel 1990). Bingham and Raffield (1995) six-step approach on price, technology, product quality, distribution, image, and service as positioning alternatives or strategies has been criticized for lack of empirical support though it partly fits well with Bennion and Redmond (1994) findings who identified four basic positioning dimensions/factors: service, product, support, and price. Some scholars also maintain that the choice and application of a certain positioning strategy is not a fixed process and that there is no single positioning strategy that works for all firms (Gulati and Garino 2000).

This discussion is an expression of the relevance of the *positioning construct*. Webster (1992) observed that though the construct has been developed in consumer marketing, it has a clear application for industrial products and services. He equates it with a firm's overall value position, which he defines as "firm's unique way of delivering value to customers." Despite the fact that academics (Hooley et al. 2001b; Kotler 1997) and practitioners (Ries and Trout 1986) have considered positioning as one of the key elements of modern marketing management, there is a dearth of a generally accepted positioning strategy typology that has empirically stood the test of time such that marketers in the multinational marketplace can use it (Alden et al. 1999). This shows that conceptualization challenges still exist in developing a positioning strategy's typology. Future studies can fill this gap.

Existing studies are criticized of being too conceptual and descriptive (Aaker and Carman 1982; Buskirk 1975), being based on limited empirical evidence (Easingwood and Mahajan 1989), and reflecting organizational practices and managerial views (Kalafatis et al. 2000) as compared to customer perceptions and many empirically derived positioning typologies have validity questions in terms of the operationalization i.e they may have been accepted without questioning their empirical basis hence many are difficult to operationalize (Kalafatis et al. 2000). Moreover, it seems quite difficult to develop a positioning strategy's typology that captures consumers' vocabulary regarding descriptions of their perceptions in terms of issues that are important for them when evaluating or considering purchases or recommending products or services to others.

While extant literature is convinced of the positive effects of a positioning strategy on a firm's performance, the importance of continued empirical examination of this relationship cannot be compromised as has, for long, been called for by several scholars including Blankson and Crawford (2012), Hooley et al. (2001a), Porter (1996). They observe that there are meager research streams documenting this relationship calling for further research. This study responds to this call. Since these scholars also maintain that positioning strategies are context-specific, this study empirically tests positioning strategies in the context of Rwanda's soft drink manufacturing industry.

2 Methods

This study adopted a descriptive cross-sectional design applying quantitative techniques of data collection and analysis. Data was collected from marketing/sales and corporate staff purposively selected from Urwibutso Enterprises Ltd. and Inyange Industries Ltd. These enterprises were selected for their background and being famous brands in the soft drink manufacturing industry. The study used the questionnaire method for collecting primary data. Perception test statements and close-ended questions were developed based on the most important theoretical areas reviewed in literature about the key study variables according to Aaker and Shansby (1982), Barney (1991), Blankson and Crawford (2012), Brooksbank (1994), Delen et al. (2013), Glick et al. (2005), James et al. (1993), Porter (1991, 1996), and Ries and Trout (1981). In all, there were 113 perception test statements (descriptors) in the initial list which were reduced to 105 after pre-testing (piloted on 10 people) and questionnaire validation by academia and industry experts. These processes were undertaken to ensure that any ambiguity with the statements was clarified prior to the first stage of data collection. For each statement, respondents were requested to indicate the extent/degree to which a descriptor (s)/statement (s) was relevant to their business positioning strategy's practices, resources/capabilities, and performance outcomes.

A 5-point *Likert scale* was used for measuring the descriptors where 5 stood for strongly agree, and 1 stood for strongly disagree; 113 responses were obtained, giving a 76% satisfactory response rate since the respondents were strictly marketing/sales and corporate staff members who understood the study's variables by theory and practice. *Non-response bias* was investigated by comparing early and late responses and through informal follow-up discussions with sales personnel. Reasons given for non-responses included (a) out of office, (b) still new in the department so did not feel confident enough filling the questionnaire, and (c) misplaced questionnaire, that is, given to wrong people in irrelevant departments. However, as researchers we were satisfied with the integrity of the data obtained.

The regression model used for estimating the level of relationship was derived using market share, sales, profitability, and market niche as market performance proxies (dependent variables) and the positioning strategy's (independent variable) proxies by product characteristics strategy, product use or application strategy, cultural symbols strategy, competitor strategy, pricing strategy, quality strategy, customization strategy, and product class strategy. The reason for adopting this positioning strategy's typology as mentioned by Aaker and Shansby (1982) is that each dimension has some bearing on the day-to-day practices and relates to consumers' perceptions of products as a basis for manipulating competition (they suggest that competition is a reference point for positioning). They largely fall under controllable managerial decision variables that are manipulated by a firm against its competitors to its favor. The adopted typology can be used for assessing positioning activities through the use of strategies (that is, factors) in a firm's communications' strategies or refinement of the tangible characteristics of the offering with the aim of creating a mental image for consumers through implied benefits of the offering (Kotler 1997).

An enterprise's management may use a strategy to either change attitudes (that is, efforts made to alter consumer beliefs or to change the market through advertising actions) or change brand products involving decisions to realistically or symbolically modify the offerings or change competition (that is, engage in actions to change the image of competing offerings from the ideal point of reference). Managers can employ all or any of the typology's items taking into account the needs, wants, and aspirations of target markets. All these are a reflection of what positioning means to different people. Aaker and Shansby (1982) relate positioning to segmentation decisions; for some others positioning is an image question (Camilleri 2018), that largely reflects on which product features to emphasize. Though scholars maintain that positioning decisions are often ad hoc and based on flashes of insights, there are systematic and research-based approaches followed for positioning decisions and this typology serves that rationale. Above all, it has been adopted and validated by others.

The multiple and simple model employed for estimating the impact of a positioning strategy on market performance of soft drink manufacturing enterprises in Rwanda is expressed in this study as

$$Y = a + bx \tag{1}$$

where

Y = Dependent variable (market performance)
a = Constant
b = Coefficient
x = Independent variable (positioning strategies)

$$MS = a + \beta_1 PCS + \beta_2 PUS + \beta_3 CSS + \beta_4 CS + \beta_5 PS + \beta_6 QS + \beta_7 CS + \beta_8 PCS + \mu \tag{2}$$

$$SZ = a + \beta_1 PCS + \beta_2 PUS + \beta_3 CSS + \beta_4 CS + \beta_5 PS + \beta_6 QS + \beta_7 CS + \beta_8 PCS + \mu \tag{3}$$

$$PF = a + \beta_1 PCS + \beta_2 PUS + \beta_3 CSS + \beta_4 CS + \beta_5 PS + \beta_6 QS + \beta_7 CS + \beta_8 PCS + \mu \tag{4}$$

$$MN = a + \beta_1 PCS + \beta_2 PUS + \beta_3 CSS + \beta_4 CS + \beta_5 PS + \beta_6 QS + \beta_7 CS + \beta_8 PCS + \mu \tag{5}$$

where

Performance is measured by market share (MS), sales (SZ), profitability (PF), market niche (MN).

β = Independent variable
a = Intercept
μ = Error terms

Positioning strategies are measured by Product characteristics strategy (PCS) = product use or application strategy (PUS) = cultural symbols strategy (CSS) = competitor strategy (CS) = pricing strategy (PS) = quality strategy (QS) = customization strategy (CS) = product class strategy (PCS).

Consequently, we put forward the following questions: Does the positioning strategy influence a firm's market performance? Do a firm's resources have a directional influence on the positioning strategy-performance relationship?

3 Results and Discussion

This study answers two questions: Does positioning strategy influence market performance? Do a firm's resources have a directional influence on the positioning strategy-performance relationship? Data for the study was collected from two soft drink manufacturing enterprises in Rwanda—Urwibutso Enterprises Ltd. and Inyange Industries Ltd. Urwibutso Enterprises Ltd. produces different soft drink products like Akandi, Akarusho, Akarabo, Urwibutso, and Agashya, whereas Inyange Industries Ltd. produces milk and milk products, juices in five different flavors, and mineral water. Both enterprises have more than 250 employees, have existed for more than 15 years, and find a market for their products in Rwanda, the East African Community, and Europe. Marketing, sales, and corporate staff members were purposively selected to increase the quality and dependability of the responses.

The study shows that managers in the two companies had several and varying perceptions about their positioning strategies and resources owned. They also gave their impressions of their actions and the impact of these actions on their enterprise's market performance.

The descriptive details in Tables 1, 2, 3, 4, 5, 6, 7, and 8 were generated using a 5-point Likert scale which was ordered such that 1 represents strongly disagree and 5 strongly agree with an issue. A mean close to 1 or 2 reflects disagreement with the issue at hand, while a mean close to 4 or 5 shows agreement with the same issue. On the other hand, a mean close to 3 reflects some uncertainty about the issue at hand. Column **N** shows how many of the respondents actually replied to the question.

The results in Table 1 show that on average, Urwibutso Enterprises Ltd. and Inyange Industries Ltd. did not have sufficient cash and capital resources (Mean = 2.11) to implement all their strategic plans and targets and their staff members had high level of managerial experience (Mean = 4.19) but were constrained by the high costs of water, electricity, and imported packaging materials (Mean = 2.15).

Table 1 Resource measurement

Resources	N	Min	Max	Mean	Std. deviation
We have enough cash and capital resources	113	2.00	5.00	2.11	0.65
The managerial experience of our executives is high	113	2.00	5.00	4.19	0.84
We have access to low cost factors of production	113	2.00	5.00	2.15	0.61
We are confident about our technical resource (patents, exclusive technologies.)	113	1.00	5.00	4.24	0.90
Our enterprise is listed on the stock exchange	113	2.00	5.00	2.15	0.66
We have a comprehensive and efficient organizational system, structure, and planning	113	1.00	5.00	4.20	0.51
We have sufficient expertise in product/service development	113	1.00	5.00	4.32	0.54
We have sufficient expertise in customer services	113	1.00	5.00	4.25	0.41
We have sufficient expertise in management	113	1.00	5.00	4.35	0.57
We have access to low cost distribution channels	113	1.00	5.00	2.15	0.54
Our enterprise's culture is supportive	113	1.00	5.00	4.32	0.61
Our reputation is good	113	2.00	5.00	4.32	0.59
All our tangible and intangible resources contribute equally to our competitive position	113	1.00	5.00	4.22	0.64
Some of our resources contribute more to our competitive position than others	113	1.00	5.00	4.17	0.53
We have the ability to implement our strategies	113	1.00	5.00	2.11	0.44

Source Authors' survey

Table 2 Capabilities measurement

Capabilities	N	Min	Max	Mean	Std. deviation
We respond to customers' needs swiftly	113	2.00	5.00	3.00	0.44
We have an appropriate managerial system with improvement capability adaptive to resource and environment changes	113	2.00	5.00	3.10	0.54
We understand technological trends and catch the changes	113	2.00	5.00	3.02	0.61
Flexibility to adapt to new industry and market trends is our secret	113	1.00	5.00	3.84	0.50
We have the necessary proactive capabilities to deal with change	113	2.00	5.00	2.55	0.46
Our resources are valuable, rare, and hard to imitate by competitors	113	1.00	5.00	2.72	0.41

Source Authors' survey

Table 3 Correlations for Resources and Capacities and the quality of the positioning strategy

Correlations			Resource and capacities	Positioning strategies
Resources and capacities	Pearson correlation		1	0.508[a]
	Sig. (2-tailed)			0.000
	N		113	113
Positioning strategies	Pearson correlation		0.508[a]	1
	Sig. (2-tailed)		0.000	
	N		113	113

Source Authors' calculations
Note [a]Correlation is significant at the 0.01 level (2-tailed)

Growing many plants such as fruits, flowers, vegetables, and bananas were found to constitute an advantage for Urwibutso Enterprises Ltd. in terms of reducing production costs, just as a strong partnership with farmers was found to Inyange Industries Ltd.'s advantage in terms of getting relatively cheap raw materials. Further, these enterprises were confident about their technical resources (patents and exclusive technologies) (Mean = 4.24). They were proud of their comprehensive and efficient organizational systems, structures, and planning systems (Mean = 4.20); expertise in product/service development, customer services and management, supportive culture, and reputation (Mean = 4.32) despite the fact that distribution costs were high and they were not listed on the stock exchange (Mean = 2.15). It was evident that they could not implement all their strategies because of insufficient resources (Mean = 2.12).

The respondents had mixed reactions and a relatively low level of confidence when responding to customers' needs, environmental changes, and catching up with the changes (Mean = 3.00, 3.10, and 3.02). An informal probe (informal talking with sales staff members) showed that some environmental changes overpowered them especially those that had to do with tax regulations and customer behavior that kept changing. Even competition seemed to be stiff where some of their capabilities were imitated by others in the industry (Mean = 2.72). This finding is contrary to Penrose's (1959) findings who argued that for a firm to have unique competitive advantages, the transfer of resources between firms should be difficult and the chance of replication by competitors should be denied since resource scarcity and inimitability secure and protect superior returns. Despite all these environmental uncertainties and being surpassed at times by changes and looking for ways to address the changes (Mean = 2.55), they were willing to adapt to new industry and market trends (Mean = 3.84). Their product varieties in milk, juices in different types and sizes, and natural mineral water constituted a big resource for these enterprises.

Table 4 Resources and capacities and market performance

Model summary[b]

Model	R	R square	Adjusted R square	Std. error of the estimate	Change statistics					Durbin-watson
					R square change	F change	df1	df2	Sig. F change	
1	0.628[a]	0.395	0.383	11.00864	0.395	33.927	1	52	0.000	1.754

Source Authors' findings
[a]Predictors: (constant), resources and capabilities
[b]Dependent variable: market performance

Table 5 Positioning strategy measurements

Strategies	N	Min	Max	Mean	Std. deviation
Using product characteristics or customer benefits					
We communicate the benefits of our products to consumers	113	2.00	5.00	4.22	0.64
Our products have manufacture and expiry dates	113	2.00	5.00	4.13	0.61
Positioning by use or application					
Our products are for office use	113	2.00	5.00	2.55	0.66
Our products are for home use	113	1.00	5.00	3.90	0.51
Our products are for social functions	113	1.00	5.00	3.70	0.54
Our products are for people on journeys	113	2.00	5.00	4.00	0.60
Positioning by cultural symbols					
We use cultural symbols in our products' design, labeling, and packaging	113	1.00	5.00	4.22	0.57
We produce products that represent cultural symbols	113	1.00	5.00	4.29	0.54
Our products' taste, flavor, and variety reflect Rwandan cultural values	113	1.00	5.00	4.32	0.84
Our product naming is cultural, for example, having some drinks named after a cow	113	2.00	5.00	4.18	0.59
Positioning by competitor					
We know our direct and indirect competitors	113	1.00	5.00	4.25	0.74
We know what our competitor does not give customers and we try to give it to them	113	1.00	5.00	4.05	0.44
Our products are the same as our competitors	113	1.00	5.00	2.03	0.54
Our products are better than our competitors	113	1.00	5.00	4.05	0.62
Our products are different from those of our competitors	113	1.00	5.00	3.65	0.49
We have geographically extended our product services as compared to our competitors	113	1.00	5.00	4.23	0.61
Our products have more functional and emotional benefits than our competitors	113	1.00	5.00	4.03	0.50
We are concerned with creating a unique position in the market	113	1.00	5.00	4.00	0.64

Source Authors' calculations

Assets (organizational assets, intellectual property assets, and reputational assets) and capabilities (human capital, networking abilities, business process related abilities, knowledge management skills, and organizational routines) were found to have a two-way directional effect on strategy formulation and enterprise performance. A strong and significant association was also found between the levels of these firms' resources and positioning decisions and targets (50.8% at the 1% significance level

Table 6 Positioning strategy measurements (continued...)

Strategies	N	Min	Max	Mean	Std. deviation
Positioning by price					
We deal with highly priced drinks (premium)	113	2.00	5.00	3.00	0.47
We deal with moderately priced drinks	113	2.00	5.00	4.23	0.61
We deal with low priced drinks	113	2.00	5.00	2.13	0.56
We tend to balance price considerations with quality considerations	113	2.00	5.00	4.33	0.66
We offer free after sale services	113	1.00	5.00	4.04	0.43
We offer discounts	113	1.00	5.00	4.00	0.54
Positioning by quality					
We use the best raw materials to ensure the quality of our products.	113	1.00	5.00	4.15	0.57
We try to meet our customers' perceived benefits	113	1.00	5.00	4.20	0.54
We tend to balance quality considerations with price considerations	113	1.00	5.00	4.33	0.64
Both tangible and intangible attributes of our products count	113	2.00	5.00	4.25	0.59
We view our products from the target customers' perspective	113	2.00	5.00	4.15	0.59
We deal in both retail and bulk product selling	113	1.00	5.00	4.35	0.64
Our product quality measurements in the laboratory have real-time process monitoring of °Brix, Sugar Inversion, percent Diet and CO_2 integrated as a standard (OEM solution) for consistent product quality and taste	113	1.00	5.00	2.15	0.44
Customized positioning					
We customize our products to suit the needs of various types of customers	113	1.00	5.00	4.32	0.54
We carry out regular market surveys to know about consumer behavior as an evaluation to control our products' image	113	1.00	5.00	2.84	0.54
We have a well-defined and known profile of our customers	113	1.00	5.00	2.45	0.50
We differentiate our products according to customers' perceptions	113	1.00	5.00	2.15	0.48
Product class strategy					
Our customers know us for our home refreshing juices	113	1.00	5.00	3.85	0.55
Our customers know us for our high-quality milk products	113	1.00	5.00	4.00	0.61
Our customers know us for our high-quality mineral drinking water	113	1.00	5.00	4.00	0.56
Our products make us unique in the market	113	1.00	5.00	4.01	0.54

Source Authors' findings

Table 7 Positioning strategies and market performance measurement

Positioning strategy-market performance relationship measurement	N	Min	Max	Mean	Std. deviation
Market share (increase in the number of customers)					
Our market share has grown because of our products' characteristics that have functional performance	113	2.00	5.00	4.19	0.60
Product use or application has helped our market share increase	113	2.00	5.00	3.90	0.61
Use of cultural symbols has positively impacted our market share	113	1.00	5.00	4.24	0.52
Managing competition has got us a good market position	113	2.00	5.00	3.55	0.66
We owe our market share to our prices that are affordable	113	1.00	5.00	4.20	0.41
We have our market share growing because of our product quality	113	1.00	5.00	4.20	0.54
Our customized product strategy has helped us increase our market share	113	2.00	5.00	2.25	0.57
Our product class has created a position for us that has increased our market share	113	1.00	5.00	2.95	0.41
We have experienced a below 20% increase in market share in the last six months in Rwanda	113	1.00	5.00	2.85	0.57
Our market share has increased by 30% in the last six months in Rwanda	113	1.00	5.00	2.85	0.54
Our market share has increased by 40% in the last six months in Rwanda	113	1.00	5.00	2.14	0.54
Our market share has increased more than 50% in the last six months in Rwanda	113	2.00	5.00	2.25	0.59
Our market share outside Rwanda has increased	113	1.00	5.00	2.15	0.64
Sales growth (customer growth rate) in the last six months					
We have experienced a below 10% increase in our sales	113	1.00	5.00	2.05	0.44
Our sales have increased by 10%	113	1.00	5.00	2.80	0.64
Our sales have increased by 20%	113	1.00	5.00	2.32	0.64
Our sales have increased by 30%	113	1.00	5.00	2.32	0.64
Our sales have increased by 40%	113	1.00	5.00	2.32	0.64
Our sales have increased more than 50%	113	1.00	5.00	2.32	0.64
Our sales have declined	113	1.00	5.00	2.25	0.64
Our sales have increased because of our products' features	113	1.00	5.00	2.35	0.64

(continued)

Table 7 (continued)

Positioning strategy-market performance relationship measurement	N	Min	Max	Mean	Std. deviation
Our sales have increased because of our product use or application	113	1.00	5.00	3.25	0.64
Using cultural symbols for our products has helped us increase the level of sales	113	1.00	5.00	4.05	0.64
The way we manage the competitive business environment has helped us increase our sales	113	1.00	5.00	3.85	0.64
Our affordable prices have helped us increase our sales volume	113	1.00	5.00	4.10	0.64
Our product quality has helped us increase our sales	113	1.00	5.00	4.22	0.64
Our sales have increased because of our customized products	113	1.00	5.00	2.15	0.64
Sales have increased because of our product class	113	1.00	5.00	3.00	0.64

Source Authors' results

of the 2-tailed test) (see correlations in Table 3). There was an observable complex interaction and interconnections between different sets of resources and capabilities in the process of creating a strategy. A 39.5% variance in these two enterprises' market performance was explained by resources and capacities (Table 4). This finding is supported by Wernerfelt (1984) and Barney (1991) who argue that internal and idiosyncratic resources at the firm-level can explain the variations in success among firms competing within the same industry. Penrose (1959) supports the view that dynamic interactions between resources and managerial decisions within an administrative framework not only provide a thorough explanation of heterogeneity between firms but also enable firms to have unique advantages relative to their competitors. This re-emphasizes the significance of assets and resources in enhancing a firm's ability to pursue market-driven strategies. Future research can look into the non-accounted for factors that explain the 60.5% variance in these enterprises' performance. However, SDMEs in Rwanda face many challenges in increasing their asset and capability levels if strategic decision making and performance are to be enhanced.

The results presented here give a grounded answer to the question: Do a firm's resources have a directional influence on the positioning strategy-performance relationship?

According to Table 5 Urwibutso Enterprises Ltd. and Inyange Industries Ltd. used product characteristic strategies and often communicated their products' benefits to their consumers (Mean = 4.22) as part of their packaging policy to indicate products' manufacture and expiry dates (Mean = 4.13). They positioned themselves as producers of soft drink products for social functions, domestic or home use, and for

Table 8 Positioning strategies and market performance measurement (continued...)

Positioning strategy-market performance relationship measurement	N	Min	Max	Mean	Std. deviation
Market niche performance					
More than 50% of the people from all age brackets consume our products	113	2.00	5.00	4.19	0.56
Only people of specific age groups consume our products	113	2.00	5.00	2.11	0.51
More than 50% of all the regions in Rwanda consume our products	113	1.00	5.00	3.00	0.60
Our products are consumed in specific regions in Rwanda	113	2.00	5.00	2.21	0.66
More than 50% of the people in cities and towns consume our products	113	1.00	5.00	2.20	0.52
Our products are consumed by both men and women	113	1.00	5.00	4.22	0.54
People from all religions in Rwanda consume our products	113	2.00	5.00	4.11	0.67
Only people from specific income groups consume our products	113	1.00	5.00	2.10	0.41
More than 50% of the people from all income groups consume our products	113	1.00	5.00	3.15	0.57
More than 50% of the educated and uneducated people consume our products	113	1.00	5.00	3.15	0.54
Only educated people consume our products	113	1.00	5.00	2.11	0.54
Profitability growth rate (in the last six months)					
Our profits have increased	113	1.00	5.00	4.20	0.64
We have experienced a 2% increase in profits	113	1.00	5.00	2.31	0.64
Our profit growth rate has been between 3 and 10%	113	1.00	5.00	2.31	0.64
Our profit growth rate has been between 10 and 20%	113	1.00	5.00	4.11	0.44
Our profit growth rate has been between 20 and 30%	113	1.00	5.00	2.31	0.64
Our profits have increased more than 30%	113	1.00	5.00	2.31	0.64

Source Authors' results

journeys (Mean = 3.90, 3.70, and 4.00, respectively). To some extent their products are also used in offices (Mean = 2.55). Cultural symbols were found to be one of the most key positioning strategies used by the two companies as their products' naming, design, labeling and packaging, taste, logo, flavor, and variety reflect Rwandan cultural values (Mean = 4.22, 4.29, 4.32, and 4.18 respectively). From the enterprises' names Inyange and Urwibutso have products names like Akarabo, Urwibutso, Akandi, Inyange juice, Inyange whole milk, Inyange pure ghee, Inyange yogurt, Inyange fresh cream, Inyange mango, Inyange apple, Inyange passion fruit, Inyange pineapple, and Inyange natural mineral water in different sizes which are purely Rwandan in origin and culture.

This study found that the competition too used positioning extensively. Quite surprising Urwibutso Enterprises Ltd. knew Inyange Industries Ltd. as its competitor and vice versa. When asked whether competition considerations guided their positioning decision making (they invest in knowing their direct and indirect competitors), the respondents expressed strong emotional feelings (Mean = 4.25). However, their emphasis was on trying to satisfy their customers' needs than what the competitor basically did (Mean = 4.05). They equally emphasized functional and emotional benefits and giving unique features to their products and trying to expand their geographical coverage regardless of what their competitors were doing (Mean = 4.03 and 4.23, respectively). They expressed satisfaction that their products were different from those of their competitors (Mean = 3.65); their position was about satisfying market needs better. This finding matches with what Brown and Sims (1976) recommend. According to them, a competitor analysis and investigating and targeting customer needs should go together. Urwibutso Enterprises Ltd. and Inyange Industries Ltd.'s sensitivity to market competitive behavior resonated well with principles of competitive advantage (Hofer and Schendel 1978). Once these competitive values are upheld for long they may help these two enterprises in attaining a pleasant competitive edge in a sustainable manner.

Price as a positioning strategy elicited various responses. Table 6 gives the results which show that the two companies neither targeted rich people in their pricing policy (Mean = 3.00), nor poor people (Mean = 2.13). They tended to balance price considerations with quality considerations and thus priced their drinks moderately (Mean = 4.33). They offered discounts and free after sales services to their business customers who bought in bulk (Mean = 4.04). Quality was a strong positioning strategy for these enterprises; they ensured that the raw materials that they used in their production were of the best quality to be able to meet their customers' perceived benefits of their products, paying attention to both tangible and intangible attributes, and viewed their products from the target customer's perspective (Mean = 4.15, 4.25, and 4.14, respectively). However, they seemed to be less aware of the technical aspects of product quality measurements (Mean = 2.15). Not all the staff members were knowledgeable about technical product information; this knowledge was confined to production personnel only.

These enterprises vehemently aspired to satisfy their customers' needs (Mean = 4.32) but the definition of their customers was broad and unspecific (Mean = 2.45), that is, they tended to largely be product-focused and did less of customer profiling since they targeted everyone. They neutrally understood the significance of market surveys (Mean = 2.84) because of financial implications.

Urwibutso Enterprises Ltd. and Inyange Industries Ltd. to a lesser extent positioned themselves according to customer classes (Mean = 2.15). They produced high-quality milk, juices, and mineral drinking water, which makes them unique in the market (Mean = 4.00).

The results in Table 7 show how these companies' strategies involved positioning themselves as producers of soft drink products for social functions, domestic use, and for journeys, capitalizing on rendering improved and better product features; and the use of cultural symbols and affordable prices influenced their market share and sales volumes (Mean = 4.19, 3.90, 4.24, and 4.20). Though the respondents acknowledged that their companies' market share was increasing, they were not sure of the extent (Mean = 2.85). They had no scientific data to that effect, but they were convinced that there had been a 10% increase in profits in the last six months. They were also unable to specifically attribute this to any of the strategies. They, however, expressed certainty about their products' quality, affordable prices, and cultural symbols to be major drivers of their increasing market share, sales, and profitability (Mean = 4.10, 4.22, and 4.05, respectively).

Kalafatis et al.'s (2000) findings are similar for the explanatory powers of product quality and price on a company's performance in terms of profits. Bennion and Redmond (1994) and Bingham and Raffield (1995), also emphasize specific positioning dimensions, for example, price and product quality. Mustapha's (2017) results also confirm that when quality products are produced by an enterprise, which are appropriately priced and efficiently distributed, it leads to better business performance in terms of profitability, increased market share, customer satisfaction, and market expansion. Urwibutso Enterprises Ltd. and Inyange Industries Ltd.'s emphasis on a few dimensions of the positioning strategy (quality, price, and cultural symbols) is also shared by Sacco (1986) who advises that companies should emphasize on only a limited number of claims when positioning a brand because using too many dimensions may lead to disbelief (Kotler 2003), confusion (Ghose 1994), or lowered memory (Meyers-Levy and Tybout 1989), often described as the enemies of positioning (Evans et al. 1996) because consumers do not have a clear picture of the brand in their minds. Trout and Rivkin (1996) maintain that the human brain has only a limited capacity to remember multiple brand associations.

From this discussion, it is clear that positioning has no rules, save for every business playing its games and resisting temptations to be all things to all people (Czepiel 1992) which these two enterprises fall prey to.

As mentioned in Table 6, product customization is less practiced since the companies direct their offerings to the whole market (young, old, educated, uneducated, rural, and urban) with their products having the same characteristics (Mean = 2.15), that is, the definition of their customers is broad and unspecific. Respondents said that their enterprises were strongly linked to the urban centers as compared to rural areas because of income and purchasing power differences. Despite their neutrality to the extent to which market shares and sales had increased, their market shares and sales had not declined (Mean = 2.25).

It was observed from the respondents' responses that the two companies did not produce for a specific group of people (Table 9). People from all religions consumed their products (Mean = 4.11). They did not target specific income groups, specific regions, or specific age groups (Mean = 2.11, 2.21). Even though they could not

Table 9 Correlations between positioning strategies and market performance Correlations

		Positioning strategies	Positioning strategies and market performance
Positioning strategies	Pearson correlation	1	0.678[a]
	Sig. (2-tailed)		0.000
	N	113	113
Positioning strategies and market performance	Pearson correlation	0.678[a]	1
	Sig. (2-tailed)	0.000	
	N	113	113

Source Authors' calculations
Note [a]Correlation is significant at the 0.01 level (2-tailed)

specifically aggregate what percentage of which income group consumed their products (Mean = 2.10), they acknowledged that their profits had increased in the last six months (Mean = 4.20) in the range of 10–20% (Mean = 4.11).

A strong and significant relationship was found between positioning strategies and market performance of the studied enterprises (67.8% at the 1% significance level in the 2-tailed test) (see correlations in Table 9). The 57.5% variance in Urwibutso Enterprises Ltd. and Inyange Industries Ltd.'s market performance can be explained by their positioning strategies (product attributes, use or application, price, quality, cultural symbols, customization, product class, and competition) (see Table 10). The result is statistically significant at $p > 0.05$ at 0.000. This means that positioning strategies influenced the companies' performance in terms of market shares, sales, and profitability. The study also found that product quality, price, and cultural symbols had a greater impact on sales, market share, and profitability as compared to the other strategies. These findings are consistent with Porter (1996) and Hooley et al. (2001b), who argue that a firm's superior competitive position comes partly from its positioning activities. Blankson et al. (2008) in their study of 1,000 executives and owner-managers of service industries in the United States, confirm that a well-formulated positioning strategy influenced a company's performance levels.

4 Summary and Conclusion

4.1 Summary

This study answered two questions, viz., (i) *Does positioning strategy influence market performance? (ii) Do a firm's resources have a directional influence on the positioning-strategy performance relationship?*

The study found a strong and significant association between the level of a firm's resources and positioning decisions and target audiences in Urwibutso Enterprises

Table 10 Positioning strategies and market performance

Model summary[b]

Model	R	R square	Adjusted R square	Std. error of the estimate	Change statistics					Durbin-watson
					R square change	F change	df1	df2	Sig. F change	
1	0.628[a]	0.575	0.563	11.00864	0.395	33.927	1	52	0.000	1.284

Source Authors' calculations
[a]Predictors: (Constant), Positioning strategies
[b]Dependent Variable: Market performance

Ltd. and Inyange Industries Ltd. (50.8% at the 1% significance level of the 2-tailed test) (see Table 3). The 39.5% variance in these enterprises' market performance is explained by their resources and capacities (Table 4). This finding is supported by Wernerfelt (1984) and Barney (1991) who argue that internal and idiosyncratic resources at the firm-level can explain the variations in firms' success (those competing in the same industry). Penrose (1959) supports the view that dynamic interactions between resources and managerial decisions within an administrative framework not only provide an explanation of heterogeneity between the firms but also enable firms to have unique advantages relative to their competitors. This re-emphasizes the significance of assets and resources in enhancing a firm's ability to pursue market-driven strategies. Future research may try to study other factors that explain 60.5% variance in a company's performance.

Positioning strategies, that is, product attributes, use or application, price, quality, cultural symbols, customization, product class, and competition were found to influence Urwibutso Enterprises Ltd. and Inyange Industries Ltd.'s market performance. How each strategy affected various performance dimensions (market share, sales, profitability, and niche) varied. Product quality, price, and cultural symbols were found to have more impact on sales, market share, and profitability than other strategies in these enterprises. Only 57.5% variance in performance was jointly explained by these positioning strategies.

4.2 Conclusion

The soft drink industry in Rwanda like in any other country in the region is among the most vibrant and growing markets. A growing middle class, increasing literacy, ever-increasing rural-urban migration, and a growing number of uses for packed soft drinks constitute a business opportunity for investors in this sector. These developments show that marketing and positioning functions remain essential for showcasing enterprises' offerings thereby informing their organizational performance through quality management, maintaining and retaining clients for the business' success, and its sustainability.

On the basis of the fact that product quality, price, and cultural symbols were found to impact sales, market share, and profitability considerably as compared to the other strategies in Urwibutso Enterprises Ltd. and Inyange Industries Ltd. SDMEs should pursue a limited number of claims (strategies) when positioning their products (Sacco 1986).

4.3 Recommendations and Future Research

The study answered two questions: Does positioning strategy influence market performance? Do a firm's resources have a directional influence on the positioning strategy-performance relationship?

First, data was limited to only Urwibutso Enterprises Ltd. and Inyange Industries Ltd. registered formal SDMEs operating in Rwanda. Further research can be carried out not only on SDMEs but also other organizations in the manufacturing and mining sectors since they are core sectors in Rwanda's economy. Second, since data collection was only limited to the use of structured questionnaires, more advanced data collection methods can be used for future research like doing comparative research, a multi-case study, and a sample study using case interviews. On the basis of the finding that these enterprises tend to be largely product-focused and doing less customer profiling for targeting specific customers and having a broad and unspecific definition of their customers, they are challenged in narrowing their focus to a specific niche that they can satisfy better.

References

Aaker, D. A., & Carman, J. M. (1982). Are you over-advertizing. *Journal of Advertising Research, 22*(4), 57–70.
Aaker, D. A., & Shansby, J. G. (1982). Positioning your product. *Business Horizons, 25,* 3.
Alden, D. L., Steenkamp, J. B. E., & Batra, R. (1999). Brand positioning through advertising in Asia, North America, and Europe: The role of global consumer culture. *Journal of Marketing, 63*(1), 75–87.
Barney, J. (1991). Firm resources and sustained competitive advantage. *Journal of Management, 17*(1), 99–120.
Bennion, M. L., & Redmond, W. H. (1994). Modeling customer response in an industrial commodity market. *Industrial Marketing Management, 23*(5), 383–392.
Bingham, F. G., & Raffield, B. T. (1995). *Business marketing management.* Cincinnati: South-Western College Publishing.
Birger, W. (1984). A resource-based view of the firm. *Strategic Management Journal, 5*(2).
Blankson, C., & Crawford, J. C. (2012). Impact of positioning strategies on service firm performance. *Journal of Business Research, 65*(3), 311–316.
Blankson, C., Kalafatis, S. P., Cheng, J. M. S., & Hadjicharalambous, C. (2008). Impact of positioning strategies on corporate performance. *Journal of Advertising Research, 48*(1), 106–122.
Bralirwa Annual Financial and Operational Reports and Accounts (2010).
Bralirwa Annual Financial and Operational Reports and Accounts (2012).
Bralirwa Annual Financial and Operational Reports and Accounts (2013).
Bralirwa Annual Financial and Operational Reports and Accounts (2014).
Bralirwa Annual Financial and Operational Reports and Accounts (2015).
Bralirwa Annual Financial and Operational Reports and Accounts (2016).
Bralirwa Annual Financial and Operational Reports and Accounts (2017).
Brooksbank, R. (1994). The anatomy of marketing positioning strategy. *Marketing Intelligence & Planning, 12*(4), 10–14.

Brown, H. E., & Sims, J. T. (1976). Market segmentation, product differentiation, and market positioning as alternative marketing strategies. In K.L. Bernhardt (ed.), *Marketing: 1776–1976 and beyond*. Educators Conference Proceedings Series No. 39, Chicago.

Buskirk, R. K. (1975). *Principles of marketing* (4th ed.). London: Dryden Press.

Camilleri, M. A. (2018). Market segmentation, targeting and positioning. In *Travel marketing, tourism economics and the airline product* (pp. 69–83). Springer.

Chernev, A. (2007). Jack of all trades or master of one? Product differentiation and compensatory reasoning in consumer choice. *Journal of Consumer Research, 33*(4), 430–444.

Cravens, D. W. (1998). Implementation strategies in the market-driven strategy era. *Journal of the Academy of Marketing Science, 26*(3), 237–241.

Czepiel, J. A. (1992). *Competitive marketing strategy*. New Jersey: Prentice Hall.

Day, G. S. (1981). Strategic market analysis and definition: An integrated approach. *Strategic Management Journal, 2*(3), 281–299.

Delen, D., Kuzey, C., & Uyar, A. (2013). Measuring firm performance using financial ratios: A decision tree approach. *Expert Systems with Applications, 40*(10), 3970–3983.

Dovel, G. P. (1990). Stake it out: positioning success, step by step. *Business Marketing, 5*, 43–51.

Easingwood, C. J., & Mahajan, V. (1989). Positioning of financial services for competitive advantage. *The Journal of Product Innovation Management, 6*(3), 207–219.

Evans, M. J., Moutinho, L., & van Raaij, W. F. (1996). *Applied consumer behaviour*. London: Addison-Wesley.

Fisher, R. J. (1991). Durable differentiation strategies for services. *The Journal of Services Marketing, 5*(1), 19–28.

Ghose, S. (1994). Visually representing consumer perceptions: Issues and managerial insights. *European Journal of Marketing, 28*(10), 5–18.

Glick, W. H., Washburn, N. T., & Miller, C. (2005). The Myth of firm performance. In *Proceedings of the Annual Meeting of American Academy of Management*.

Grant, R. M. (1991). The resource-based theory of competitive advantage: Implications for strategy formulation. *California Management Review, 33*(3), 114–135.

Gulati, R., & Garino, J. (2000). Get the right mix of bricks & clicks. *Harvard Business Review, 78*(3), 107–107.

Hamel, G., & Prahalad, C. K. (1990). The core competence of the corporation. *Harvard Business Review, 68*(3), 79–91.

Hayes, H. M., Jenster, P. V., & Aaby, N. E. (1996). *Business marketing: Global perspective*. Richard D: Irwin.

Hofer, C. W., & Schendel, D. (1978). *Strategy formulation: Analytical concepts*. St. Paul: West Pub. Co.

Hooley, G. J., Möller, K., & Broderick, A. J. (1998). Competitive positioning and the resource based view of the firm. *Journal of Strategic Marketing, 6*(2).

Hooley, G., Fahy, J., & Cadogan, J. (2001a). Market-focused-resources, competitive positioning and firm performance. *Journal of Marketing Management, 17*, 5–6.

Hooley, G., Greenley, G., Fahy, J., & Cadogan, J. (2001b). Market-focused resources, competitive positioning and firm performance. *Journal of Marketing Management, 17*(5–6), 503–520.

James, B. T., Clark, S. M., & Dennis, A. G. (1993). Strategic sense-making and organizational performance: Linkages among scanning, interpretation, action, and outcomes. *The Academy of Management Journal, 36*(2).

Kalafatis, S. P., Tsogas, M. H., & Blankson, C. (2000). Positioning strategies in business markets. *Journal of Business & Industrial Marketing, 15*(6), 416–437.

Kotler, P. (1997). *Marketing management: Analysis, planning, implementation and control*. Upper Saddle River. NJ: Prentice-Hall.

Kotler, P. (2003). *Marketing management* (11th ed.). New Jersey: Prentice Hall.

Meyers-Levy, J., & Tybout, A. M. (1989). Schema congruity as a basis for product evaluation. *Journal of Consumer Research, 16*(1), 39–54.

Mustapha, B. (2017). Effects of marketing mix strategy on performance of small scale businesses in Maiduguri Metropolitan, Bomo State Nigeria. *Journal of Marketing and Consumer Research, 31*(1), 1–6.
Penrose, E. T. (1959). *The theory of the growth of the firm.* Oxford: Basil Blackwell.
Porter, M. E. (1991). Towards a dynamic theory of strategy. *Strategic Management Journal, 12*(S2), 95–117.
Porter, M. E. (1996). What is strategy? *Harvard Business Review, 74*(6), 61–78.
Ries, Al, & Trout, J. (1981). *Positioning: The battle for your Mind.* New York: Warner Books.
Ries, A., & Trout, J. (1986). Marketing warfare. *Journal of Consumer Marketing, 3*(4).
Ries, A., & Trout, J. (2001). *Positioning: The battle for your mind* (The 20th anniversary ed.). New York, NY: McGraw-Hill.
Sacco, J. (1986). Rosser Reeves' lost chapter. *Advertising Age, 17.*
Solomon, M. R., Marshall, G. W., & Stuart, E. W. (2006). *Marketing: Real people, real choices* (4th ed.). New Jersey: Pearson Education.
Solomon, M. R. (2007). *Consumer behavior* (7th ed.). Upper Saddle River, NJ: Pearson Prentice Hall.
Sophia, K., & Söderbom, M. (2013). *Constraints and opportunities in Rwanda's Industrial Sector.* Working paper by International Growth Centre (IGC), London School of Economic and Political Science, Houghton Street, London WC2A 2AE.
Trout, J., & Rivkin, S. (1996). *The new positioning.* New York: McGraw-Hill.
Webster, F. E., Jr. (1992). The changing role of marketing in the corporation. *Journal of Marketing, 56*(4), 1–17.
Wernerfelt, B. (1984). A resource-based view of the firm. *Strategic Management Journal, 5*(2), 171–180.

Chapter 12
Determinants of Productivity of Rwandese Food and Beverage Processing Sector: Do Tax Incentives Matter?

Etienne Ndemezo and Jean Bosco Ndikubwimana

Abstract This study discusses the main determining factors of capacity utilization in the food and beverage manufacturing industries which are likely to be positively affected by tax incentives. It uses data from the manufacturing industry comprehensive survey carried out by the Rwandese Ministry of Trade and Industry (MINICOM) in 2013–14. The model it uses is derived from an augmented Cobb–Douglas production function. The key findings of the study are: (i) in the food processing industry the main factors which undermine firms' capacity utilization are shortage of raw materials, lack of specialized technologies, poor tax administration and standards; (ii) in the beverage manufacturing industry, drivers of capacity utilization are firm experience (age) and its material-intensive characteristics. Four factors harm the capacity utilization of beverage manufacturing firms—oversize in terms of fixed assets, lack of working capital, standards and insufficient demand. Thus, policymakers in Rwanda need to focus on non-tax measures to boost the food and beverage processing sectors.

Keywords Capacity utilization · Tax incentives · Food and beverage · Processing productivity

JEL Classification Codes D24 · H32 · L66

1 Introduction

In Rwanda, the largest number of firms in the manufacturing industry is in the food and beverage processing sectors (NISR 2016). Further, according to MINICOM (2012), food processing firms remain the most productive among the manufacturing firms contributing 19.1% to GDP while the contribution of the beverage and tobacco manufacturing industry is 12.4%. The manufacturing industry contributes 14% to

---

E. Ndemezo (✉)
Department of Economics, University of Rwanda, Kigali, Rwanda
e-mail: ndemo.etcroix@gmail.com

J. B. Ndikubwimana
Department of Applied Statistics, University of Rwanda, Kigali, Rwanda

© Springer Nature Singapore Pte Ltd. 2020
G. G. Das and R. B. Johnson (eds.), *Rwandan Economy at the Crossroads of Development*, Frontiers in African Business Research,
https://doi.org/10.1007/978-981-15-5046-1_12

GDP as a whole. The other sub-sectors of the manufacturing industry make negligible contributions to GDP.

However, despite their productive performance, Rwandese food and beverage manufacturing firms are not competitive both internally and externally. All food exports are resource-based (NISR 2016) and this is like a general rule for all goods exported. Most of the agro-based food and beverages sold in Rwanda are imported from neighboring countries, mainly from Kenya and Uganda. As reported in NISR (2011), this low competitiveness of the food and beverage processing industries is because of their low capacity utilization as most of them are agro-processing firms and are commonly faced with problems of unreliable supply of inputs. This is supported by Lai (2015) for the Canadian food manufacturing industry. His study concluded that capacity underutilization can be one of the reasons for firms' productivity growth slowing down.

The industrial capacity utilization rate can be defined as the ratio of actual production of output to the maximum or potential capacity output (Lai 2015). This index measures an industry's ability to provide its products to consumers. Barbour (2005) categorizes incentives into two types: fiscal and non-fiscal. Fiscal incentives can be direct or indirect. Direct incentives are direct instruments like government subsidies as direct cash payments or as payments-in-kind. Indirect incentives are when the government uses tax instruments like reduction in taxes, tax holidays, accelerated depreciation allowances, and investment tax allowances or deductions of qualifying expenses. Non-fiscal incentives include exemptions from certain rules and regulations.

In literature, fiscal incentives are among the instruments used by governments to boost firms' investments, productivity, and competitiveness (Mayende 2013; Ohaka and Agundu 2014). However, most of these studies are restricted to the role of taxes in investments (Kransdorff 2010; Wentzel and Steyn 2014) and only a few studies question the effects of fiscal incentives on firms' capacity utilization and competitiveness.

Ndemezo and Baye (2016) recommend using tax incentives for improving poor households' welfare in Rwanda. They suggest reducing taxes on manufactured food items. This can be done downstream or upstream, that is, at the manufacturer level or at the consumer level. At the manufacturer level, the target of fiscal incentives should be reducing production costs and ensuring the availability of enough manufactured food items. At the consumer level, the emphasis should be on lowering living costs by reducing manufactured food items' final prices. However, because downstream fiscal incentives decrease production costs and allow availing these incentives on enough products, they can also result in reducing consumers' living cost. Consequently, it is better to reduce taxes on manufactured food items on the production side.

This study determines the circumstances under which tax incentives can help enough food and beverage products in Rwanda. This study's specific objective is determining the main factors of capacity utilization in the food and beverage manufacturing industries which are likely to be positively affected by indirect tax incentives.

This study covers Rwandese food and beverage manufacturing firms as they use agricultural products. Consequently, the study does not include mineral water and beer brands like *Brasseries et Limonaderies* du Rwanda (BRALIRWA) and SKOL International. The firms were selected using 4-digit classification as specified in the 3rd edition of the International Standard Industrial Classification of all Economic Activities (UNSD 2002).

To address its objective, the study used data from the manufacturing industry survey carried out by the Rwandese Ministry of Trade and Industry from October 2013 to February 2014 covering fiscal year 2012 and three quarters of 2013. It uses the augmented Cobb–Douglas production function estimated using the OLS regression technique.

The key outcomes of the study are: (i) in the food manufacturing industry, the main factors which undermine firms' capacity utilization are shortages of raw materials, lack of specialized technologies, poor tax administration and standards; no factors positively and significantly influence their capacity utilization; (ii) the drivers of capacity utilization in the beverage manufacturing industry are firms' experience (age) and their material-intensive characteristics. However, four factors reduce firms' capacity utilization—oversize in terms of fixed assets, lack of working capital, standards and insufficient demand. Consequently, no taxes are advisable for boosting production in the food and beverage manufacturing sectors. However, we suggest simplifying tax compliance rules and subsidizing young and small firms to help them acquire appropriate technology and standards. To deal with the shortage of agro-raw materials, we recommend using non-fiscal measures to avail agro-inputs thus reducing their costs.

The rest of the study is organized as follows. The next section gives the literature review and the third section discusses the methodology. The fourth section presents the empirical findings, while the last section summarizes the findings and gives a conclusion.

2 Literature Review

The industrial capacity utilization rate can be defined as the ratio of actual production output to the maximum or potential capacity output (Lai 2015). Capacity utilization can be studied following two definitions: the technical-based definition and the economic-based definition. Technically, full capacity refers to the maximum production of output from a specific bundle of the quasi-fixed inputs without restriction on the availability of variable inputs (Johansen 1968). Consequently, technical potential output represents the maximum amount of output that can be produced in the short run with the existing capital stock (Nelson 1989). Thus, technical-based capacity utilization is one or less than one.

The difference between the technical-based definition and the economic-based definition relies on measuring the potential output. Economically, potential output is the optimum level of output at which short-run average total costs are minimized.

There are two alternative ways of calculating the potential output—minimizing costs or maximizing profits (Färe et al. 1989). This study uses the technical-based definition of capacity utilization.

According to these two approaches, the determinants of capacity utilization influence the actual output and not the potential output either positively or negatively. Thus, these factors can be in a firm's internal or external business environment. Internal factors can be corporate governance mechanisms like the quality of leadership and organization of the company. External factors can be the market structure and competition, availability and quality of inputs, market demand and prices, public and private infrastructure, and business rules and regulations.

Recently, many studies have analyzed the relationship between capacity utilization or the productivity of food and beverage processing firms and its determinants. In Iran, Afrooz et al. (2011), used the Cobb–Douglas production function to analyze the determinants of labor productivity in the food industry during the period 1995–2006. They found that the main driver of productivity in the Iranian food industry was workers' specialization. The other variables that influenced the productivity of the food processing industry in Iran were educational levels of the workers, capital per worker, firm size, and wages. The gender variable (ratio of women workers to men workers) had a negative effect on labor productivity.

In India, Ali et al. (2009) used the non-parametric data envelopment analysis (DEA) to analyze particular reasons for inefficiency and low productivity across various segments of the food processing industry and found that technology was the key to enhancing growth and efficiency in the food processing sector. However, they observed that the growth in output was largely driven by the incremental use of input doses. Thus, in contrast to the Iran food processing industry, in India the capital input was the main driver of productivity.

Analogously, Shamsudin et al. (2011) used the same approach in the context of Malaysia and found that research and development (R&D), employee training, and public infrastructure were the main determinants that positively affected total factor productivity growth of the food processing industry.

Using the parametric statistical method and applying it to Malaysia's food manufacturing sector, Ahmed (2012) observed that factors affecting output growth in the Malaysian food sector were individual contributions of capital, labor, and materials as well as the combined contribution of the quality of these inputs. Consequently, he explains the low productivity levels seen prior to 1987 in the food manufacturing industry by the low quality of inputs used by the industry.

Further, another study on the Malaysian food manufacturing industry by Yodfiatfinda et al. (2012) showed that the significant drivers of productivity growth and efficiency of large scale enterprises that were significant were public infrastructure, information technology (IT) expenditure, and foreign ownership; while energy prices were a determinant with a negative relationship. These authors used the data envelopment analysis (DEA) approach.

In Nigeria, Ohaka and Agundu (2014) used financial (secondary) data obtained from a net sample of 58 firms quoted on the Nigerian Stock Exchange to confirm that tax incentives were among the determinants of their financial performance. However, they only used firm productivity, especially in the food manufacturing industry.

In Uganda, Mayende (2013) analyzed the effects of tax incentives on the performance of manufacturing firms in terms of gross sales and value-added using panel data estimation techniques and showed that firms with tax incentives performed better. Another finding of Mayende's study was that the education level of managers, firm size, and firm experience had a positive impact on a firm's performance. In Kenya, Heshmati and Rashidghalam (2016), used the World Bank's Enterprise Survey database for 2013 and found that capital intensity and wage significantly and positively affected labor productivity in terms of sales and value added.

Apart from these studies which focus on manufacturing firms' performance determinants, there are no studies that emphasize the role of fiscal incentives for boosting production levels of the food and beverage manufacturing industries in the sub-Saharan region to the best of our knowledge. Hence, this study goes beyond productivity and financial performance and analyzes how fiscal incentives can help to raise capacity utilization of food and beverage manufacturing firms.

3 Methodology and Data

3.1 The Model

Like Afrooz et al. (2011), Ahmed (2012), and Heshmati and Rashidghalam (2016), this study uses the Cobb–Douglas production function. According to this approach, the production of the ith firm in the food or in the beverage manufacturing industry can be represented by a production function as

$$Q_i = F(K_i, L_i, M_i, Z_i) \qquad (1)$$

where output Q is a function of industrial capital input K, labor input L, intermediate input M, and other factors Z. The variable Z can designate raw materials' cost and quality, company experience, specific technology, skills of the labor force, and managers' efforts. These variables interact and mutually condition one another in determining firms' production levels.

To explain, we refer to the Cobb–Douglas production function defined as

$$Q = AK^\beta L^\rho \qquad (2)$$

where Q is the amount of products; K and L are the level of capital and labor inputs respectively; and variable A designates other production factors, namely, raw materials, market demand, and a qualified workforce. Parameters β and ρ can be defined as elasticities of the quantity produced with respect to capital and labor, respectively.

Further, we define *capacity utilization* as the ratio of actual production output and potential production output as

$$cu = \frac{Q}{Q^*} \tag{3}$$

where cu represents capacity utilization, Q the actual output level, and Q^* is potential output.

Combining Eqs. (2) and (3), we obtain the following capacity utilization expression:

$$cu = \frac{A}{Q^*} K^\beta L^\rho \tag{4}$$

All variables are defined as earlier. Here the ratio $\frac{A}{Q^*}$ designates the input–output ratio, and measures how the firm is material-intensive. This ratio is a standardization and allows us to consider the heterogeneity of the sub-sectors within the food and beverage manufacturing sectors. To consider more determinants of capacity utilization, we use the augmented Cobb–Douglas production function.

Thus, the relationship between capacity utilization and economic factors characterizing the firms is described as

$$q_i = \alpha + \beta a_i + \varphi k_i + \rho l_i + \delta m_i + \omega sh_i + \sum \gamma_i Z_i + \varepsilon_i \tag{5}$$

Variable ε_i is the error term possessing all traditional characteristics. Variables q, a, k, l, m, sh, and Z are capacity utilization, input–output ratio, capital, labor, cost of raw materials, share of raw materials sourced in Rwanda, and other factors influencing capacity utilization, respectively; subscript i designates a firm unit. Variables are in log form, except the qualitative determinants of capacity utilization. The last is considered as dummy variables and have a value 1 when they are considered as a problem limiting the production of the firm and value 0 when they are not considered a problem. Parameters α, β, φ, ρ, δ, ω, and γ are estimates of the model.

Variables in dummy form and not specified here are insufficient demand, shortage of qualified labor, shortage of raw materials, shortage of power and electricity, shortage of water, shortage of road infrastructure, lack of specialized technology, lack of working capital, old equipment, tax rates, tax administration, and standards. We considered companies' reports on their perceptions about each variable as a limiting factor of their capacity utilization. Each limiting factor was assessed using three levels of painfulness: not a problem; a moderate problem; and a significant problem. We considered a limitation factor as a problem if it was reported as a moderate or a significant problem. Otherwise, we considered that it was not a problem for the company. The model (Eq. 5) was estimated using the ordinary least squares technique. The same technique has also been used in literature (see Afrooz et al. 2011; Ahmed 2012).

3.2 Data

This study used data from the manufacturing industry's survey by the Rwandese Ministry of Trade and Industry (MINICOM) from October 2013 to February 2014. This survey covered the period corresponding to fiscal year 2012 and three quarters of 2013. The survey collected information about employees, fixed assets, capacity utilization and its limiting factors, years of operation in the sector, and inputs used and their sources. In this study, the data meets the variables in Eq. (5), that is, estimated capacity utilization, input–output ratio, capital, labor, cost of raw materials, share of inputs sourced in Rwanda, and other variables. The estimated capacity utilization was reported by companies. This reported capacity utilization is preferred because it considers the firms' production seasonality. The input–output ratio was computed using the input volume required if the firm operated using 100% machine capacity per day and the total installed capacity per day. For capital and labor inputs, we used total fixed assets and total employees in 2012. We calculated the costs of raw materials by multiplying the value of intermediate inputs used per day and the intermediate input volume used per day. The share of inputs sourced in Rwanda was also reported by the companies.

4 Empirical Findings and Interpretation

We start by giving the descriptive statistics of the keys variables, i.e. number of employees, share of inputs sourced in Rwanda and experience (age) of a company.

4.1 Descriptive Statistics

4.1.1 Permanent Employees

Most of the food and beverage manufacturing companies are small in size. During the survey period, the average number of employees was 15 and 9, respectively, in the food and beverage manufacturing firms. Using the MINICOM (2010) categorization,[1] in the beverage manufacturing sector, out of 60 enterprises which reported their workforce status, 27.27% were micro-enterprises, 66.67% were small enterprises, 6.06% were medium enterprises, and there were no large firms. In the food processing sector, of the 127 firms which reported their workforce status, only 1.57% were large, 5.52% were medium, 61.41% were small, and 31.50% were micro-enterprises.

---

[1] Through the SMEs' development policy, Ministry of Trade and Commerce defines a micro-enterprise as a company having less than 4 employees; a small enterprise between 4 and 30 employees; a medium enterprise between 31 and 100 employees; and a large enterprise having more than 100 employees.

Consequently, we can observe that most of the firms were micro and small sized in the two sectors. With reference to literature (Atmaja 2008; Hanazaki and Liu 2007) these small firms are usually family controlled and face severe internal financing constraints which restrict their investments and competitiveness. Further, they face agency problems which raise conflicts between minority and large shareholders that negatively impact their entrepreneurial activities and probably also their capacity utilization.

4.1.2 Companies' Experience

When it comes to age (experience) the firms in the two sectors, were mostly young. Their average age was 5.17 and 3.57 operating years in the food and beverage sectors, respectively. In these two sectors, a large number of firms had been operating for five years or less in 2014 or 77.51% and 84.27%, respectively, in the food and beverage sectors. The oldest firm in the food sector had been operational for 79 years (only one company), while the oldest firm in the beverage sector had been operating for 15 years (also one firm). These figures show that most of the firms in the two sectors had entered the industry recently. In food processing, less than 7% of the firms had more than 10 years of operating experience, whereas in the beverage processing industry less than 3% had been in operation for more than 10 years. Thus, in comparison with beverage manufacturing firms the food processing firms had relatively more experience.

4.1.3 Share of Inputs Sourced in Rwanda

Surprisingly, almost all the firms used inputs from the domestic market—89.5 and 96.07% firms manufactured their products using 100% inputs from Rwanda in the food and the beverage sectors, respectively. Further, 50% or more of the inputs from Rwanda were used for manufacturing products by 96.31 and 98.69% firms in the food and beverage sectors, respectively. This shows that the food and beverage manufacturing industry is heavily dependent on the Rwandese internal market, not only for selling its products but also for procuring inputs.

Consequently, conditions in the domestic business environment determine firms' capacity utilization in these two sectors. Given that all these firms use inputs from the agriculture sector, we assume that the main determinant of their capacity utilization is the availability of agro-raw materials during their working period, that is, for their production and distribution.

4.2 Determinants of Capacity Utilization in the Food Manufacturing Industry

Table 1 summarizes the regression results obtained using Eq. (5). In the table, we can see that four variables negatively influenced capacity utilization: shortage of raw materials, shortage of specialized technologies, limited infrastructure, tax administration, and standards.

Table 1 Determinants of capacity utilization of food manufacturing firms in Rwanda

Variables	Coefficients	P-values
Log (input–output ratio)	−0.0405608	0.197
Log (fixed assets)	0.0443998	0.357
Log (employees)	0.0069612	0.939
Log (company age)	0.0634462	0.654
Log (share of inputs sourced in Rwanda)	−0.3731546	0.256
Log (raw materials cost)	−0.0044456	0.928
Insufficient demand (dummy)	0.0402074	0.825
Shortage of qualified labor (dummy)	0.4888373	0.021
Shortage of raw materials (dummy)	−0.2930969	0.083
Shortage of power electricity (dummy)	0.394466	0.049
Shortage of water (dummy)	−0.0421137	0.843
Lack of road infrastructure (dummy)	0.5337161	0.002
Lack of specialized technology (dummy)	−0.6229921	0.003
Lack of working capital (dummy)	0.1741905	0.334
Old equipment (dummy)	0.0429775	0.827
Tax rates (dummy)	0.1319389	0.603
Tax administration (dummy)	−0.5649931	0.007
Standards (dummy)	−0.4832884	0.015
Constant	4.749787	0.006
Number of obs	105	
F (18, 86)	3.76	
Prob > F	0.000	
R-squared	0.4407	
Adj R-squared	0.3236	
Root MSE	0.65421	

Source Authors' computation using data from the MINICOM manufacturing industry survey (2013–14)

According to Table 1, a shortage of raw materials undermines food manufacturing firms' capacity utilization in Rwanda. According to NISR (2016), this shortage is because of agriculture seasonality and the high costs of intermediate goods and services. Food manufacturing is the second industry using costlier intermediate materials after the electricity, water, and waste management industry. Consequently, food processing firms that use more raw materials are much more affected than those which use less. Coefficients of the variables 'input–output ratio' and 'input costs' are negative even if they are statistically not significant and relatively small. This is another explanation for the significance of raw materials in the food and beverage manufacturing industry. Incentives in this area are non-fiscal because till now agro-raw materials are not taxed in Rwanda. These incentives can be measures which guarantee availability of agro-raw materials throughout the year which will help firms reduce their costs.

Considering coefficients and statistical significance levels, food processing firms face three major challenges: lack of specialized technologies, tax administration, and standards. Here, we observe that tax incentives can boost capacity utilization of manufacturing firms through tax administration and compliance, for example, by simplifying tax assessments and returns, tax audits, and tax payments. Lowering tax rates is not yet a problem in boosting capacity utilization of food processing firms.

In contrast, two technical problems remain a big challenge for the food processing industry which are also interlinked: lack of specialized technologies and standards. As seen earlier, most of the food processing firms are young and very small. They are family companies, which use undeveloped technologies and suffer because of poor standards. Consequently, they have to face competition from bigger firms in the local market and are also unable to enter the international market because of fierce competition. Here, all kinds of subsidies are advisable to help them in raising their technology levels and standards. However, EAC[2] regulations must be examined closely and carefully. Although the beverage manufacturing industry has the same structure as the food processing industry, it faces different challenges.

4.3 Determinants of Capacity Utilization in the Beverage Manufacturing Industry

In the beverage manufacturing industry, two factors influence capacity utilization positively while four factors impact it negatively. The input–output ratio and company experience are factors which support beverage manufacturing firms' ability to produce more. However, a firm's fixed assets, shortage of demand, lack of working capital, and standards are negative drivers of capacity utilization in this industry.

---

[2]EAC is the East African Community, an inter-regional organization comprising Burundi, Kenya, Rwanda, Tanzania, and Uganda (recently, South Sudan joined the Community).

The input–output ratio is high in this industry[3] and, according to NISR (2016), it grows with the size of the manufacturing firm as given by the number of full-time employees. Even if companies report that they face a shortage of raw materials, this does not undermine their capacity utilization. Thus, being material-intensive is not a disadvantage for beverage manufacturing firms. Further, experience in beverage manufacturing boosts capacity utilization. For improving their experience by 100% firms need to increase their capacity utilization by 114%. This shows that as the firms grow in age, they are able to improve their technology and their management methods (Table 2).

In contrast, two factors are negatively interlinked and harm beverage manufacturing firms' capacity utilization. They are insufficient demand and product standards. As mentioned earlier, the beverage manufacturing industry has the same structure as the food processing industry. Firms are young and are almost small craft industries. Thus, they face problems of standards and as a consequence of demand. The problem of standards can be understood through the problem of lack of qualified labor. Here, the coefficient is negative and nearly significant. The appropriate incentives are those suggested for the food manufacturing sector, namely, subsidizing young and small firms.

Two other challenges are also interlinked: big fixed assets and lack of working capital. Capacity utilization is reduced as a firm is oversized in terms of fixed assets. Thus, more money is required for using its installed capacity in full. Here, action needs to be taken for easing access to finance for firms involved in beverage manufacturing activities, particularly the bigger ones. As compared to the food manufacturing firms, the capacity utilization of beverage manufacturing firms cannot be raised by any kind of tax incentives. Even if they report significant T-statistics, improving tax instruments like tax rates and administration will not raise capacity utilization in this industry.

Further, even if the sign of the coefficient of inputs' share sourced inside Rwanda is negative, it is not statistically significant. It is the same for input costs which have a positive coefficient, meaning that it does not damage the capacity utilization of beverage processing firms. Thus, tax reductions for inputs sourced in Rwanda for boosting capacity utilization of local beverage manufacturing firms is not required.

5 Summary and Conclusion

The objective of this study was determining factors of capacity utilization in the food and beverage manufacturing sectors. The data used was collected by the Ministry of Trade and Industry of Rwanda from October 2013 to February 2014, covering fiscal year 2012 and three quarters of 2013. The model used was derived from an

---

[3] According to NISR (2016), the input-output ratio is valued at 82.7% in the beverage and tobacco manufacturing sector, while the average for the entire manufacturing industry is 81.2%.

Table 2 Determinants of capacity utilization of beverage manufacturing firms

Variables	Coefficients	P-values
Log (input–output ratio)	0.1899247	0.001
Log (fixed assets)	−0.2435112	0.013
Log (employees)	0.1867568	0.257
Log (company experience)	1.142225	0.012
Log (input cost)	−0.2292847	0.626
Log (share of inputs sourced in Rwanda)	0.0968313	0.235
Insufficient demand (dummy)	−0.8886207	0.01
Shortage of qualified labor (dummy)	−0.4983392	0.182
Shortage of raw materials (dummy)	0.8597989	0.011
Shortage of power electricity (dummy)	−0.2573813	0.518
Shortage of water (dummy)	0.3344376	0.399
Lack of road infrastructure (dummy)	0.9260447	0.021
Lack of specialized technology (dummy)	−0.1055031	0.762
Lack of working capital (dummy)	−0.6334258	0.063
Old equipment (dummy)	−0.3111244	0.353
Tax rates (dummy)	0.7073018	0.048
Tax administration (dummy)	0.6879884	0.099
Standards (dummy)	−0.9269832	0.02
Constant	5.676852	0.026
Number of obs	84	
F (18, 65)	6.96	
Prob > F	0.000	
R-squared	0.6585	
Adj R-squared	0.5639	
Root MSE	1.0469	

Source Authors' computation using data from the MINICOM manufacturing industry survey (2013–14)

augmented Cobb–Douglas production function and was estimated using the OLS regression method.

The key results of the study include: (i) in the food manufacturing industry the main factors which undermine firms' capacity utilization are shortages of raw materials, lack of specialized technologies, tax administration, and standards; (ii) in the beverage manufacturing industry, the drivers of capacity utilization are firm experience and its material-intensive characteristics. However, four factors harm the capacity utilization of beverage manufacturing firms—being oversized in terms of fixed assets, lack of working capital, standards, and insufficient demand.

To boost capacity utilization of the food and beverage manufacturing sectors, only non-tax incentives are advisable. In particular, we suggest simplifying and easing the tax administration and compliance instruments in the food manufacturing sector. For addressing shortages of agro-raw materials, it is advisable to resort to non-tax measures, particularly those which guarantee availability of agro-raw materials throughout the year which will help reduce costs. We also suggest subsidizing firms, particularly young and small ones, to help them acquire appropriate technology and raise standards in the two sectors. These subsidies could focus mainly on R&D or related expenses. Further, it is recommended that financial regulations should be simplified to allow the beverage manufacturing firms to fund their working capital needs.

References

Afrooz, A., Rahim, K. B. A., & Edalati, A. (2011). Determinants of productivity in food industries of Iran. *Production Management, 38*, 4253–4256.
Ahmed, E. M. (2012). Malaysia's food manufacturing industries productivity determinants. *Modern Economy, 3*, 444–453.
Ali, J., Singh, S. P., & Ekanem, E. (2009). Efficiency and productivity changes in the Indian food processing industry: Determinants and policy implications. *International Food and Agribusiness Management Review, 12*(1), 43–66.
Atmaja, S. L. (2008). Corporate governance in family firms. *Journal Management Bisnis, 1*(1), 103–115.
Barbour, P. (2005). *An assessment of South Africa's investment incentive regime with a focus on the manufacturing sector* (ESAU Working Paper no. 14). Overseas Development Institute.
Färe, R., Grosskopf, S., & Kokkelenberg, E. C. (1989). Measuring plant capacity, utilisation and technical change: A non-parametric approach. *International Economic Review, 30*(3), 655–666.
Hanazaki, M., & Liu, Q. (2007). Corporate governance and investment in East Asian firms: Empirical analysis of family-controlled firms. *Journal of Asian Economics, 18*(1), 76–97.
Heshmati, A. & Rashidghalam, M. (2016). *Labour productivity in Kenyan manufacturing and service industries* (Working Paper IZA DP No. 9923).
Johansen, L. (1968). Production functions and the concept of capacity, in CERUN, *Recherches Récentes sur la Fonction de Production*. Facultés Universitaires N.-D. de la Paix, Collection 'Economie Mathématique et Econométrie' 2, 49–72.
Kransdorff, M. (2010). Tax incentives and foreign direct investment in South Africa. *Consilience: The Journal of Sustainable Development, 3*(1), 68–84.
Lai, Z. (2015). *Capacity utilization and productivity analysis in the Canadian food manufacturing industry*. M.Sc thesis, University of Guelph, Guelph, Ontario, Canada.
Mayende, S. (2013). The effects of tax incentives on firm performance: Evidence from Uganda. *Journal of Politics and Law, 6*(4), 95–107.
MINICOM. (2012). *Rwanda Industrial Survey 2011*. Kigali: MINICOM.
Ndemezo, E., & Baye, M. F. (2016). Evaluation of redistributive and welfare impacts of indirect taxes reform in Rwanda. In A. Heshmati (Ed.), *Poverty and well-being in East Africa: A multi-faceted*

economic approach. economic studies in inequality, social exclusion and well-being Series, XV (pp. 165–195). Switzerland: Springer International Publishing.

Nelson, R. A. (1989). On the measurement of capacity utilisation. *Journal of Industrial Economics, 37*, 273–286.

NISR. (2011). *Establishment census 2011: Analytical report*. Kigali: NISR.

NISR. (2016). *Integrated Business Enterprise Survey report 2014*. Kigali: NISR.

Ohaka, J., & Agundu, P. U. C. (2014). Tax incentives for industry synergy in Nigeria: A pragmatic proprietary system advocacy. *African Research Review, 6*(3), 42–54.

Shamsudin, M. N., Yodfiatfinda, M. Z. A., Yusop, Z., & Radam, A. (2011). Evaluation of market competitiveness of SMEs in the Malaysian food processing industry. *Journal of Agribusiness Marketing, 4*, 1–20

UNSD (2002). *International Standard Industrial Classification of all economic activities (ISIC Rev. 3.1)*. New York: UN.

Wentzel, M. S. I., & Steyn, M. (2014). Investment promotion in South African manufacturing industry: Incentive comparisons with Malaysia and Singapore. *AJEMS NS, 17*(3), 319–335.

Yodfiatfinda, N. M. S., Zainalabidin, M., Ariff, M. H., Zulkornain, Y., & Alias, R. (2012). The empirical evaluation of productivity growth and efficiency of LSEs in the Malaysian food processing industry. *International Food Research Journal, 19*(1), 287–295.

Chapter 13
Tax Incentives and Growth of SMEs in Rwanda: A Case Study of Small and Medium Enterprises in Nyarugenge District

Daniel Twesige, Faustin Gasheja, and Jonas Barayendema

Abstract This study analyzes the effect of tax incentives on the growth of SMEs in Rwanda taking SMEs in Nyarugenge as a case study. It uses both qualitative and quantitative research approaches. The population is 49,000 SMEs from agricultural, industrial, service, and tourism sectors operating in Nyarugenge district. The study uses a sample of 136 SMEs using Silovin and Yemen's formula of sample size by using the simple random and purposive sampling techniques. The dataset is analyzed using descriptive statistics and a multiple regression analysis is used for explaining the relationships between the variables. The results show that 75.7% of the respondents knew the tax laws and 78.7% knew the tax incentives available to SMEs. The results further show that wear and tear, loss carried forward, and value-added tax (VAT) refunds are tax incentives available to Rwandan SMEs as evidenced by 100%, 94.1%, and 95.6%, respectively, of the respondents receiving the benefits. The study also shows that there is a strong, positive, and significant relationship between tax incentives and the growth of small and medium enterprises in Rwanda as the coefficients of correlation are 88.8% of R-square. This means that only 11.2% of the variations in the growth of SMEs is outside the tested variables. The study concludes that tax incentives are the key to sustainable growth of SMEs. Hence, the government should design policies that specifically address issues related to SMEs' sustainable growth.

Keywords Tax · Tax incentives · SMEs · Growth

Code 126

D. Twesige (✉) · F. Gasheja · J. Barayendema
School of Business, University of Rwanda CBE, Kigali, Rwanda
e-mail: twesiged@yahoo.com

© Springer Nature Singapore Pte Ltd. 2020
G. G. Das and R. B. Johnson (eds.), *Rwandan Economy at the Crossroads of Development*, Frontiers in African Business Research,
https://doi.org/10.1007/978-981-15-5046-1_13

1 Introduction

The theory behind using tax incentives for promoting SMEs comes from the finance theory of the net present value (NPV) decision rule. The rule states that firms continue to spend on capital assets and R&D as long as the present value from an additional unit of capital or R&D is equal to or exceeds the cost of the additional unit. Consequently, it is assumed that businesses will consider tax implications in their calculations of the value of their expenditure decisions since any reduction in the cost of capital because of a tax policy leads to an equal increase in expenditure (Hansson and Brokelind 2014).

SMEs play a vital role in a country's economic development. Studies have shown that SMEs contribute more than 50% to the GDP of many developing countries. Further, SMEs are the largest employers as they employ more than 90% of the workforce.

In a bid to stimulate growth among SMEs, a number of countries have used tax incentives for both investors and listing firms for promoting activities on the SMEs' boards. Tax incentives for investors are a common approach, particularly in advanced markets (Mintz and Chen 2011). For instance, Poland adopted a policy of encouraging investments in SMEs by removing the so-called 'back-end' taxes, which are taxes levied on profits made when selling a security.

In South Korea and India, investors benefit from reduced capital gains taxes on SMEs' equity investments. This is done via the cutting of short-term capital gains tax to half, from 30 to 15% for SMEs' shares that are listed. UK and Spain have adopted tax incentive policies where retail investors may deduct a set percentage of the value they invest in shares in SMEs' equity.

Though these policies have been adopted, their possible outcomes may not significantly affect entrepreneurs as their interest lies in the capital influx from equity offerings in SMEs (Bertrand and Mullainathan 2003).

Belgium offers several investment allowances. The general investment deductions for SMEs amount to 10.5% of the depreciation taken for assets. This rate has varied between 10.5 and 12.5% since 2009. These incentives are restricted to companies with fewer than 20 employees. Additionally, an allowance of 20.5% is granted to SMEs for investments in safety measures either in the year of the investment or the following year. The same rules apply for carryforwards. A national interest deduction of 4% of qualifying equity is available for all Belgian companies. SMEs, however, are allowed to deduct an additional 0.5%. Since 2012, carryforwards are no longer allowed (De Wit and De Kok 2014; Devereux et al. 2014).

Austria does not offer special tax incentives for SMEs at the firm level. There is only an adjusted minimum tax for newly founded companies of € 1,092 that only benefits low-income companies. On the shareholder level, Austria grants full exemption to income from participation in unlisted European SMEs (that is, dividends, capital gains, and interest payments) for so-called intermediary investors. Intermediary investors must be corporate entities financed with equity capital. For individual investors, dividends from such intermediary investors are exempt from income taxation up to € 25,000. Enterprises are exempt from the value-added tax (VAT) if their turnover is less than € 35,000. Moreover, enterprises with less than a € 100,000 turnover in the preceding year only have to file VAT returns and make VAT payments on a quarterly basis (instead of monthly). Suppliers with a turnover of less than € 110,000 may pay VAT on a cash basis (De Wit and De Kok 2014).

Bulgaria does not have special tax incentives for SMEs. Small companies are subject to administrative relief though. Enterprises whose net sales in the previous year were below BGR 300,000 (≈€ 150,000) do not have to make advance tax payments and those with net sales below BGN 3,000,000 (≈€ 1,500,000) only have to make quarterly advance payments (instead of monthly). In addition, simplified accounting standards apply to SMEs. VAT registration is only required for enterprises with more than BGN 50,000 in turnover (De Wit and De Kok 2014; Fletcher 2003; Bahizi 2013).

Croatia provides comprehensive incentives for investments in new undertakings. Income from new investments (also by existing enterprises) can be subject to corporate income tax rates that are reduced by up to 100% for 10 years. The exact amount of the reduction depends on the size of the investment and on the number of newly created jobs related to the investment: 100% reduction if there is an investment of at least € 3 million and related to 15 new employees; 75% reduction if the investment is at least € 1 million and related to 10 new employees; and 50% reduction if investment is less than € 1 million and related to five new employees (De Wit and De Kok 2014).

Finland does not have tax incentives specifically targeted at SMEs. There is a regime of accelerated depreciation for fixed assets being used in production activities (200% of the usual depreciation rate on machinery, equipment, and industrial buildings). The regime was restricted to SMEs till 2013 but is now available for all enterprises. Moreover, with a super deduction of 100% for salary costs incurred for R&D projects being capped at € 400,000, SMEs should benefit more than large enterprises. Businesses with less than € 8,500 in turnover are exempt from VAT. If the turnover is below € 25,000, only yearly VAT payments need to be made and if it is below € 50,000 only quarterly payments are required (instead of monthly). Moreover, SMEs are subject to reduced documentation requirements with regard to transfer prices (De Wit and De Kok 2014).

Zimbabwe provides investment incentives with six objectives: employment creation; small business development; industrial development; export promotion; spatial development; and 'upliftment' of the disadvantaged. Many of the incentives take the form of financing arrangements, which operate through the Ministry of Industry and International Trade, the Industrial Development Corporation, and the Zimbabwe Investment Center. The most extensive tax incentives accrue to exporters. Under the Export Processing Zone Act of 1995, enterprises in manufacturing, processing, or services are licensed by an EPZ (Kaplan 2001). Authority to operate in an EPZ is related to obtaining a 5-year tax holiday, followed by a rate of 15% Corporate income tax. EPZ companies also receive standard duty-free access to imports and refunds on sales tax for domestically procured goods and services. In addition, they are exempt from capital gains tax, shareholder's tax, and non-resident tax on interest, fees, royalties, and remittances. Other exporters outside EPZs qualify for a rebate or drawback of certain duties on imported inputs. Since January 2003, manufacturers who export 50% or more of their volumes are taxed at 20%. Finally, exporters can take a double deduction for export marketing costs. Tax holidays apply to other activities as well. Tourism operators in approved tourist development zones benefit from a 5-year corporate income tax holiday, followed by a 15% reduction in the tax rate. The same provisions apply to industrial park developers. Build-own-operate-transfer projects have a 5-year corporate income tax holiday, followed by 15% corporate income tax rate for 5 years, 20% for 5 years, and then the normal tax rate. In growth point areas, approved manufacturers get a 10% tax rate, while certain infrastructure projects get a 15% rate. Special investment allowances also apply to a limited set of beneficiaries (Kaplan 2001).

The aim of Tanzania's tax incentive programs is attracting productive investments, creating employment, and enhancing exports. The Tanzania Investment Act of 1997 provides the basic framework for promoting investments though associated tax measures are incorporated into the respective tax legislations. A major change was made in 1997 to end income tax holidays outside export processing zones, in favor of expensing capital assets and remissions from customs duty on capital goods for holders of a Certificate of investment from Tanzania (Zee et al. 2002).

Tax incentives in Kenya can be grouped into investment-promotion incentives and export promotion incentives. Investment-promotion incentives include an investment deduction allowance which was introduced in 1991 to encourage investments in physical capital such as industrial buildings, machinery, and equipment. Industrial building allowances were introduced in 1974 with the objective of encouraging investments in buildings used for industrial purposes like hotels and manufacturing plants. A mining deduction allowance which was introduced to encourage investors to venture into the mining industry which is very capital intensive and farm works deductions were introduced in 1985 to encourage investments in the agricultural sector.

The export promotion incentives program has three main schemes—export processing zones (EPZs), manufacture under bond (MUB), and the Tax Remissions and Exemption Office (TREO). EPZs' objective is generating and encouraging economic activities and foreign direct investments while MUB and TREO are meant to encourage investors to manufacture for export (Githaiga 2013).

The Rwanda fiscal policy provides various tax incentives with the aim of enhancing business and foreign direct investments. The Rwanda Investment Board provides tax incentives such as accelerated depreciation of 50% for investments in new or used assets, a preferential corporate income tax rate of 0 and 15% for registered investors, and tax holidays of seven and five years. In addition to the tax incentives provided for investments, a number of tax incentives are also provided in the fiscal tax law. These include loss carried forward for a period of five years and exemption of some income and allowance for some expenses like research and development. All these incentives are aimed at promoting businesses in Rwanda (MINECOFIN 2012).

SMEs play a very important role in many developing countries. Young (2009) observes that in developing countries, in particular, the health of the economy as a whole has a strong relationship with the health and nature of SMEs. In Rwanda, for example, SMEs contribute more than 60% to the new jobs created. Due to the importance of SMEs in the Rwandan economy, the Government of Rwanda has made notable interventions by putting in place measures like the Umurenge SACCOs that are geared toward promoting and developing SMEs (MINICOM et al. 2017).

A study by MINICOM et al. (2017) showed that 99.9% of the population was employed by small and medium enterprises and only 0.1% by large enterprises. This implies that a large workforce was employed by SMEs. Despite their significance and the financial support given to them, the SMEs are faced with a threat of failure with past statistics indicating that three out of five fail within the first few months of starting operations. According to MINCOM et al. (2017), only a fraction of the establishments started in 2010–17 remain operational. The effects of SMEs shutting down are loss of jobs and assets as well as GDP. However, despite the importance of sustainability and continuity of SMEs, studies solely focusing on whether tax incentives affect SMEs' growth in developing countries, particularly in Rwanda, seem to be very limited and scarce. It is in this context, that researchers want to investigate the effects of tax incentives on the growth of SMEs in Rwanda.

This study answers two main questions:

1. *Do Rwanda's tax laws provide tax incentives that support the growth of SMEs?*
2. *Are there significant effects between tax incentives and SMEs' growth?*

2 Theoretical and Conceptual Framework

2.1 Neoclassical Theory

The neoclassical economic theory argues that providing tax incentives to one group of investors rather than another violates one of the principal tenets of a good tax system, that of horizontal equity. This inequality distorts the price signals faced by potential investors and leads to an inefficient allocation of capital (Comanor 1967). The justification that is most often given for special incentives is that there are market failures surrounding the decisions to invest in certain sectors and locations which justify government intervention.

Market failures result in either too much or too little investment in certain sectors or locations. A key market failure most often cited is positive externalities not internalized in a project's rate of returns that are higher in certain sectors than in others. An example is research and development where investments yield a higher social rate of returns than a private rate of returns because not all the technological knowledge can be effectively patented and as such there exists a justification for subsidizing investments in research and development (Kaplan 2001).

Colmar (2005) points out that there are other purported benefits of tax incentives such as symbolic signaling effects and the need to compensate for inadequacies in the investment regime elsewhere. Investment incentives are provided either as tax relief or cash grants. International experience shows that such incentives play only a minor role in investment decisions. Firms take investment decisions based on many factors including projections for future demand, certainty about future government policies, prevailing interest rates, and moves by competitors. In general, neo-classics see incentives as 'nice to have' but not deal-breaking. Yet incentives remain a popular policy in both developed and developing countries.

2.2 Agency Theory of Tax Incentives

According to Zee et al. (2002), despite lack of evidence to support the efficacy or efficiency of fiscal incentives, governments continue to offer them. Tax incentives offer an easy way to compensate for other government-created obstacles in the business environment. In other words, fiscal incentives respond as much to government failures as they do to market failures. It is far harder and takes far longer, for governments from the developing countries to tackle the investment impediments themselves like a low skill base and regulatory and compliance costs than to put in place a grant or tax regime to help counterbalance these impediments. Although it is a second-best solution to providing a subsidy to counteract an existing distortion, this is what often happens in practice.

Agency problems also exist between government agencies responsible for attracting investments and those responsible for a more generic business environment. While investment-promotion agencies can play an important role in coordinating government activities to attract investments, they often argue for incentives without taking into account the costs borne by the economy as a whole (Zee et al. 2002).

2.3 Tax Incentives Theory

UNCTAD (2003) defines tax incentives as instruments that reduce the tax burden for a party to induce it to invest in particular projects or sectors. They are exceptions to the general tax regime and include reduced tax rates on profits; tax holidays; accounting rules that allow accelerated depreciation and loss carryforwards for tax purposes; and reduced tariffs on imported equipment, components, and raw materials, or increased tariffs to protect the domestic market. The Kenya Revenue Authority (KRA) defines tax incentives as a provision that grants any person or activity favorable conditions that deviate from the normal provisions of the tax legislation. Tax expenditures refer to revenue losses that a government incurs by providing tax exemptions, deductions or allowances, tax credits, preferential tax rates or deferral of tax payments legally to any party in the economy (Gravelle 2013).

A government's budget deficit is a form of a negative saving and a reduction in the deficit can positively influence the net national savings more than any feasible changes in tax policies and encourage savings within an economy which will then stimulate investments (Goolsbee 2004). Keen (2013) defines tax incentives as all measures and strategies which provide for more favorable tax treatment to certain activities or sectors; he goes on to describe the following to be typical tax incentives:

i. Tax holidays: temporal exemptions in business investments from certain specified taxes, typically at least corporate income tax. Partial tax holidays offer reduced obligations rather than full exemption.
ii. Special zones: are placed in geographically limited areas where qualified companies can locate and hence benefit from various exemptions in taxes or administrative requirements.
iii. Investment tax credit: deduction of some fraction of an investment from tax liability.
iv. Investment allowance/accelerated depreciation: deduction of some fraction of an investment from taxable profits (in addition to depreciation).
v. Reduced tax rates/preferential tax rates: reduction in a tax rate, specifically the corporate income tax rate.
vi. Exemptions from various taxes: exemptions from certain taxes, most of the time those collected at the border such as tariffs, excise, and VAT on imported inputs.
vii. Financing incentives: reductions in tax rates for fund providers, for example, reduced withholding taxes on dividends.
viii. Loss carried forward: when a business has a loss, the loss can be carried forward to offset the business' future profits.

2.4 SMEs' Growth

Countries that have tax incentives for SMEs claim that preferential tax treatment creates a large number of jobs and enhances the level of entrepreneurship that is associated with flexibility, speed, risk-taking, and innovations (Chen et al. 2002). Berger and Udell (1998) emphasize that SMEs are key drivers of economic success because they are job creators, sales generators, and a source of tax revenue. These authors base their assertions on the fact that a large percentage of SMEs contribute to various countries' gross domestic product, they employ a large percentage of the workforce, and lead to high ratios of small businesses vis-à-vis large businesses in the countries concerned.

According to Berger and Udell (1998), SMEs represent a fertile ground for the development of large, profitable, tax-paying employers, and SMEs experience high growth rates in comparison to large enterprises. However, tax policies that are aimed at promoting the economic growth of small businesses should be evaluated judiciously because the inherent characteristics of small businesses can make a specific differentiated tax policy undesirable. Studies undertaken in this regard have come up with the following findings: a majority of the SMEs have limited growth potential; small businesses vary in terms of productivity, job growth, wages, innovations, and export performance within the same industry subgroups. Small businesses also do not follow the same growth patterns. Certain small businesses will remain small for most of their existence and it is for this reason that it is not obvious why a tax system influences the growth process. Such interventions, to the extent that they do not act in a lump-sum way, influence marginal decisions and could lead to excessive risk-taking and overinvestments (Heshmati 2001).

2.5 Business Environment in Rwanda

The World Bank's Doing Business Report (2013) ranked Rwanda 32nd out of 189 countries which was a significant jump up by 22 positions from the previous year. The country excelled in registering property and starting businesses by entering the top 10 countries worldwide. In Rwanda, it takes only 12 days to register a property and 2 days to start a business, which is far less than the regional averages and even the OECD average. Several reforms have contributed to improving the business environment. For example, in recent years, Rwanda has reduced the time required to obtain a registration certificate for starting a business. It has also eased transferring property by eliminating the requirement for a tax clearance certificate and by implementing the web-based Land Administration Information System for processing land transactions. Privatization of state-owned enterprises and reforming to come up with a pro-investment policy has been done for attracting foreign direct investments (FDI). However, despite no limits on foreign investments, participation, or control of enterprises, FDI levels are still low.

Businesses in Rwanda are categorized into four depending on their level of sales. If the annual turnover ranges from FRW 2,000,000 to 12,000,000 the business is classified as a micro business; if it has an annual turnover of 12,000,001 to 20,000,000 it is classified as a small business; and if it has an annual turnover of FRW 20,000,001 to 200, 000,000 it is classified as a medium business. A business with an annual turnover of FRW 200,000,000 is classified as a large business. The micro and small businesses are taxed under a lump-sum tax regime whereas the medium and large businesses are taxed under a real tax regime.

This study developed a conceptual framework which represents a synthesis of literature on how to explain a phenomenon. It illustrates actions required given other researchers' points of view and the author's own observations to show the relationship between the variables (Fig. 1).

As illustrated in Fig. 1 the independent variables, that is, those variables which are believed to play a role in the growth of SMEs as measured by an increase in their assets, retained earnings, and a sustainable growth rate are: investment allowance, loss carried forward, and wear and tear. However, for the relationship to hold, government

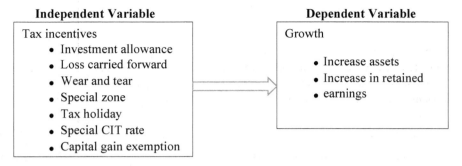

Fig. 1 Conceptual framework of the study. *Source* Author's formulation (2019)

policy and economic conditions must also be considered. Therefore, this study defines them as intermediate variables.

3 Research Methodology

This section describes the research methodology and instruments used in the study. It covers the research design, survey population, sample size, sampling procedures, sources of data, data collection instruments, validity and reliability of the research instruments, a measurement of research variables, and a measurement of research instruments. It also shows how the research was processed, analyzed, and presented.

3.1 Research Design

The study design is based on a multi-method strategy which used both qualitative and quantitative research approaches. It used a case study and a survey strategy, and this helped in the triangulation of different strategies. According to Kothari (2000) a multi-method strategy is followed when more than one research approach and data source are used in a study of a social phenomenon. A multi-method approach can be undertaken within a single research strategy by using multiple sources of data or across research strategies (Kothari 2000). A combination of qualitative and quantitative design approaches has been recommended and used by researchers in situations where one of the approaches is insufficient to show all that is required to be known about a phenomenon (Kothari 2000).

3.2 Study Population

Study population is a group of elements/items/or people in which the study is interested. The study population of this study was 49,000 SMEs in Nyarugenge district registered with RRA. However, the study targeted managers/owners and accountants/directors of finance of the SMEs.

3.3 Sample Size and Sampling Procedure

In selecting a sample an optimum sample size was considered. According to Kothari (2000), an optimum sample is one which fulfills the requirements of efficiency, representativeness, reliability, and flexibility. To determine the sample size, the study used Solvin and Yamen's formula ($n = N/(1 + N(e)^2)$), where 136 SMEs were selected from 49000 SMEs.

3.4 Data Source and Research Instruments

Both primary and secondary data was used in this study. The primary data was obtained through questionnaires while documentary techniques were used for collecting secondary data. The questionnaires were close-ended and self-administered. Close-ended questionnaires are recommended in social science research due to their advantages over open-ended questionnaires.

3.5 Data Processing and Analysis

Data was first collected through a primary survey after which a secondary survey was compiled, sorted, edited, and coded to have the required quality accuracy and was analyzed statistically using the Statistical Package for Social Scientists (SPSS). A principal component analysis approach and varimax rotation methods were used to determine the factors that explain tax incentives. The results of the analysis were put in tables for interpretation. Pearson's correlation was used for establishing the relationship between tax incentives and SMEs' growth. A multiple regression analysis was used for examining the model on tax incentives and growth of SMEs. A T-test was used to examine the variability of each variable of tax incentives.

The model's equations are
Growth $(G) = F$ (tax incentives (TI))

$$G = \beta_0 + \beta_1 \text{TI} + \alpha \qquad (1)$$

TI = F (accelerated depreciation (AD), loss carried forward (LC), wear and tear (WT), research and development (RD), and capital gain exemption (CE)
Capital gain exemption

$$TI = \beta_0 + \beta_1 AD + \beta_2 LC + \beta_4 WT + \beta_5 RD + \beta_6 LCF + \beta_7 ST + \beta_8 CE + \alpha \quad (2)$$

Substituting Eq. (1) gives

$$G = \beta_0 + \beta_1 AD + \beta_2 LC + \beta_4 WT + \beta_5 RD + \beta_6 LCF + \beta_7 ST + \beta_8 CE + \alpha \quad (3)$$

4 Results and Discussion

This section presents the results and a discussion of the survey.

Table 1 shows the type of industry of the responding SME, where respondents in the agriculture sector constituted 0%; commerce constituted 47.8%; services constituted 36%; consultancies constituted 10.3%; and education constituted 0%. As seen, most of the respondents were involved in the commerce sector.

Table 2 gives the results of an enquiry about the understandability of tax laws in Rwanda, where 30.9% of the respondents said that they strongly agreed, 44.8% agreed. and 24.3% disagreed when asked if they understood the tax laws in Rwanda.

Table 1 Type of industry all tables need to be mentioned in text

Type of industry		Frequency	Percent	Valid percent	Cumulative percent
Valid	Agriculture	0	0	0	0
	Commerce	73	53.7	53.7	53.7
	Service	49	36	36	83.8
	Consultancy	14	10.3	10.3	94.1
	Education	0	0	0	100.0
	Total	136	100.0	100.0	

Source Primary data (2019)

Table 2 Respondents' views on understanding the tax laws in Rwanda

		Frequency	Percent	Valid percent	Cumulative percent
Valid	Strongly agree	42	30.9	30.9	30.9
	Agree	61	44.8	44.8	75.7
	Disagree	33	24.3	24.3	100.0
	Total	136	100.0	100.0	

Source Primary data (2019)

Table 3 Respondents' views on awareness about the tax incentives available in tax laws

		Frequency	Percent	Valid percent	Cumulative percent
Valid	Strongly agree	39	28.7	28.7	28.7
	Agree	68	50	50	78.7
	Disagree	29	21.3	21.3	100.0
	Total	136	100.0	100.0	

Source Primary data (2019)

The results of the survey show that a majority of the respondents understood the tax laws (75.7% of the answers). The results of the survey conform with Vann and Holland's (1998) findings. These findings show that taxation means contribution imposed by the government on its people or on an individual or on companies for the use of services or facilities that it provides (Vann and Holland 1998).

Table 3 gives responses to the question whether they were aware of the tax incentives available in tax laws. The results show that 28.7% of the respondents strongly agreed, 50% agreed, and 21.3% disagreed. So, a large number of respondents were aware of the tax incentives available in tax laws. The results relate to Keen's (2013) findings. According to Keen (2013), tax incentives are seen as measures and strategies which provide more favorable tax treatment to certain activities or sectors.

Table 4 shows the tax incentives enjoyed by SMEs in Rwanda, where 42.6% of the respondents mentioned that they accelerated depreciation; 100% respondents mentioned wear and tear; 94.1% mentioned loss carried forward; and none of the respondents mentioned tax holiday, special CIT and special zones and listed shares as tax incentives; 58.8% of the respondents mentioned research and development and capital gain exemptions. The results show that SMEs' enjoy various tax incentives. However, the ones that they enjoy the most include wear and tear loss carried forward, and accelerated depreciation (Table 4). The results relate to the findings of UNCTAD (2003). The UNCTAD study showed that there were various tax incentives available in the tax laws that supported SMEs. The study by UNCTAD defines tax incentives as any incentive that reduces the tax burden of any party to induce it to invest in particular projects or sectors. These are exceptions to the general tax regime and may include, reduced tax rates on profits; tax holidays; accounting rules that allow

Table 4 Distribution of respondents by tax incentives enjoyed by SMEs

Tax incentive	Frequency	Percentage
Accelerated depreciation/investment allowance	58	42.6
Wear and tear	136	100
Loss carried forward	128	94.1
Research and development	80	58.8
Capital gain exemption	58	42.6

Source Primary data (2019)

Table 5 Level of SMEs' sales and profits

Years	Sales (FRW)	Profits (FRW)
2013	6,765,146,070	135,302,934
2014	14,710,080,125	323,621,763
2015	19,052,671,910	476,316,798
2016	23,462,405,030	610,022,531
2017	31,050,521,520	838,364,081
2018	40.050,935,745	1,241,579,000

Source Primary data (2019)

accelerated depreciation and loss carryforwards for tax purposes; reduced tariffs on imported equipment, components, and raw materials; or increased tariffs to protect the domestic market.

Table 5 shows the level of sales and profits of SMEs in 2013–18 where sales and profits increased year to year. Based on these results from their financial statements the SMEs' financial performance was good. As profitability is a measure of the amount by which a company's revenues exceed its relevant expenses, the results show that an increase in sales raised the profitability of SMEs during the study period. This means that tax incentives had an effect on SMEs' sales and profitability. The findings also relate to Külter and Demirgüneş' (2007) findings which show that SMEs' revenue and profitability were affected by tax incentives.

Table 6 shows the level of investments in assets in SMEs in 2013–18. As shown in the table, the level of investments in assets increased indicating that SMEs' performance was good. The findings conform with previous studies, for example, Goolsbee (2004), that assets are probable future economic benefits obtained or controlled by a particular entity as a result of past transactions or events.

Table 6 Level of investments in SMEs' assets

Years	Assets (FRW)
2013	29,471,200,000
2014	38,901,984,000
2015	44,673,981,200
2016	49,451,730,600
2017	57,321,545,100
2018	68,345,217,000

Source Primary data (2019)

4.1 Relationship Between Tax Incentives and Growth of SMEs in Rwanda

Considering the effect of tax incentives on the growth of SMEs in Rwanda, this study established the statistical relationship between tax incentives and promotion of SMEs in Rwanda using Pearson's correlation analysis using the Pearson moment correlation coefficient as given in Table 7.

Table 7 provides both the coefficient of determination which is adjusted R-squared and the coefficient of correlation which is R. The coefficient of determination ($R^2 = 0.788$) explains the explanatory power of the model and indicates that 78.8% of the variations in SMEs' growth is explained by the variations in the explanatory variables of investment allowance, loss carried forward, listing shares, and tax holidays. However, the adjusted R-square of 62.2% shows that there are other variables that affect SMEs' growth such as government policy and economic conditions which are not captured by the model formulated for the study that accounts for about 37.8% variations not explained by the model. The coefficient of correlation ($R = 0.888$) is greater than 0.5. This shows that there is a strong positive and moderate relationship between tax incentives and growth of SMEs. The results relate to findings by previous studies. Colmar (2005) identified a strong relationship between tax incentives and growth of SMEs. Similar findings are also seen in Chukwumerije Akinyomi's (2011) study.

Table 7 Model summary

Model	R	R-square	Adjusted R-square	Std. error of the estimate
1	0.888[a]	0.788	0.622	0.24618

[a]Predictors:(constant), investment allowance, loss carried forward, wear and tear, tax holiday
Source Primary data (2019)

Table 8 Estimated coefficients of the model

Model		Unstandardized coefficients		Standardized coefficients	T	Sig.
		B	Std. error	Beta		
1	(Constant)	0.821	0.301		2.727	0.004
	Investment allowance	0.636	0.216	0.822	2.941	0.037
	Loss carried forward	0.773	0.289	386	2.674	0.000
	Research and development	0.664	0.234	0.469	2.874	0.056
		0.686	0.272	0.356	2.522	0.001
	Wear and Tear Capital gain	0.715	0.281	0.427	2.544	0.057

[a]Dependent variable: SMEs assets
Source Primary data (2019)

Table 8 shows the estimated coefficients of the regression model used in this study. From the findings, all the coefficients are statistically significant considering the positive values of the coefficients and a significance level greater than 0.05. Specifically, there is a correlation between investment allowance and growth of SMEs ($b = 0.636$, sig $= 0.037$) indicating that the investment allowance itself explains 63.6% of the variations in the effectiveness of the growth of SMEs. Moreover, there is a significant and strong positive relationship between loss carried forward and evaluations with SMEs' growth ($b = 0.773$, sig $= 0.000$) indicating that 77.3% of the variations in SMEs' growth is explained by loss carried forward. Research and development has a significant and positive relationship with the growth of SMEs ($b = 0.664$, sig $= 0.056$) indicating that 66.4% of the variations in the growth of SMEs is explained by tax holidays. Wear and tear has a significant and positive relationship with the growth of SMEs ($b = 0.686$, sig $= 0.001$) indicating that 68.6% of the variations in the growth of SMEs is explained by listing shares. Capital gains have a significant and positive relationship with the growth of SMEs ($b = 0.715$, sig $= 0.057$) indicating that 71.5% of the variations in the growth of SMEs is explained by capital gains. These results relate to Chukwumerije and Akinyomi's (2011) findings which showed a significant effect of investment allowances, loss carried forward, tax holidays, listing shares, and preferential tax rates on SMEs' assets.

5 Conclusion and Recommendations

This section gives the general conclusions and some recommendations.

5.1 *Conclusion*

This research confirms that tax incentives are germane to the growth, development, and continued sustenance of small and medium enterprises. This is evidenced by a strong correlation between tax incentives and SMEs growth and the significance of tax incentive variables as shown in Tables 7 and 8. The results further revealed that most of the tax incentives that are available in tax laws are not enjoyed by SMEs; only the large taxpayers enjoy most of the tax incentives. Tax incentives play a vital role in ensuring that small and medium enterprises thrive because the government has made tax holidays for pioneer companies available, and the government also provides a number of general and industry-specific incentives. Finally, for many SMEs, the decision to remain informal is deliberate because the costs and procedural burdens of joining the formal sector outweigh the benefits of staying in the informal sector.

5.2 Recommendations

On the basis of the findings of this study the following recommendations are made:

i. The government can address the direct need for a start-up fund for SMEs by providing incentives for SMEs' funding.
ii. The government needs to use tax holidays as a major tax incentive for newly established small and medium enterprises because these stimulate their investing power thereby exempting them from other tax liabilities.
iii. The government should promote the growth of small and medium enterprises by creating necessary enabling frameworks and relax the burden of regulating measures and ensure that their efforts are geared toward granting tax incentives to micro, small, and medium enterprises.
iv. Building SMEs' capacity through the localization of supply chains requires leadership at the top. Localizing value creation through engagement with SMEs is a key area that large corporations can contribute to as this will bolster their license to operate by creating a positive local impact, considering partnerships across segments, and sharing business planning skills.
v. Small and medium enterprises should emphasize on tax incentives so that their operations continue to be more efficient and effective.
vi. The government should start campaigns to explain the role of taxation in the development of the country and help small and medium enterprises to understand tax laws in Rwanda.

Putting all these measures in place will go a long way in ensuring that the tax incentives granted to the SMEs have a significant impact on their growth.

References

Bahizi, K. A. (2013). *The impact of tax incentives on the promotion of SMEs.* Kigali: MIT Press.
Berger, A. N., & Udell, G. F. (1998). The economics of small business finance: The roles of private equity and debt markets in the financial growth cycle. *Journal of Banking & Finance, 22*(1), 613–678.
Bertrand, M., & Mullainathan, S. (2003), Enjoying the quiet life? Corporate governance and managerial preferences. *Journal of Political Economy, 111*(5), 1043–1075.
Broersma, L., & Gautier, P. (1997). Job creation and job destruction by small firms: An empirical investigation for the Dutch manufacturing sector. *Small Business Economics, 9*(3), 211–224.
Chen, D., Lee, F. C., & Mintz, J. (2002). *Taxation, SMEs and entrepreneurship.* Tokyo: Prentice Hall.
Chukwumerije, T., & Akinyomi, O. (2011). The impact of tax incentives on the performance of small-scale enterprises. *Journal of Accounting and Finance, 23*(15), 104–136.
Colmar, B. (2005). *Measuring the tax compliance costs of small and medium sized businesses.* Harlow: Pearson Education Ltd.
Comanor, W. S. (1967). Market structure, product differentiation and industrial research. *The Quarterly Journal of Economics, 81*(4), 639–657.

De Wit, G., & De Kok, J. (2014). Do small businesses create more jobs? New evidence for Europe. *Journal of Small Business Economics, 42*(2), 283–295.

Devereux, M. P., Liu, L., & Loretz, S. (2014). The elasticity of corporate taxable income: New evidence from UK tax records. *American Economic Journal: Economic Policy, 6*(2), 19–53.

Fletcher, K. (2003). *An evaluation of marginal effective tax rates on domestic investment in South Africa between 1994 and 2002.* Johannesburg: Pearson Education.

Githaiga, I. (2013). *The impact of tax incentives on foreign direct investments inflows of firms listed at the Nairobi Securities Exchange* (unpublished MBA Project), University of Nairobi, Kenya.

Goolsbee, A. (2004). The impact of the corporate income tax: Evidence from state organizational form data. *Journal of Public Economics, 88*(11), 2283–2299.

Gravelle, J. (2013). Corporate tax incidence: Review of general equilibrium estimates and analysis. *National Tax Journal, 66*(1), 185–214.

Hansson, A., & Brokelind, C. (2014). Tax incentives, tax expenditures theories in research and development: The case of Sweden. *World Tax Journal, 6*(2), 168–200.

Heshmati, A. (2001). On the growth of micro and small firms: Evidence from Sweden. *Small Business Economics, 17*(3), 213–228.

Kaplan, D. (2001). Rethinking government support for business sector research and development in South Africa: The case for tax incentives. *The South African Journal of Economics, 69*(1), 72–73.

Keen, M. (2013). *Taxation and development: Critical issues in taxation and development.* Cambridge: MIT Press.

Kothari, C. R. (2000). *Research methodology: Methods and techniques* (2nd ed.). New Delhi: Pearson Education Ltd.

Külter, B., & Demirgüneş, K.(2007). Determinants of profitability in retailing firms: An empirical study on ISE listed retailing firms. *Journal of Çukurova University and Institutions of Social Sciences, 2*(34), 445–460.

MINECOFIN. (2012). *The Rwanda investment board provides tax incentives.* Kigali: MINECOFIN.

MINICOM, NISR, MIFOTRI, & PSF. (2017). *Small and medium enterprise development policy in Rwanda.* Kigali: MINICOM.

Mintz, J., & Chen, D. (2011) Small business taxation: Revamping incentives to encourage growth. *University of Calgary—School of Public Policy Research Papers, 4*(7), 1–31.

The World Bank. (2013). *Report on doing business.* World Bank Publications.

UNCTAD. (2003). *The financial grants to encourage investment and employment in non-traditional sectors.* New York: UNCTAD.

Vann, R. J., & Holland, D. (1998). Income tax incentives for investment. *Tax Law Design and M Drafting, 2*(1), 986–1020.

Young, J. F. (2009). *Decision-making for small business management* (4th ed.). Florida: Krieger Publishing Company.

Zee, H. H., Stotsky, J. G., & Ley, E. (2002). Tax incentives for business investment: A primer for policy makers in developing countries. *World Development, 30*(9), 1497–1516.

Author Index

A
Aaby, N. E., 194
Aaker, D. A., 191, 196–198
Abdul, R., 80
Acemoglu, D., 2, 75
Achtenhagen, L., 6, 115, 119, 128, 134
Acs, Z. J., 174
Adha, A., 61
Adham, K. A., 115, 118, 128
AFR, 37
Afrooz, A., 220–222
Aghion, P., 2, 79
Agundu, P. U. C., 218, 220
Ahlburg, D. A., 75
Ahmad, M., 26, 37
Ahmed, E. M., 220–222
Aissa, M. S. B., 2
Akinyomi, O., 244, 245
Alden, D. L., 196
Alexanderson, O., 118, 128
Alias, R., 220
Ali, J., 220
Ali, M., 44, 49
Ali, S., 80, 90
Al-Yousif, Y., 75
Amin, A., 80, 90
Amir, Z. B., 44, 49
Anghel, M. G., 49
Angrist, J. D., 27
Ansong, D., 22, 23
Anudjo, E. Y., 81
Arcury, T. A., 140
Ariff, M. H., 220
Arifin, J., 172
Arora, S., 23
Aryeetey, E., 4, 24

Asghar, T., 26, 37
Athukorala, P. C., 25, 26
Atmaja, S. L., 224
Attanasio, O. P., 22, 24
Audretsch, D. B., 100
Axelsson, B., 117
Ayyagari, M., 173
Azémar, C., 151

B
Bahizi, K. A., 233
Baines, S., 117
Baker, D., 74
Balachandran, V., 100
Ball, M. O., 141
Banks, K., 22
Baran, D., 177
Barbour, P., 218
Bardhan, P., 2
Barney, J. B., 206, 212
Barr, A., 118, 119, 127, 128
Barrientos, A., 23
Barro, R. J., 2, 75
Basu, K., 2
Bates, R. H., 2
Batra, R., 196
Baye, M. F., 218
Begovic, N., 22
Bell, E., 180
Bennett, M., 162, 164
Bennion, M. L., 195, 196, 209
Berger, A. N., 237
Bernanke, B. S., 58
Bertrand, M., 232
Beverly, S. G., 25

Bhattacharyya, S., 2
Biggiero, L., 118, 128
Bingham, F. G., 196, 209
Binns, T., 2
Birger, W., 193
Birgül, C., 57
Bjuggren, P. O., 175, 176
Blankson, C., 193–195, 197, 210
Blinder. A. S., 58
Bloom, D. E., 74
Blouin, J. L., 150
Boadu, E. A., 77, 90
Boserup, E., 75
Bourbonnais, R., 60
Boutilier, J. J., 141
Bouzahzah, M., 74
Bradač, B., 117–119, 128
Braga, A., 100
Brata, A. G., 22
Braun, R. E., 24
Brenda, S. L., 115, 118, 128
Broderick, A. J., 193, 196, 197
Broersma, L., 246
Brokelind, C., 232
Bronwyn, H. H., 103
Brooksbank, R., 193, 195, 197
Brooks, C., 49
Brooks, S. C., 141
Brown, F., 103
Brown, H. E., 196, 208
Brundin, E., 6
Brunninge, O., 135
Bryman, A., 180, 181
Buick, J. E., 141
Bulere, T., 51
Buskirk, R. K., 196
Byers, A., 141

C
Cadogan, J., 193, 197
Cain, L. P., 76
Cameron, A. C., 27
Camilleri, M. A., 198
Campo, C., 181
Canning, D., 74
Carter, M. W., 140
Carter, S., 180
Cartwright, N., 1
Catenaro, M., 74
Cevik, S., 58
Chell, E., 117
Chen, D., 232, 237
Cheng, K. C., 56
Chernev, A., 195

Chitonge, H., 2
Cho, J., 140
Chowa, G. A., 22, 23
Chowdhury, M., 78
Chrisman, J. J., 178
Chua, J. H., 176, 178
Chukwumerije, T., 244, 245
Ciftcioglu, S., 22
Clark, G., 1, 2
Clark, S. M., 197
Clausing, K. A., 150, 155, 164
Collier, P., 2, 3, 14
Collins, D., 23
Collins, S. M., 59
Colmar, B., 236, 244
Comanor, W. S., 235
Corcos, G., 151
Cote, M. J., 140
Covelo, S., 100
Covin, J. G., 117
Cravens, D. W., 195
Crawford, J. C., 193–195, 197
Crépon, B., 99, 100, 102, 104, 112
Cristea, A. D., 150
Crossley, T. F., 25
Czepiel, J. A., 195, 209

D
Dalberg, H., 178
Darrat, A. F., 75
Das, G. G., 2
Das, J. R., 24
Daskin, M. S., 141, 142, 144, 146, 147
Dauda, M. I., 81, 90
Davidson, P., 25
Davis, J. A., 175, 178
Davis, J. C., 76
Day, G. S., 194
Deaton, A., 1
De Kok, J., 232, 233
De la Croix, D., 74
Delen, D., 197
Delong, J. B., 74
Demirguc-Kunt, A., 173
Demirgüneş, K., 243
Dennis, A. G., 197
Dercon, S., 37
Desai, M., 157
Desai, S., 174
Devereux, M. P., 232
De Wit, G., 232, 233
Deyuan, Z., 80
Dieden, S., 29
Dionco-Adetayo, E. A., 178

Author Index

Dirschmid, W., 26
Dischinger, M., 157
Donatus, M., 116
Dovel, G. P., 196
Drine, I., 2
Duflo, E., 2
Duguet, E., 102
Duh, M., 175, 176
Dupas, P., 23
Durbin, J., 29, 202, 211
Dwivedi, D. N., 57

E

Easingwood, C. J., 196
Easton, G., 117
Economist, The, 1, 13
Edalati, A., 220, 221
Edwards, S., 59
Egger, P., 157
Eggert, W., 157
Ejigu, F., 22
Ekanem, E., 220
Ekone, A. F., 58, 68
Eli, H. T., 81, 90
Emenuga, C., 58
Emmerson, C., 25
Engel, C., 157
Engelhardt, G. V., 26
Engle, R. F., 49, 51, 60
Entrekin, L., 115, 118, 128
Éva, K., 59
Evans, M. J., 195

F

Fadare, S. O., 57
Fahy, J., 193, 196, 197, 210
Färe, R., 220
Feliu, N., 174
Fisher, R. J., 193
Fletcher, K., 233
Floro, M. S., 26
Fofack, 2, 4
Foley, F., 157
Ford, D., 116, 117, 119, 121
Fosu, A., 2, 4
Frazer, 5
Freedman, C., 56
Friedman, B. M., 56
Friedman, M., 25, 57
Fritsch, M., 100
Furuoka, F., 81

G

Gachanja, P. M., 77, 82, 90
Gaertner, M., 47
Galia, F., 102
Galor, O., 2
Garino, J., 196
Gautier, P., 246
Gedela, S. P. R., 26
Gerry, C., 100
Gersick, K. E., 174, 175, 178
Gertler, M., 58
Gesler, W. M., 140
Ggombe, 5
Ghauri, P., 120
Ghose, S., 195, 209
Giang, P., 100, 103
Gilding, M., 178, 180
Gispert, C., 178
Githaiga, I., 234
Glick, W. H., 197
Glover, D. R., 75
Goins, R. T., 140
Goolsbee, A., 237, 243
Granger, C. W. J., 49, 51, 60, 66, 67, 81, 82
Grant, R. M., 193
Gravelle, J., 236
Griffith, R., 102
Groen, A., 117
Grosskopf, S., 220
Grubert, H., 157
Gujarati, D. N., 27, 29, 49, 84
Gulati, R., 196
Günes, S., 57
Gupta, K. L., 25
Gustafsson, J., 121
Guzman, A., 103

H

Hadjicharalambous, C., 210
Håkansson, H., 116, 117, 119, 121
Hall, B. H., 101
Hameed, G., 60
Hameed, I., 57
Hamel, G., 195
Hamori, S., 82, 90
Hanazaki, M., 224
Handler, W. C., 175
Hanna, S., 26
Hansson, A., 232
Harjes, T., 23
Hausman, J. A., 12, 29
Havnes, P.-E., 117–119, 121
Hayes, H. M., 194

Heady, D. D., 74
Heidhues, F., 24
Heijdra, B. J., 74
Hejase, A., 159, 160
Hejase, H., 159, 160
Henderson, J. V., 76
Hernantes, J., 140
Heshmati, A., 2, 103, 105, 106, 221, 238
Hickey, S., 2, 4
Hines, J., 157
Hoddinott, J., 23
Hodge, A., 74
Hogan, K., 141
Holland, D., 242
Homer, S., 56
Hooley, G., 193, 196, 197, 210
Hossain, M., 78
Howitt, P., 2, 79
Hromadkova, F., 102
Huergo, E., 102
Hughes, J., 76
Huizinga, H., 157
Hulme, D., 23

I

Inyang, B. J., 191, 197, 199, 201, 206–210, 212, 213
Iragena, J., 23
Islam, A., 37
Islam, N., 2
Iturriza, M., 140

J

Jacobsen, S. K., 141
James, B. T., 197
Janmohamed, A., 141
Jenster P. V., 194
Johannisson, B., 118, 128
Johansen, L., 219
Johansen, S., 63
Johnson, S. H., 59
Junanker, P. N., 44

K

Kakkonen, M. L., 177
Kalafatis, S. P., 194, 196, 209
Kamin, S. B., 98
Kaplan, D., 233—235
Karlan, D., 22, 36
Kaseorg, A., 178
Kasomo, D., 181
Kasongo, A., 22

Keen, M., 237, 242
Keilbach, M. C., 100
Kelley, A. C., 74, 77
Kelly, R., 22, 37
Kennedy, P., 63
Keuschnigg, C., 157
Keynes, J. M., 24, 25, 29
Kibet, L. K., 25, 26, 37
Kigabo, T. R., 61
Kim, S. J., 140
Kirsipuu, M., 176, 177, 179
Klasen, S., 74
Klau, M., 58
Koduru, B. P. K., 81, 90
Koe, W. L., 173, 178, 179
Kokkelenberg, E. C., 220
Kothari, C. R., 181, 239, 240
Kothari, S. P., 181, 239, 240
Kotler, P., 195, 196, 198, 209
KPMG, 151
Kraay, A., 26
Kransdorff, M., 218
Kremer, M., 12
Krugman, P. R., 74
Kulkarni, K., 74
Külter, B., 243
Kumhof, M., 56

L

Labaka, L., 140
Laeven, L., 157
Lai, Z., 218, 219
Lanis, R., 150, 155, 164
Lansberg, I., 175, 178
Lavers, T., 2, 4
Lawson, D., 74
Laxton, D., 56
Lee, F. C., 237
Legros, D., 102
Lehmann, E. E., 100
Leicester, A., 25
Levine, R., 75
Lewis, A., 1, 16
Ley, E., 234, 236
Lim, G.J., 140
Linden, E., 74
Lin, F. L., 141
Lin, J., 2
Littunen, H., 179
Liu, L., 224, 232
Liu, Q., 224
Loayza, N., 22
Loaza, N., 56
Lööf, H., 103, 105, 106, 109

Lotti, F., 103
Lucas, R. E. Jr., 75
Lucian, L. A., 61
Lury, D. A., 2
Lusardi, A., 25, 37
Lussier, R. N., 176, 178, 179
Lutz, C., 120

M

Maasoumi, E., 2
Maddison, A., 74
Mahajan V., 196
Mairesse, J., 101, 102
Maitra, P., 37
Majid, I. A., 172, 179
Majid, M. Z. A., 58, 172
Maksimovic, V., 173
Malaney, P. N., 76
Malinen, P., 176
Malthus, T., 74, 78
Marlow, S., 180
Marques, C. S., 100
Marshall, G. W., 194
Masa, R. D., 22, 23
Mason, A., 77, 90
Mavrotas, G., 22, 37
Mayende, S., 218, 221
Mazzarol, T., 119
Mburu, D. M., 26
McKinnon, R. I., 23, 24
Meier zu Selhausen, F., 26
Melese, N., 22
Melin, L., 119, 127, 128, 134
Menike, H. R., 76
Miller, C. C., 197
Miller, M. H., 25
Miller, W. R., 172
Mills, L. F., 105, 109, 110, 125
Mintz, J., 156–158, 232
Mishkin, F. S., 58, 68
Mishra, P. K., 24
Mishra, S. K., 24
Modigliani, F., 25
Mohnen, P., 101
Möller, K., 193, 196, 197, 210
Monga, C., 2
Montalto, C., 26
Montiel, P., 58
Moore, K., 23
Morduch, J., 23
Morrar, R., 102
Mosbah, A., 180

Moutinho, L., 195, 209
Mueller, P., 100
Mugenda, A. G., 181
Mughal, K., 60
Mullainathan, S., 232
Mulyungi, P., 26
Muradoglu, G., 22
Murindahabi, E., 23
Murphy-McGreevey, M., 37
Musinguzi, J., 26
Mustapha, B., 209
Mutai, B. K., 25, 26, 37

N

Nabi, M. S., 2
Nayyar, D., 2
Ndemezo, E., 218
Ndulu, B. J., 2
Nelson, R. A., 219
Newfarmer, R., 5
Ngoc, N., 100, 103
Nguyen, D. X., 150
Nhan, N., 100, 103
Nicodµeme, G., 157
Nigar, S., 26, 37
Niño-Zarazúa, M., 2, 4
Niyibizi, O., 154, 162
Norman, M. S., 172, 174, 175
Nowicki, K., 118, 128
Nsengiyumva, E., 26
Ntaganira, E., 26
Nweze, C., 3, 11
Nyamulinda, B., 37

O

O'Connell, S. A., 2
Obayelu, O., 22
Obere, A., 77, 82, 90
Ocran, M. K., 22
Odhiambo, N. M., 24
OECD, 2
Ogunmuyiwa, M. S., 58, 68
Ohaka, J., 218, 220
Okonjo-Iwela, N., 2, 3
Omar, R., 178
Onyeiwu, C., 56
Opreana, A., 44
Osipian, A., 75
Ostry, J., 59
O'Sullivan, A., 56
Ouma, D. E., 25, 26, 37

Ouma, S. A., 25, 26, 37
Ouyang, M., 147
Owuor, G., 25, 26, 37

P
Pandey, I. M., 25
Park, T., 1
Pascal, M., 61
Penrose, E. T., 201, 206, 212
Peter, A., 74, 76, 81, 90
Peters, B., 102
Peterson, E., 74
Pierrard, O., 74
Piketty, T., 74
Pischke, J. S., 27
Porter, M. E., 49, 192
Pounder, P., 175
Powers, J. M., 140
Prahalad, C. K., 195
Preisser, J. S., 140
Premaratine, S., 119, 128
Price Waterhouse Coopers., 54
Pritchett, L., 4
Pryma, K., 149, 150

R
Radam, A., 220
Raffield, B. T., 196, 209
Rahim, H. A., 74
Rahim, K. B. A., 220–222
Rahim, S., 60
Rajan, R. G., 59
Ramirez-Pacillias, 2
Rashidghalam, M., 221
Rashid, I. M., 74
Ratan, A. L., 22, 36
Raudsaar, M., 178
Rautamäki, H., 177
Razin, O., 59
Readhead, A., 154
Reddy, S., 2
Redmond, W. H., 195, 196
Renelt, D., 75
ReVelle, C., 141
Rha, J. Y., 26
Rialp, J., 178
Richardson, G., 150, 155, 164
Ries, A., 193, 194, 196, 197
Rivkin, S., 195, 209
Robin, A., 113
Robin, S., 102

Robinson, L. A., 2
Robson, P., 2
Rodrik, D., 1, 2, 4
Roelen, K., 37
Rohan, K., 78
Rohwedder, S., 24, 38
Rollnick, S., 172
Romer, P. M., 83
Romp, W. E., 74
Rotehr, P. C., 74
RRA, 13, 152, 165, 166, 171, 181, 240
Rurangwa, E., 26
Rusuhuzwa, T. K., 14
Rutherford, D., 23, 44
Rutherford, S., 23
Ruthven, O., 23

S
Sa'ari, J. R., 189
Sacco, J., 195, 209, 212
Sakthivelan, M. S., 100
Sala-i-Martin, X., 2
Sanya, S., 47
Sarriegi, J. M., 140
Saunders, B. R., 180, 181
Saunders, M., 180, 181, 189
Schaltegger, S., 179
Schendel, D., 196, 208
Schmidt-Hebbel, K., 22
Schmidt, K. H., 56
Schmidt, R. M., 74, 77
Schrieder, G., 24
Schulenburg, D., 118
Schultz, T. P., 25
Schumpeter, J. A., 44
Seekings, J., 2, 4
Seguino, S., 26
Seidman, J. K., 150
Sen, A. K., 2
Senik, C., 115, 118, 128
Sen, K., 25
Senneseth, K., 117, 119, 121
Serief, S. R., 180
Servén, L., 22
Shaari, M. S., 74
Shamshad, A., 57
Shamsudin, M. N., 220
Shansby, J. G., 197, 198
Sharma, M., 175, 176, 189
Sharma, P., 175
Shawa, K. C., 23
Shaw, E. S., 23, 24

Sheffrin, S. M., 56
Sherraden, M., 25
Shwab, G., 74
Silberg, U., 179
Simon, J. L., 75
Sims, J. T., 196, 208
Singh, S. P., 220
Širec, K., 117–119, 128
Skirbekk, V., 74
Slevin, D. P., 117
Smart, M., 157
Smith, A., 14
Sneessens, H. R., 74
Snyder, L. V., 141
Söderbom, M., 192
Solomon, M. R., 194
Solovieva, T., 140
Solow, R., 79, 90
Soludo, C. C., 2
Sonfield, M. C., 176, 178, 179
Song, S., 74
Sophia, K., 192
Spencer, S. M., 140
Steenkamp, E. M. S., 196
Stephens, M., 181
Stern, E., 141
Steyn, M., 218
Stiglitz, J., 2
Stotsky, J. G., 234, 236
Strulik, H., 76
Stuart, E. W., 215
Subramanian, A., 59
Sulong, Z., 172
Sund, L. G., 175, 176
Swasdpeera, P., 25, 41
Syed, H., 26, 37
Sylla, R., 56
Székely, M., 22

T
Tambunan, T., 120
Tandoh, A., 24, 29, 36
Tartiyus, E. H., 74, 76
Taskin, F., 22
Tausch, A., 2
Taylor, G., 150, 155, 164
Taylor, J., 58
Teksoz, K., 58
Tesfom, G., 120
Thirlwall, A. P., 77
Thuku, G. K., 77, 82, 90
Trivedi, P. K., 27
Trout, J., 193–197, 209

Tsai, P. L., 26
Tsogas, M., 194, 196, 209
Tuan, N., 100, 103
Tybout, A. M., 195, 209

U
Udell, G. F., 237
Ullah, S., 26, 37
Ume, A., 57
United Nations Conference on Trade and Development (UNCTAD), 120, 128, 134, 236, 242
Uwimbabazi, H., 154

V
Van Biesebroeck, 5
Vann, R. J., 242
van Raaij, W. F., 195, 209
Van Stel, A., 100
Velickaite, R., 177
Vincent, B., 180, 181
Von Braun, J., 24

W
Wagner, M., 179
Wahab, K. A., 180
Waheed, A., 103
Wan, G., 2
Wang, F., 77, 78, 90
Wang, Y., 120
Wanjohi, M., 176
Washburn, N. T., 197
Waygood, S., 44
Webster, F., 196
Welter, F., 116
Wentzel, M. S. I., 218
Werker, E., 4
Wernerfelt, B., 192, 206, 212
Wesley, F., 74
Williams, K. A., 140
Wincent, J., 118
Winner, H., 157
Wooldridge, J. M., 27, 29
World Bank, 2, 5, 9, 99, 100, 106–111, 124, 128, 221, 238
Wu, D. M., 29

Y
Yabara, M., 47
Yao, W., 82, 90

Yazid, A. S., 172
Yin, R. K., 121
Yodfiatfinda, M. Z. A., 220
Yodfiatfinda, N., 220
Young, A., 2
Young, J. F., 235
Yusop, Z., 220

Z
Zainalabidin, M. S., 220
Zaman, T., 44, 49
Zee, H. H., 234, 236
Zeller, M., 24
Zemplinerova, A., 102
Zhan, C., 141
Zinman, J., 22, 36
Zulkornain, Y., 220

Subject Index

A
Aaker and Shansby's model, 191
Accelerated depreciation, 218, 233, 234, 236, 237, 241–243
Accelerator principle, 44
Access to finance, 22, 25, 26, 120, 126, 133, 136, 178, 227
Access to market information, 116, 118, 129–133
Adoption, 2, 12, 151
Africa, 1–6, 11, 14, 45–47, 120, 123, 139, 142, 155, 157
Africa capital markets watch report, 45, 47
Africa growth initiative, 2
African Union Agenda 2063, 3
Age, 23–26, 30, 32–36, 74, 77, 78, 90, 106–108, 112, 207, 209, 217, 219, 223–225, 227
Ageing population, 78
Agency costs, 155
Agency theory, 149, 155, 156, 236
Agent-based models, 140
Aggregate production function, 79, 83
Agro-raw materials, 219, 224, 226, 229
Akaike Information Criterion (AIC), 54, 62, 65
Analysis of Variance, 161–164
ANOVA test, 161, 164
Anti-development traps, 2
Anti-Malthusian, 12
Appropriate technologies, 2, 116, 129, 131–133, 179, 219, 229
A-R-A framework, 117
Arithmetic progression, 80
Arm's length principle, 151, 152, 154, 156, 163, 166
Atlas of economic complexity, 12
Augmented Dickey–Fuller test, 64
Automated External Defibrillators (AEDs), 141
Automotive solutions, 122
Autoregressive distributed lag, 80, 81, 84

B
Back-end taxes, 232
Balance of payments equilibrium, 56, 59
Bank lending rate, 59, 61, 65, 68–70
Beverage manufacturing industry, 217–219, 221, 224, 226, 227, 229
Bottom billion, 14
Bottom-up, 2, 7
Bounds testing approach, 80
Box–Jenkins approach, 63
Bralirwa annual reports, 192
Branch and bound algorithm procedure, 141
Broad money, 55, 57, 61
Broad money supply, 55, 61
Build-own-operate-transfer projects, 234
Business climate, 1, 3, 9
Business process related abilities, 203
Business' sustainability, 10, 171, 181, 182, 184–187

C
Capabilities, 2, 9, 11–13, 119, 120, 179, 191–193, 197, 200–203, 206
Capacity utilization, 11, 13, 106, 108, 109, 111, 112, 217–229
Capital accumulation, 22, 59, 76
Capital gain exemption, 241, 242

Capital gains, 26, 232, 244, 245
Capital gains taxes, 232, 234
Capital intensity, 78, 221
Capital markets, 6–8, 12, 43–48, 52, 58
Catching up, 3
Causality, 60, 66, 67, 76, 80–82
CDM method, 102
Change theory, 75
Child labor, 77
Chi-square, 36, 182–186
Chi-square test, 171, 181–186
Chow test, 66
Civil war, 5
Climate change, 1
Cobb douglas production function, 104, 105, 217, 219–222, 228
Coefficient of determination, 52, 161, 163, 244
Cointegration, 8, 49, 60, 63–65, 69, 80–82, 84
Collinearity statistics, 160
Combination approach, 171, 180
Competition, 13, 100, 103, 105, 118, 120, 193, 194, 198, 201, 205, 208, 210, 212, 220, 226
Competitive market structure, 155
Competitiveness, 5, 9, 59, 100, 106, 108, 112, 179, 218, 224
Competitor strategy, 197, 199
Congestion effect, 141
Consumer price index, 82, 90, 92
Contraceptives, 80
Contractionary and expansionary policies, 58
Control variables, 61, 87, 89, 92
Convergence, 3, 60, 75, 115
Corporate governance, 45, 155, 177, 220
Corporate profits, 150, 156, 159, 162, 164, 165, 191, 197, 237
Corporate strategy, 195
Correlational test, 60
Correlation coefficient, 67, 161, 163, 244
Cost of capital goods, 232
Cost of finances, 158
Costs of doing business, 116, 120
Crepon, Duguet and Mairesse Method, 102
Cross-sectional data, 29
Cultural symbols, 11, 191, 203, 205–207, 209, 210, 212
Cultural symbols strategy, 197, 199
Cumulative sum of squares (CUSUM squares), 90
Customization, 11, 197, 199, 210, 212
Customization strategy, 197, 199, 212

D
Dallas–fort worth metroplex, 194
Data unit root (ADF), 60, 62–64, 81, 83, 88
Degree of industrialization, 82
Democracy, 154
Demographic change, 8, 75, 76
Demographic dividend, 77
Demographic transition, 78
Dependency ratio, 25, 26
Devaluation, 59
Dichotomy, 116
Diminishing returns, 78
Disease traps, 2
Disequilibrium, 49, 90
Divergence, 3, 76
Drone, 8, 9, 13, 139–146
Drone-aided healthcare services, 139, 146
Dummy variables, 105, 106, 222
Durbin–Wu–Hausman specification test, 29
Dynamic interactions, 206, 212

E
East African Community (EAC), 3, 47, 199
East Asia, 22
ECM approach, 63
ECM coefficient measures, 48
Econometric analysis, 55, 70
Econometric estimation, 60
Econometric technique, 8
Economic crisis, 4
Economic development, 1, 3–5, 7–9, 12, 14, 21–23, 36–38, 73–78, 80–84, 90, 92, 120, 172, 173, 232
Economic development and poverty reduction strategy 3, 3
Economic development-induced population growth, 81
Economic freedom, 4
Economic growth, 2, 7–9, 21–24, 55–61, 68, 69, 73–83, 86–90, 99, 100, 237
Economic miracle, 3, 11
Economic reforms, 3, 5
Economic welfare, 9, 22
Economies of scale, 76
Education, 10, 12, 23–26, 30, 31, 34, 35, 37, 77, 80, 171, 178, 185–187, 221, 241
Education Research and Policy Network (NERPNET), xxi
EICV5 cross-section survey data, 27
Employment, 3, 9, 11, 13, 45, 57, 59, 77, 78, 100, 107, 116, 120, 172–174, 192, 234
Employment creation, 1, 9, 13, 177, 233

Subject Index 259

Enabling environment, 246
Endogeneity, 23, 29, 84
Engle–Granger (EG) method, 49
Engle–Granger Tau-statistic, 51
Engle–Granger two-step method, 49, 51, 60, 66
Entrepreneurial skills, 116, 129–133, 179
Entrepreneurship, 2, 6–10, 13, 99, 100, 116, 118, 172, 173, 176–178, 181, 187, 237
Entrepreneurship sustainability, 10, 13, 171–173, 178, 179
Equity investments, 232
Error Correction Method (ECM), 43, 49, 52, 55, 60, 63, 65, 66, 84
Error correction model, 55, 62, 63, 65, 81, 84, 90
Error terms, 21, 27, 29, 48, 52, 61, 66, 83, 84, 160, 199, 222
Evidence-based policy making, 14
E-Views, 48
Exchange rate policy, 8
Export, 3–6, 12, 59, 68, 69, 106, 111, 112, 126, 127, 134, 150, 177, 218, 233, 234, 238
Export Processing Zone (EPZ) Act, 233, 234
Export Processing Zones (EPZs), 233, 234
Export promotion, 3, 233, 234

F
Family business, 7, 10, 11, 13, 171–181
Family entrepreneurship, 7, 10, 13, 171, 173, 176, 178, 179, 181, 187
Family planning, 81, 86
Family shareholders, 175
Financial depth, 58
Financial development, 7, 9, 12
Financial intermediation, 58, 69
Financial openness, 2
Firm dynamics, 9
Firm growth, 115, 116
Firm heterogeneity, 2, 12, 206, 212, 222
Firm innovation, 103
Firm performance, 6
Firm size, 102, 103, 108, 220, 221
Firm's productivity, 6, 7, 12, 101–103, 218, 220, 221
First difference, 43, 51, 62, 63, 84
First 10-year plan, 3
Fiscal policy, 56, 234
Fiscal sustainability, 74
Fisher effects, 8

Five-point likert scale, 197, 199
Flexible exchange rate regime, 58
Food and beverage processing, 7, 11, 217, 218, 220
Foreign aid, 86
Foreign currency risk, 156
Foreign Direct Investment (FDI), 10, 13, 23, 74, 82, 83, 87, 88–90, 92, 103, 150, 234, 238
Foreign exchange rate, 157–159, 165
Foreign policy, 3
Functional and emotional benefits, 203, 208
Further Offers (FOs), 45

G
Gender, 24, 26, 36, 112, 173, 220
Generalized tobit model, 105
Genocide, 1, 4, 5, 44, 85, 86, 120
Geography, 2
Gini index, 4
Globalization, 2, 149, 150
Global Positioning System (GPS), 122, 134
Governance, 2–4
Granger causality test, 66
Gross Domestic Product (GDP), 4, 12, 45, 47, 57, 59, 61, 76, 77, 81–83, 86, 89, 172, 173, 192, 217, 218, 232, 235
Growth aspirations, 119, 128
Growth debacles, 2
Growth engines, 13
Growth miracles, 2

H
Health and education, 1, 2, 77, 81
Health care services, 7, 9, 10, 13, 77, 140
Heteroscedasticity, 90, 91
High-Yield (HY), 45
HIV/AIDS, 141
Homoskedasticity, 52
Horizontal equity, 235
Household living survey, 8
Household size, 24–26, 30, 35, 37
Human and non-human wealth, 25
Human capital, 2, 4, 6, 9, 10, 12, 13, 22, 75, 203
Human capital accumulation, 22, 76

I
Import competing sectors, 59
Impulse-response, 8, 43, 82
Inclusive growth, 2, 3, 6, 9

Industrial building allowances, 234
Industrial development, 10, 99, 233
Industrial development corporation, 233
Industrialization policy, 2
Inflation rate, 13, 61
Inflation targets, 57
Informal credit, 118
Information asymmetries, 118
Initial Public Offerings (IPOs), 45, 46
Innovation, 5–7, 9, 10, 12, 13, 44, 69, 99–106, 109–112, 171, 177, 179, 185–187, 196, 237, 238
Input-output models, 146
Input-output ratio, 222, 223, 225–228
Institutions, 2, 3, 22, 37, 46, 47, 117–119, 122–129, 131, 133, 135, 179
Instrumental variable, 23, 27, 29
Instrumental variables (IV) regression model, 23, 27, 29
Intangible assets, 150, 157, 164
Integer linear programming, 9, 139, 146
Integrated household living conditions surveys, 21
Intellectual property assets, 203
Interest rate pass-through, 57
Intermediate goods, 76, 226
Internal capabilities, 119
International standard industrial classification, 219
International standard industrial classification of all economic activities, 219
Intra-firm trade, 151
Intra-group transactions, 10, 149, 157–165
Inverse mills ratio, 105, 106, 109
Investment deduction allowance, 234
Investment-Grade (IG), 45
Investment projects, 13, 234, 236
Inyange industries ltd, 191, 197, 199, 201, 206, 208–210, 212, 213
IP holding company, 157
IV-2SLS estimates, 29

J
Job creation, 3, 4, 7, 13, 24
Joblessness, 79
Johansen cointegration, 60, 64
Johansen cointegration test, 60, 64, 81

K
Keynesian macroeconomics, 8
Keynesian model, 29
Keynesian theory, 55

Know-how, 118, 156, 176
Knowledge-based economy, 3
Knowledge management skills, 203

L
Lagged value, 66
Lagrange-multiplier, 91
Lag selection, 52, 62
Land administration information system, 238
Landlocked, 14, 120
Law of motion, 79
Life care systems, 75
Life expectancy, 90
Likelihood estimation, 105
Likelihood function, 79
Likelihood-ratio test, 182–186
Linear regression modeling, 52
Long-run cointegration, 49, 64
Long-run equilibrium, 63, 65, 81
Long-run relationship, 43, 51, 52, 55, 60, 62, 64, 65, 69, 81, 84, 88, 89
Long-run welfare, 8
Long-term equilibrium, 49
Long-term growth, 3, 59, 134
Loss carried forward, 231, 234, 237, 238, 241, 242, 244, 245
Low technological capabilities, 120

M
Macroeconomic policies, 6
Macroeconomic stability, 2
Macro-variables, 56, 58, 62, 69
Made in Rwanda, 4
Malaria, 141
Malthus' theory of population, 90
Manufacture Under Bond (MUB), 234
Manufacturing enterprises, 7, 11, 191, 192, 198, 199
Marginal efficiency of capital, 44
Marginal propensity to consume, 25
Market capitalization, 43, 46, 48, 50–52
Market competitive behavior, 208
Market-driven strategies, 206, 212
Market performance, 7, 191, 192, 194, 197–199, 202, 205–207, 210–213
Maternal mortality, 10, 139, 141, 142
Mathematical modeling, 48, 139, 141, 144
Mathematical network theory, 147
Maximal covering location model, 141
Maximum Likelihood Estimation (MLE), 105

Subject Index

McKinnon–Shaw hypothesis, 58
McKinnon–Shaw model, 58
Medium of exchange, 56
Micro-enterprises, 223
Micro-foundations, 8
Middle-income, 4, 5, 7, 11
Mining deduction allowance, 234
Ministry of finance, 59
Missing variables, 21, 29
Mittelstand businesses, 172
Monetary aggregates, 56, 57, 61
Monetary policy, 7–9, 12, 13, 55–61, 68, 69
Monetary transmission mechanism, 8, 57
Money supply, 55–58, 60, 61, 65, 68, 70
Money supply (M3), 59, 61, 68
Moral suasion, 80
MPTM effects, 59
Multicollinearity, 160
Multinational companies, 7, 10, 13, 123, 149, 150, 154, 156, 159, 161, 165
Multinational corporations (MNCs), 6, 10, 149, 150, 154, 157
Multiplier effect, 56
Multi-stage modeling method, 112

N

National Bank of Rwanda, 59
National Institute of Statistics of Rwanda (NISR), 27, 48, 59, 159, 173, 192, 217, 218, 226, 227
National Police and the Rwanda Utilities Regulating Authority, 122
National strategy for transformation, 3
Needs ratio, 77
Neoclassical theories, 8, 25, 235
Net Present Value (NPV), 232
Network-based growth, 119, 128, 134
Networking abilities, 203
Networks, 2, 6–10, 12, 13, 115–136, 139, 141, 147, 166
Neutrality of money, 59
NGOs, 3, 13
Nobel memorial prize in economic sciences, 1, 14
Nominal exchange rate, 55, 59, 61, 65, 67–70
Non-fiscal incentives, 218
Non-parametric data envelopment analysis (DEA), 220
Normality assumption, 160

O

OECD countries, 151, 172
One-size-fits-all, 3

Operations research, 140
Optimal lagrangian relaxation algorithm, 141
Ordinary Least Squares (OLS), 27, 29, 37, 60, 159, 219, 228
Organizational assets, 203
Organizational routines, 203
Out-of-Hospital Cardiac Arrests (OHCAs), 141
Over-communicated society, 193

P

Pension systems, 74
Personal networks, 117, 118, 123, 124, 126, 128, 129, 133
Phenomenology approach, 180
Phi-value, 181, 182, 184–186
P-Median Problem (PMP), 141
Population densities, 76
Population dynamics, 9
Population growth, 7, 12, 73–90, 92
Positioning strategies, 6, 7, 11–13, 191, 193–199, 201, 203–213
Positioning strategy's typology, 196, 197
Positive checks, 80
Positivism, 171, 180
Postpartum Hemorrhaging (PPH), 141
Poverty, 3, 4, 8, 13, 23, 27, 32, 36–38, 75, 77, 120, 173
Poverty reduction, 3, 23
Precautionary motives, 25
Preferential tax rates, 236, 237, 245
Price and product quality, 195, 209
Price, quality, 11, 195, 196, 204, 206, 208–210, 212, 220
Price rigidities, 57
Price Waterhouse Coopers (PWC), 45–47, 54
Pricing strategy, 197, 199
Principal and agents, 155
Principal component analysis, 240
Private sector federation, 123, 134, 173
Product attributes, 210, 212
Product characteristics strategy, 197, 199
Product class, 197, 199, 204–206, 210, 212
Product class strategy, 197, 199, 204
Product customization, 209
Product use or application strategy, 197, 199
Profitability, 44, 153, 175, 191, 195, 197, 199, 207, 209, 210, 212, 243
Profit maximization, 155
Profit sharing, 6
Profit shifting, 7, 149, 150, 153, 154, 156, 157, 159, 161, 162, 164, 165

Pro-investment policy, 238
Public policy, 4, 7, 9
Public transport, 122
P-value, 33, 50–52, 64–67, 109–111, 162–164, 182, 184, 185
Python language, 144

Q

Quality-ladder, 12
Quality strategy, 197, 199
Quasi-fixed inputs, 219

R

Rabies, 141
Ramsey, 91
Regional cooperation, 3
Regulatory framework, 120, 122
Replacement investments, 43
Reputational assets, 203
Reserve money, 57
Resource-Based Theory (RBT), 192
Risk sharing arrangement, 118
Robustness, 75
Role model, 4, 13
Royalty expenses, 149, 157–159
R-square, 231, 244
Rural poor, 6, 8, 23, 33–38
Rwanda Development Board (RDB), 44
Rwanda Management Institute (RMI), 122, 123, 134
Rwanda Revenue Authority (RRA), 13, 149, 152, 153, 159, 165, 166, 171, 181, 240
Rwanda stock market, 23
Rwandese ministry of trade and industry, 217, 219, 223

S

Savings, 4, 6–9, 12, 13, 21–27, 29, 30, 32–38, 58, 79, 82, 141, 237
Schooling, 77
Segmentation decision, 198
Selection bias, 100, 105, 109
Self-reliance, 4
Shared prosperity, 2, 13
Short-run model, 66, 84
Short-run relationship test, 60
Simple random sampling, 159, 171, 181
Simulation, drones, 139, 140, 144, 146
Simulations, 8, 140
Simultaneous equations model, 21, 27, 37

Skill scarcity, 2
Small and Medium Enterprises (SMEs), 6, 7, 9–11, 13, 103, 107, 115–121, 127–136, 171–173, 178, 179, 181, 231–233, 235, 237, 238, 240, 242–246
Small business development, 233
SmartPLS, 144
Smokestack industries, 7
Social capital, 76
Soft Drink Manufacturing Enterprises (SDMEs), 11, 191, 192, 198, 199, 206, 212, 213
Soft drinks, 11, 191, 192, 197–199, 206, 209, 212
Solovian paradigm, 8
Solvin and Yamen's formula, 240
Southeast Asia, 1, 14
Spacing of childbirths, 80
Spatial development, 233
Special CIT rate, 242
Special zone, 237, 242
Specific product positioning, 194
Speculative motives, 25
Stabilization programs, 13
Stable state growth, 75
Standard deviation, 32, 33, 87, 160
Standard of living, 1
State failure, 2
State-owned enterprises, 120, 238
Stationarity test, 48, 50, 63, 82
Stationary, 43, 50, 51, 60, 62–64, 83, 88
Stationary data, 83
Stationary time-series, 60, 63, 82, 83, 88
Stationary trend, 43, 48, 62
Statistical Package for Social Scientists (SPSS), 159, 181, 240
Steady-state growth, 75, 78
Stochastic shocks, 55
Stock exchanges, 44, 47, 48, 52, 200, 201, 220
Stores of value, 25
Strategic alliances, 117
Strategic roadmap, 3
Structural break, 66
Structural diversification, 2, 4, 12
Structural equation model, xxii
Sub-Saharan Africa (SSA), 4, 5, 22, 23, 47, 118, 140
Sub-Saharan SMEs, 4, 5, 22, 23, 46, 140, 221
Subsidiary firms, 155
Supply-side determinants, 59

Subject Index

Sustainable development, 13, 45, 140, 173, 177
Sustainable Development Goals (SDGs), 3, 45
Sustainable economic growth, 56

T

Tanzania investment act of 1997, 234
Tax administration, 151, 152, 154, 165, 166, 217, 219, 222, 225, 226, 228, 229
Tax benefits, 6, 11
Tax credit, 236, 237
Tax holiday, 218, 233, 234, 236, 237, 242, 244–246
Tax incentives, 7, 8, 10, 11, 13, 217, 218, 221, 226, 227, 229, 231–237, 240–246
Tax Remissions and Exemption Office (TREO), 234
Technical know-how, 118
Technological invention, 76
Technological progress, 59, 78, 83
Technology gap, 75
Technology intensity, 106, 112
Telehealth, 140
Three-stage least squares, 105, 106
Time-series data, 63, 83
Top-down, 2, 7
Total Factor Productivity (TFP), 12, 82, 220
Trade, 2, 3, 5, 9, 10, 12, 13, 44, 59, 75, 122, 134, 156, 194, 227
Traded goods, 50, 59
Tramigo, 123, 124, 127, 131
Transaction motives, 25
Transfer pricing, 7, 10, 13, 149–151, 153–157, 161, 163–166
Transmission channels, 58
Transmission mechanisms, 55, 56, 58, 61, 69
Transparency, 3
Transportation model, 9, 139
Transportation problem, 142, 143, 146
Transport technology, 122
T-test, 21, 29, 33, 34, 36, 52, 240
Tuberculosis, 141
Turn over ratio, 47, 48
Two-stage technique, 112

U

Umurenge Saving and Credit Cooperative (Umurenge SACCO) program, 23, 37, 235
Unanticipated monetary shocks, 56

Uncapacitated Fixed-charge Location Problem (UFLP), 141
Underemployment, 80
Unit root test, 60, 83, 84
Universal Health Coverage (UHC), 140
Unrestricted Error Correction Model (UECM), 84
Upliftment of the disadvantaged, 233
Urbanization, 76
Urban population, 80
Urwibutso Enterprises Ltd., 191, 197, 199, 201, 206, 208–210, 212, 213

V

Value Added Tax (VAT), 11, 231, 233, 237
VAR-based cointegration tests, 63
Variance, 34, 48, 52, 160, 206, 210, 212
Variance decomposition, 82
Variance Inflation Factor (VIF), 160
Varimax rotation methods, 240
VAR/VEC model, 62
VAR/VEC order, 62
VEC model, 62
VEC stability roots, 62
VEC stability test, 62
Vector Auto Regression (VAR) model, 49
Vector error correction model, 62
Vision 2020 Umurenge program (VUP), 4, 37
Vision 2050, 3

W

Wear and tear, 11, 231, 238, 241, 242, 244, 245
Well-being, 6, 13, 75, 76
Working-age population, 77, 90
World bank's doing business report, 238
World bank's enterprise survey database, 221
World commission on environment and development, 172
World Development Indicators (WDI), 73, 81, 82, 92
World Health Organization, xxii

Z

Zigama Credit and Savings Society (Zigama CSS), 23
Zimbabwe investment centre, 233
Z-statistic, 51

CPSIA information can be obtained
at www.ICGtesting.com
Printed in the USA
LVHW060850200721
693180LV00004B/97